ARTIFICIAL NEURAL SYSTEMS

Principle and Practice

Authored By

Pierre Lorrentz

University of Kent

United Kingdom

advertisements or ideas contained in the Work.

Limitation of Liability:

In no event will Bentham Science Publishers, its staff, editors and/or authors, be liable for any damages, including, without limitation, special, incidental and/or consequential damages and/or damages for lost data and/or profits arising out of (whether directly or indirectly) the use or inability to use the Work. The entire liability of Bentham Science Publishers shall be limited to the amount actually paid by you for the Work.

General:

1. Any dispute or claim arising out of or in connection with this License Agreement or the Work (including non-contractual disputes or claims) will be governed by and construed in accordance with the laws of the U.A.E. as applied in the Emirate of Dubai. Each party agrees that the courts of the Emirate of Dubai shall have exclusive jurisdiction to settle any dispute or claim arising out of or in connection with this License Agreement or the Work (including non-contractual disputes or claims).
2. Your rights under this License Agreement will automatically terminate without notice and without the need for a court order if at any point you breach any terms of this License Agreement. In no event will any delay or failure by Bentham Science Publishers in enforcing your compliance with this License Agreement constitute a waiver of any of its rights.
3. You acknowledge that you have read this License Agreement, and agree to be bound by its terms and conditions. To the extent that any other terms and conditions presented on any website of Bentham Science Publishers conflict with, or are inconsistent with, the terms and conditions set out in this License Agreement, you acknowledge that the terms and conditions set out in this License Agreement shall prevail.

Bentham Science Publishers Ltd.
Executive Suite Y - 2
PO Box 7917, Saif Zone
Sharjah, U.A.E.
Email: subscriptions@benthamscience.org

BENTHAM SCIENCE

CONTENTS

ARTIFICIAL NEURAL SYSTEMS

FOREWORD

Neural Networks, Fuzzy Logic and Evolutionary Computing are members of Soft Computing class of techniques. The techniques are capable of identifying and handling inexact solutions for complex tasks and can deal with the real life uncertainties within the computational framework. Soft Computing has significantly matured over the years and we can find significant applications of soft computing in industry and research environment. Neural Networks is the most mature of other techniques in the Soft Computing. The networks have also benefitted from integrated Fuzzy Logic based systems to model complex engineering systems with the human expert knowledge and through robust system modelling.

Evolutionary Computing helps to optimise the design a Neural Network. Each members of the Soft Computing has several algorithms and concepts that need better understanding for application development.

This book on 'artificial neural networks – principle and practice' provides necessary foundation to understand the basics of Neural Networks and how to develop real life applications. From basic definitions to relevant theorems the book presents an algorithm approach to describe the foundations.

The book also emphasises systematic approach to Intelligent System analysis and design. In order to build a Neural Network or Artificial Neural Network application, one needs to apply knowledge of probability based methods as well as fuzzy sets for more uncertain aspects of the problem. The book then explains the motivation from our neural system to develop the Neural Networks.

Description of other network-based approaches using nodes and edges also strengthens the understanding about the Neural Networks. A major strength of the book is the fundamentals of quantum logic for emerging Neural Network development. This is major area for future development. A discussion on Neural Network hardware would have strengthened the book.

The second part of the book presents detailed discussion on learning algorithms, current and emerging Neural Network structures and application development. The chapters also present metrics to evaluate effectiveness of the network. Selection and integration of multiple Neural Networks to solve a real life and complex problem is a major aspect of the book. As mentioned before there are several algorithms and approaches to solve a problem, the systematic approach presented in the book is of major interest. Application of the network to solve a complex modelling task usually requires significant volume of data. A further discussion on the modelling approaches with less data would be very helpful.

The emphasis on probability based neural network and its application is significant because of its popularity. But the real strength of this part of the book is in describing the Quantum Neural Networks and the Deep Belief Network (DBN).

Finally the book also outlines the research and development in Neural Networks. Future Neural Networks are learning from specialised parts of our neural system and trying to scale up to solve even more complex engineering applications.

Rajkumar Roy
Cranfield University, UK

PREFACE

An intelligent system is that which exhibit characteristics of learning, adaptation, and problem-solving, among others. The group of intelligent system, conceived and designed by human, is loosely termed Artificial Neural Network (ANN) System. Such ANN system is the theme of the book. The book also describe nets (also called network or graphs), evolutionary methods, clustering algorithm, and others nets, most of which are complementary to ANN system.

The term "practice" in the title refers to design, analysis, performances assessment, and testing. The design and analysis may be facilitated by the explanations, equations, diagrams, and algorithms given. Performance assessments occur in any section that bear the name and apply to any ANN system because they are standard independent methods and most ANN system has an associated error feedback. Testing is exemplified by case studies and is given toward the end of most chapters.

An interest in artificial neural sciences is a sufficient requirement to understand the content of the book, though knowledge of signal processing, mathematics, and electrical/electronic communication is an advantage. The book specifically takes a developmental perspective, making it more beneficial for professionals. The book adopts a spiral method of description whereby various topics are revisited several times; each visit introduces fresh material at increasing level of sophistication. Each visit to a specific ANN type may also introduce new ANN system(s) and/or new algorithm(s) as the case may be.

The book is divided into two parts (I and II). Part I contain five chapters. Chapter 1 introduce the biological neurons and basic artificial neurons. From these, chapter 2 derive better neurons and introduce statistical methods. Chapter 3 describe a framework of dynamic fuzzy-neuron, and explain the fundamental principle governing the design and analysis of ANN system. To distinguish other algorithms (*e.g.* clustering algorithm) from learning algorithms, chapter 4 describe fundamentals of genetic algorithm, clustering algorithms, and those other algorithms complementary to ANN systems. Neural network is in chapter 3 introduced by graph. Chapter 5 concludes part 1 by introducing quantum neural network, quantum maths and logic. The chapter also describe Hodgkin-Huxley neuron, and memristance.

Similarly, part II consists of six chapters. In Chapter 6, artificial neuromorphic network, and Widrow-Hoff learning are visited; so is fuzzy ANN system. While chapter 7 describes the usual weighted, weightless ANN systems. It also introduces Bayesian ANNs, and discusses general performance assessment methods. On the other hand, chapter 8 considers various selection and combination strategy for ANN systems. Chapter 9 is dedicated to Bayesian networks. There are some promising ANN systems being considered in the research arena, and also now in chapter 10, these ANN may revolutionize ANN throughput in future. In chapter 11 implementation issues regarding Monte Carlo algorithm is visited, and also implementation issues regarding neuromorphic networks is revisited.

The book attempts to impart considerable knowledge of know-how of ANN to the reader in order to facilitate a novel development and research. Albeit also improve an ad-hoc ANN. This may encourage and help a developer to meet any industrial increasing demand for novel ANNs' implementation and application.

Pierre Lorrentz
University of Kent,
United Kingdom

Part 1

Principles

CHAPTER 1

Neurons

Abstract: The aim of this chapter is to explain what a natural biological neuron is, and what an artificial neuron is. To this end, the first section introduces the biological neuron, explains its structure and its information transmission methods. The second section explains how an artificial neuron may be obtained from a corresponding biological neuron. The resources for the artificial neuron may be purely electrical in nature and the behaviour of the resulting electric circuit is expected to be similar to that of information transmission of a biological neuron.

Keywords: Active transport, Axon, Calcium, Conduction, Conductance, Central nervous system, Dendrites , Diffusion, Depolarization, Electrogenesis, Ganglia, Hyperpolarization, Motor, Myelin sheath, Neurotransmitter, Neuron, Potassium, PRVP, Sodium, Soma, Sheath.

A BIOLOGICAL NEURON

Neurons form the fundamental components of the central nervous system (CNS) and the ganglia of the Peripheral nervous system (PNS). Neurons are also found in other locations which may accord them a corresponding name *e.g.* sensory neurons, motor neurons, and interneurons.

As shown in Fig. (**1**), a normal neuron has a soma (cell body), dendrites, and an axon. The term neurite refers to an axon, any dendrite, or other protrusions from the soma of the neuron without paying attention to their differences. Axon emerges from the soma at a base called the axon hillock and usually extends a longer distance than any dendrite of the neuron. Neurons do not undergo cell division but are generated by stem cells. Biology and Bio-scientific researchers have confirmed that the main features that distinguish a neuron are: (1) electrical excitability, and (2) the presence of synapses which are complicated junctions that permit signals to travel to other cells.

Pierre Lorrentz

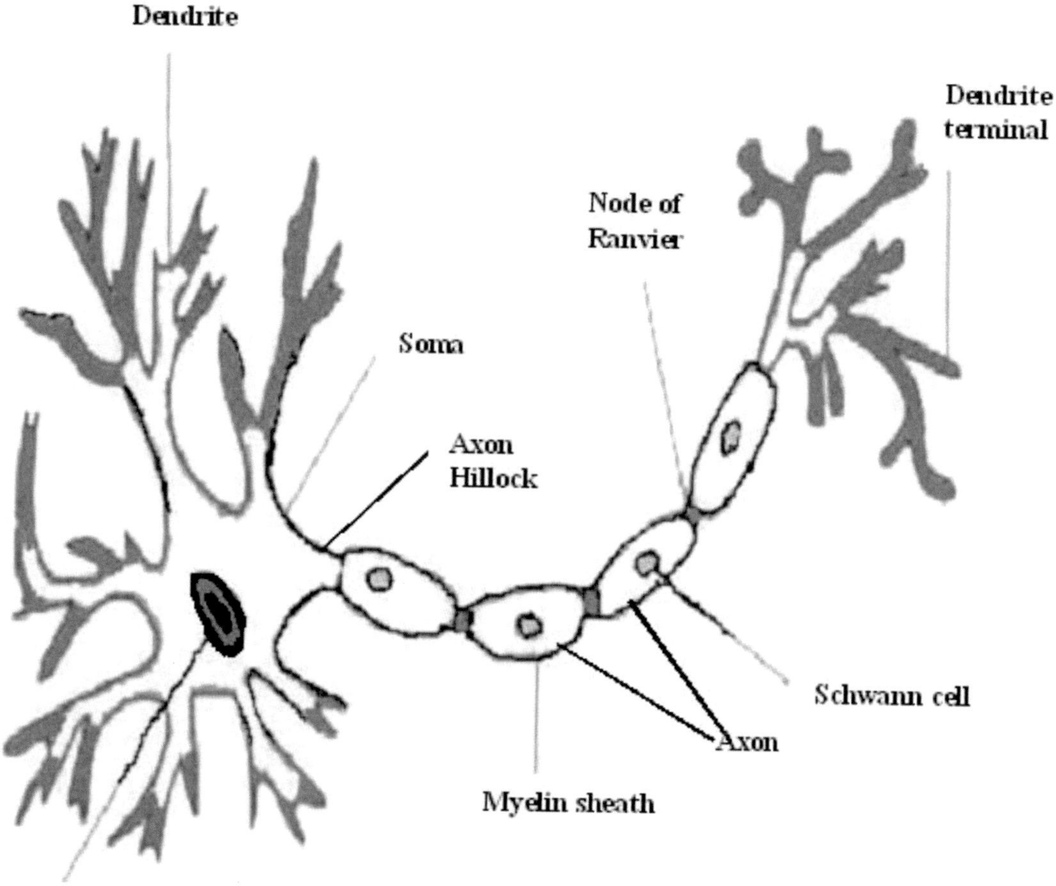

Fig. (1). A natural biological neuron.

Dendrites normally branched profusely from both the soma and the axon. Every neuron has only one axon which maintains the same approximate diameter throughout its length. The myelin sheath provides a protective coating around the axon. The myelin sheath allows the action potential to propagate faster than it would have been if compared with another axon of equal diameter. Neurons performs various specialized functions depending on their location and event received, Events are received by communication which is effected in two ways. One is by the release/absorption of neurotransmitter from the surrounding; this is a partly chemical process called neurotransmission. The second is the synaptic transmission. These modes of communication and the associated energy required for the communication is common to all natural biological neurons.

Synaptic Transmission

Synaptic signal is either excitatory or inhibitory. If the net signal excitation exceeds certain threshold and is sufficiently large, it generates a brief electrical pulse called action potential which originates at the soma. The action potential propagates down the axon as follows.

There are pores not covered by myelin sheath (see Fig. **2**) through which ion exchanges occur between the axon and the extrinsic fluid; these pores are known as nodes of Ranvier. The ion exchanges are responsible for the production of action potential. The action potential at one node is most often sufficient to initiate another action potential at a nearby node. A signal thus travels discretely rather than continuously along an axon. This mode of transmission along the axon is termed saltatory conduction.

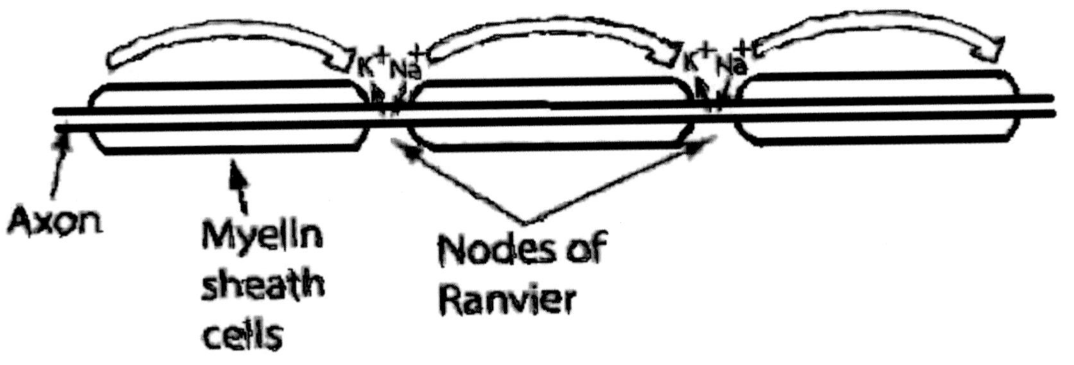

Fig. (2). A section of axon showing saltatory conduction.

TRANSMISSION ACROSS SYNAPSES

A presynaptic action potential propels the calcium Ca^{2+} ions through the voltage-gated calcium channel.

As depicted in Fig. (**3**), a Presynaptic Releasable Vesicle Pool (PRVP) constitutes the active synaptic region of the dendritic terminal ends. The concentration of the Ca^{2+} causes the PRVP vesicles to fuse with the membrane and release the neurotransmitters into the synaptic region. The neurotransmitters move by diffusion and binds with postsynaptic current (PSC). The electrical current I_N (t) that is released from a unit amount of neurotransmitter at $t \geq t_s$ is given by:

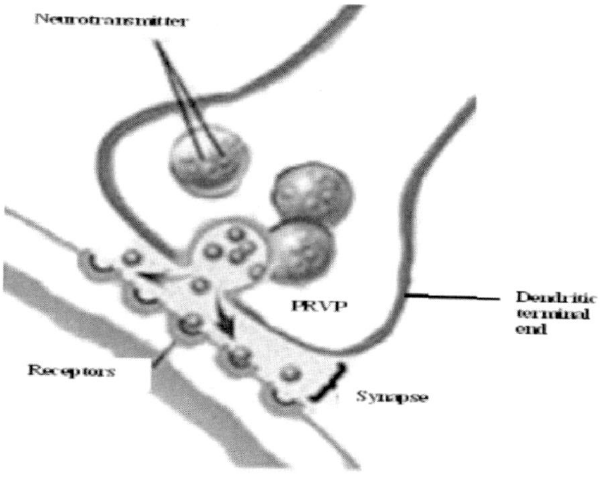

Fig. (3). Synaptic transmission by discharge of neurotransmitter.

$$I_N(t) = g_N[v(t) - E(t)] \quad \textbf{(1)}$$

Where

V(t) = postsynaptic membrane potential;

E(t) = reversal potential of ion channel;

and the activities of the neurotransmitters and other effects may be the conductance change g_N (t).

Because the conductance of the synapse that connects one neuron to another neuron is very important, several experiments were performed by several eminent researchers [1 - 4]. Some results of the conductivity at synaptic junctions are:

$$g_N(t) = \overline{g}_N\left(\frac{t-t_s}{\tau}\right)\exp\left(\frac{t-t_s}{\tau}\right) \quad \textbf{(2)}$$

$$g_N(t) = \overline{g}_N\left(\frac{\tau_1\tau_2}{\tau_1-\tau_2}\right)\left[\exp\left(-\left(\frac{t-t_2}{\tau_1}\right)\right) - \exp\left(-\left(\frac{t-t_2}{\tau_2}\right)\right)\right] \quad \textbf{(3)}$$

Equations (2) and (3) are obtained by modelling experimental data of natural biological neuron *e.g.* the axon and soma of a giant squid. The movement of Calcium Ca^{2+} ion and other ligands in the soma or axon of the giant squid may be confirmed by injection of fluorescent dyes into the substrate before or during the experiment which is often performed at low temperature.

The main fundamental structure and function of a single natural neuron has been described, so also its connections to other neighbouring neurons. They are common to all biological neurons. There are also very many neurons in the CNS.

It is noteworthy that equations (2) and (3) are also solutions of a second-order damped wave oscillator given by:

$$\tau_1\tau_2 \frac{\partial^2 g}{\partial t^2} + (\tau_1 + \tau_2)\frac{\partial g}{\partial t} + g = \bar{g}_N x(t) \qquad \textbf{(4)}$$

AN ARTIFICIAL NEURON

In this section, we would like to design an artificial neuron from a natural biological neuron of section 1. Basic resources such as resistance, capacitance, voltage sources, and basic electric circuit analysis are employed in this design. Inside the soma and axon are called the intracellular medium. The intracellular medium is higher in sodium (Na^+) and potassium (K^+) ion concentration as compared to extracellular fluid. Other ions present include, but not limited to, chlorine (Cl^-), Phosphate ($Ph0^-_4$), Magnesium (Mg^{2+}). Delimiting the neuron from the surrounding is the cell membrane which consist mainly lipids. The cell membrane may be impermeable to water and ions but permeate ion only at the ion channels and pumps. Because each channel is selectively permeable, when positive ions are concentrated on one side of a membrane as a result, it induces a corresponding negative charge on the opposite side which is the behaviour of a capacitor. For this reason, the neuron cell membrane shall be represented by capacitance. Charged particles in the intracellular fluid do not accelerate despite the field potential, but moves with certain average velocity. This is due to frequent collision with other element which obstructs their movement. Also at the ion pumps, energy is supplied by the hydrolysis of Adenosine triphosphate (ATP), in a process called *Electrogenesis*, to Adenosine diphosphate (ADP). The sodium-potassium exchanger is an example of ionic pumps that pushes K^+ into the intracellular fluid against its concentration gradient.

Because energy is supplied and resistances are present in the intracellular fluid, the electrical representation of the intracellular fluid is shown in Fig. (**4**). This is similar for other active pump and ion channels. A schematic representation of one section of a neuron is shown in Fig. (**5**).

Fig. (4). Resistance and voltage source as electric model of ionic pump and active conduction.

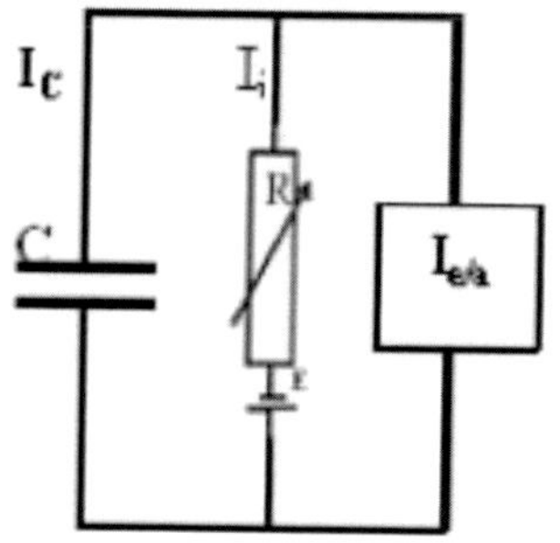

Fig. (5). A simple electric model of a neurite.

By Kirchhoff's current law [5] the algebraic sum of current at a junction is given by:

$$I_{e/a} = I_c + I_i \quad \textbf{(5)}$$

Where

$$I_i = g_m\left(V - E_m\right) = \frac{\left(V - E_m\right)}{R_m} \quad \textbf{(6)}$$

And

$$I_c = C_m \frac{\partial V}{\partial t} \tag{7}$$

Substituting equations (7) and (6) into (5) and re-arranging gives

$$I_{e/a} = I_c + I_i = C_m \frac{\partial V}{\partial t} + \frac{(V - E_m)}{R_m} \tag{8}$$

$$I_{e/a} - \frac{(V - E_m)}{R_m} = C_m \frac{\partial V}{\partial t} \tag{9}$$

$$C_m \frac{\partial V}{\partial t} = \frac{(E_m - V)}{R_m} + \frac{I_e}{a} \tag{10}$$

The equation (10) is a first-order Ordinary Differential Equation (ODE) of the membrane potential V. This equation is valid for an isolated section of part of a neuron. Following the standard method of solution to first-order ODE, the solution to equation (10) may be represented as:

$$V(t) = E_m + (V_0 - E_m)\exp\left(-\frac{(t - t_0)}{R_m C_m}\right) \tag{11}$$

This is a rise and fall exponential solution. The initial increase of V(t) from resting potential is known as *depolarization*. The product $R_m C_m$ is called the time constant of the membrane. When t→∞ the steady state value of V (t) is given by:

$$V(t) = E_m + \frac{R_m I_e}{a} \tag{12}$$

When the membrane re-charges its capacitance to regain the resting potential, it is termed *repolarization*. By injecting current or voltage from an external source, it is always possible to drive the membrane below the resting potential; this phenomenon is known as *hyperpolarization*. Fig. (**6**) shows an extension of Fig. (**5**) to make a complete neuron in an extracellular fluid with both continuity and boundary conditions included.

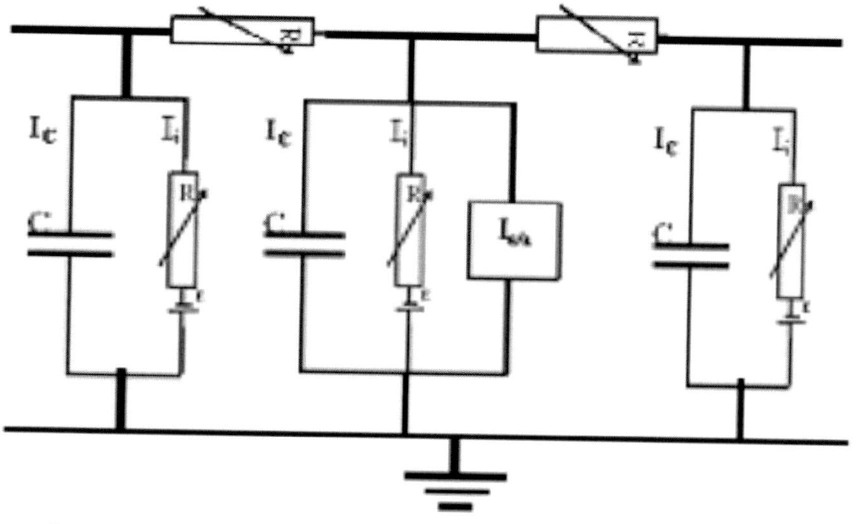

Fig. (6). A complete electric model, with boundary condition, of a section of a neuron.

These cases will now be considered. The axial resistance of cross-section of an axon is proportional to its length l and inversely proportional to cylindrical crosssectional area $\pi r^2 = \pi\left(\frac{d}{2}\right)^2$. Specific axial resistivity (in Ωcm) is denoted by R_a so that axial resistance R is calculated as follows.

Recall that resistivity $\rho$is defined by $R\frac{A}{l}$

$$\text{that is } \rho = R\frac{A}{l} = R\frac{\pi r^2}{l} = R\frac{\pi\left(\frac{d}{2}\right)^2}{l} \tag{13}$$

$$\text{Specific axial resistivity } R_a = \rho = R\frac{\pi\left(\frac{d}{2}\right)^2}{l} \tag{14}$$

(15)

$$R_a = R\frac{\pi\left(\frac{d}{2}\right)^2}{l}$$

$$l R_a = R\pi\left(\frac{d}{2}\right)^2$$

$$4l R_a = R\pi d^2$$

(16)

$$\frac{4l R_a}{\pi d^2} = R$$

Also, the membrane current I_a now flows both to the left and to the right; the sum is given by:

(17)

$$I_{j,a} = \frac{V_{j+1} - V_j}{4R_a l / \pi d^2} + \frac{V_{j-1} - V_j}{4R_a l / \pi d^2}$$

We have now included voltages from other membrane sections and indexed them by j as show in equation (17). Modifying equations (8) by substituting equation (17) into it we have;

(18)

$$\pi dl C_m \frac{\partial V}{\partial t} = \frac{E_m - V_j}{R_m / \pi dl} + \frac{V_{j+1} - V_j}{4R_a l / \pi d^2} + \frac{V_{j-1} - V_j}{4R_a l / \pi d^2} + I_{c,j}$$

The surface area "a" of a cylindrical axon is πdl. Dividing (18) by πdl gives;

(19)

$$C_m \frac{\partial V}{\partial t} = \frac{E_m - V_j}{R_m} + \frac{\partial}{4R_m}\left(\frac{V_{j+1} - V_j}{l^2} - \frac{V_{j-1} - V_j}{l^2}\right) + \frac{I_{c,j}}{\pi dl}$$

Equation (19) is a second-order difference equation making it suitable for numerical integration. To derive a continuous version of equation (19) replace the length l by x δ x and evaluate it in the limit δx→0.

$$C_m \frac{\partial V}{\partial t} = \frac{E_m - V(x,t)}{R_m} + \frac{d}{4R}\left[\frac{1}{\delta x}\left(\left(\frac{V(x+\delta x,t)-V(x,t)}{\delta t}\right)-\left(\frac{V(x,t)-V(x-\delta x,t)}{\delta t}\right)\right)\right] + \frac{I_c(x,t)}{\pi d} \quad \textbf{(20)}$$

$$\frac{\partial^2 V(x,t)}{\partial x^2} = \lim_{\delta x \to 0} \frac{1}{\delta x}\left(\left(\frac{V(x+\delta x,t)-V(x,t)}{\delta t}\right)-\left(\frac{V(x,t)-V(x-\delta x,t)}{\delta t}\right)\right) \quad \textbf{(21)}$$

Substitute (21) into (20)

$$C_m \frac{\partial V}{\partial t} = \frac{E_m - V}{R_m} + \frac{d}{4R_a}\frac{\partial^2 V}{\partial x^2} + \frac{I_c}{\pi d} \quad \textbf{(22)}$$

The equation (22) gives a more accurate description of an artificial neuron than equation (10). This is the first example of an artificial neuron obtained by modelling natural neuron directly. This method whereby an attempt is made to produce a morphological, and structural equivalent of a neuron, and watch for the same behavioural pattern, is termed *neuromorphic*. When Equation (22) is constructed as a neuromorphic neuron, it may be verified if it possesses equivalent information-transmission characteristics by checking against that of biological neuron data. Additional design issue may be the choice of capacitances, variable resistance ranges, and initial calibration. Equation (22) is usually refers to as the cable [6] equation and also bear much semblance to wave equation.

CONFLICT OF INTEREST

The author confirm that this chapter contents have no conflict of interest.

ACKNOWLEDGEMENTS

Cited works are appreciated.

REFERENCES

[1] Hodgkin AL, Huxley AF, Katz B. Measurement of current-voltage relations in the membrane of the giant axon of loligo. J Physiol 1952; 116: 424-48. [http://dx.doi.org/10.1113/jphysiol.1952.sp004716] [PMID: 14946712]

[2] Koch C. Biophysics of computation: information processing in single neurons. New York: Oxford University Press 1999.

[3] Goldman DE. Potential, impedance, and rectification in membranes. J Gen Physiol 1943; 27: 37-60. [http://dx.doi.org/10.1085/jgp.27.1.37] [PMID: 19873371]

[4] Hodgkin AL, Katz B. The effect of sodium ions on the electrical activity of giant axon of the squid. J Physiol 1949; 108: 37-77. [http://dx.doi.org/10.1113/jphysiol.1949.sp004310] [PMID: 18128147]

[5] Charles A, Mathew NO. Fundamentals of electric circuits. Singapore: McGraw-Hill International Edition 2000.

[6] David S, Bruce G, Andrew G, David W. Principles of computational neuroscience. New York, USA: Cambridge University Press 2011.

CHAPTER 2

Basic Neurons

Abstract: The aim and objectives of this chapter is to present other types of artificial neuromorphic neurons with capability of reset and recovery. For this reason, the first section starts with the integrate-and-fire neuron, which has the propensity for reset. The second section introduces probability theory owing to the fact that many processes in the brain and central nervous system obey probability laws. The third section introduces another artificial neuromorphic neuron which employs a Poisson process and is closer in behaviour to a biological neuron.

Keywords: Bayes theorem, Binomial, Bernoulli, Charging, Depolarization, Density function, Excitatory, Expected-value, Inhibitory, Mean, Moment, ODE, Pseudo-random-number-generator, Poisson, Steady-state, Synaptic strength, Spike, Threshold potential, Uniform distribution, Variance.

The first chapter has introduced one biological neuron and one artificial neuron. One advantage of developing ANN from principle is that reproduction is assured with minimal loss of resources and a target performance may often be achieved. Since the book is more about artificial neural network systems, chapter 1 contains the last item on biological neuron. Most development throughout the book however depends, directly or indirectly, on the biological neuron so that it may be regarded as an introduction to the rest of the book.

INTEGRATE-AND-FIRE NEURON

There is another version of artificial neuron model known as integrate-and-fire model; this is a version of figure 5 chapter 1 neuron with an inclusion of spike generation and reset. It states that when the membrane potential [1, 2] reaches or exceeds a threshold potential θ, firing an action potential [3] and discharging occurs. After that, it reset and (re-)build its potential again. The charging proceeds as follows.

Pierre Lorrentz

$$C_m \frac{\partial V}{\partial t} = -\left(\frac{V - E_m}{R_m}\right) - I_v \tag{1}$$

Multiplying (1) by R_m;

$$\tau_m \frac{\partial V}{\partial t} = -V + E + R_m I \tag{2}$$

where $\tau_m = R_m C_m$

Equation (2) is a first-order ODE, whose solution is given by:

$$V(t) = E_m + R_m I\left(1 - \exp\left(-\frac{T_s}{\tau_m}\right)\right) \tag{3}$$

One may be interested at what frequency $f(I)$ does the neuron fire. The neuron fire whenever the voltage V equals θ the threshold voltage or exceed it. Setting $Em = 0$ and $V = \theta$ in equation (3);

(4)

$$\theta = R_m I\left(1 - \exp\left(-\frac{T_s}{\tau_m}\right)\right)$$

$$\frac{\theta}{R_m I} = 1 - \exp\left(-\frac{T_s}{\tau_m}\right)$$

$$\left(\frac{\theta}{R_m I} - 1\right) = -\exp\left(-\frac{T_s}{\tau_m}\right)$$

$$\left(1 - \frac{\theta}{R_m I}\right) = \exp\left(-\frac{T_s}{\tau_m}\right)$$

$$Ln\left(1 - \frac{\theta}{R_m I}\right) = -\frac{T_s}{\tau_m}$$

$$-\tau_m Ln\left(1 - \frac{\theta}{R_m I}\right) = T_s$$

$$f(I)=\frac{1}{T_s+\tau_s}=\frac{1}{\tau_s-\tau_m Ln\left(1-\frac{\theta}{R_m I}\right)} \quad \textbf{(5)}$$

where I is the injected current.

In order to apply this artificial neuron to model a stereo-typical situation found in CNS of some animals, a *distribution* known as *Poisson distribution* shall be introduced. A relevant introductory probability theory is presented now.

PROBABILITY

Definition 1.1: Probability is a set function *p* that assigns to each datum x_i in the sample space X a number $p(x_i)$ called the probability of the datum x_i, such that the following properties hold:

1) $p(x_i) \geq 0$

2) $p(X) = 1$

3) If x_1, x_2, x_3, ...are data and $x_i \cap x_j = \emptyset$, $i \neq j$, then

$p(x_1 \cup x_2 \cup ... \cup x_k) = p(x_1) + p(x_2) + ... + p(x_k)$, for each positive integer *k*, and $p(x_1 \cup x_2 \cup x_3 \cup ...) = p(x_1) + p(x_2) + p(x_3 + ...)$, for an infinite, but countable number of data. For any datum x_i,;

$$p(x_i)=1-p(x_i^{'}); \text{ where } x_i^{'} = \text{complement of } x_i \quad \textbf{(6)}$$

If x_i and y_i are any two independent databases with no data in common, then:

$$p(x_i \cup y_i)=p(x_i)+p(y_i) \quad \textbf{(7)}$$

Otherwise;

$$p(x_i \cup y_i)=p(x_i)+p(y_i)-p(x_i \cap y_i) \quad \textbf{(8)}$$

In this case $p(x_i \cap y_i)$ is defined as;

$$p(x_i \cap y_i) \equiv p(x_i \mid y_i)p(y_i) \tag{9}$$

$p(x_i \mid y_i)$ is called *conditionalprobability*. $p(x_i \mid y_i)$ reads "the probability that x_i occurs given that y_i occurs". The $p(x_i)$ and $p(y_i)$ are examples of *priorprobability*, while the conditional probability is an example of a *posteriorprobability*.

Bayes Theorem: Let $x_1, x_2, x_3, \ldots x_m$ be a partition of the database X such that $x_i \subseteq X$ and $x_i \cap x_j = \emptyset, i \neq j$, by mixing database x_i with y_i, databases x_i and y_i are said to intersect. The intersection of x_i and y_i ($y_i \subseteq Y$) may be written as:

$$Y = (x_1 \cap Y) \cup (x_2 \cap Y) \cup \ldots \cup (x_m \cap Y) \tag{10}$$

Given that:

$$p(Y) = \sum_{i=1}^{m} p(x_i \cap y_i) \tag{11}$$

And by the defining equation (9)

$$p(Y) = \sum_{i=1}^{m} p(y_i \mid x_i)p(x_i) \tag{12}$$

If p(x_i) ≥ 0, *then*

$$p(x_i \cap y_i) \equiv p(y_i \mid x_i)p(x_i) \tag{13}$$

Recall that $y_i \subseteq Y$; and $x_i \subseteq X$; therefore,

$$p(Y \mid X) = \frac{\sum_{i=1}^{m} p(x_i \cap y_i)}{p(X)} = \frac{p(X \mid Y)p(Y)}{p(X)} \tag{14}$$

$$p(Y \mid X)p(X) = p(X \mid Y)p(Y) \tag{15}$$

Equation (15) is referred to as *Bayes Theorem.*

Probability Density Function (p.d.f.): If x_i is allowed to take any value ranging from 0 to 1 inclusive, it is said to be a random variable. If it is discovered that x_i follows certain pattern when assuming any value whatsoever, then this "certain pattern" is a distribution. Since the pattern is certain, it is representable by a function which is called a probability density function (p.d.f.) $f(x_i)$ As $f(x_i)$ moves (*i.e.*; assume values) in space, it trace out what is called a distribution. Let $f(x_i)$ be the p.d.f. of a the random variable x_i, and let R be the space of X. since $f(x_i)=p(X= x_i)x_i \in R$, $f(x_i)$ must be positive for $x_i \in R$.

Definition 1.2: The p.d.f $f(x_i)$ of a random variable X is a function that satisfy the following prorperties:

a. $f(x_i) > 0; x_i \in R$

b. $\sum_{x_i \in R} f(x_i) = 1$ or $\int_{x \in R} f(x_i) = 1$

c. The probability P ($x_i \in R$) of data $x_i \in R$ is given by:

$$p(x_i) = \int_{x_i \in R} f(x_i)$$

$$\text{or } p(x_i \in R) = \sum_{x \in R} f(x_i)$$

In (b) and (c) above, whether to use summation or integral is often experiment dependent. Thus probability can often be written as a distribution, that is, as an integral or sum of $f(x_i)$. In nature, $f(x_i)$ takes various forms. We are also interested in the space R for which $f(x_i)$ is a density function. Recall that x_i ($x_i \subseteq X$) is a random variable subset of X on space R. Luckily, there is a systematic way of analysing $f(x_i)$. The systematic way is by multiplying $f(x_i)$ by an exponential function and summing or integrating – the result of which is called the moment-generating function M(t).

Definition 1.3: Let X be a random variable with p.d.f $f(x_i)$. If there is a positive number h such that either:

$$E(e^{tX}) = \sum_{x_i \in R} e^{tX} f(x_i) \tag{16}$$

or $$E(e^{tX}) = \int_{-\infty}^{\infty} e^{tX} f(v)dv \tag{17}$$

exists and is finite for $-h<t<h$, then the function of t defined by M(t) = E(e^{tX}) is called the moment-generating function of X.

The choice of whether to use equation (16) or (17) is often experiment dependent. Theoretically, it is possible to find the moment-generating function M(t) of any function whose integral (or sum) is finite. If the result obtained is observed in nature, we are lucky. The procedure commonly followed is to map the (any) function to a p.d.f. f(x_i) whose integral (or sum) equals 1. Once the M(t) is obtained as shown in definition 1.3, it becomes a simple matter to explain the properties of the distribution as follows:

i. **The mean of $f(x_i)$:** The mean of $f(x_i)$, denoted by μ , is obtained from M(t) by differentiating M(t) to give M'(t) and evaluating M'(t) at t = 0. That is:

$$M'(t)|_{t=0} = M'(0) = \mu$$

This equation is true only if X is sufficiently large as explained previously. The μ also equals the expected value of x_i, E(e^{tx_i}) in the limit $i \to \infty$. But note that a single value of x_i may never equal the mean μ exactly.

ii. **Variance:** The variance, denoted by Var(x) or σ^2 , is the square of the standard deviation, σ . The variance σ^2 , is obtained from the moment-generating function M(t) by first calculating both the first- and the second-order derivative of M(t).

Then:

$$Var(X) = M''(0) - [M'(0)]^2 = \sigma^2 \tag{18}$$

Where M"(0) = second-order derivative of M(t) at t = 0.

Both the mean μ and variance σ^2 of a distribution are very important properties of a space described by its density function. Notable examples of some p.d.f. $f(x_i)$ that satisfy definition 1.2 will now be given to illustrate the properties of a distribution obtainable from $f(x_i)$ *via* M(t).

Example 3: Uniform distribution: Let X be a uniform distribution on [a, b], then the moment generating function M(t) is given by

$$M(t) = \int_a^b (1/(b-a))e^{tv}dv \quad \textbf{(19)}$$

$$M(t) = \int_a^b (-((e^{tv})/(a-b)))dv = -(1/(a-b))\int_a^b e^{tv}dv$$

$$\int e^{tv}dv = (1/t)e^{tv}$$

$$\int_a^b e^{tv}dv = [(1/t)e^{tv}]_{v=a}^{v=b} = (1/t)e^{bt} - (1/t)e^{at}$$

$$M(t) = (-(1/(a-b)))((1/t)e^{bt} - (1/t)e^{at}) = ((e^{at} - e^{bt})/(at - bt)) \quad \textbf{(20)}$$

$$M(t) = ((e^{at} - e^{bt})/(at - bt)) \quad \textbf{(21)}$$

$$M(0) = 1$$

A special case of (21) is when a = 0 and b = 1, it is called *pseudo-randomnumber generator.*

Example 4: Binormial distribution: Let X have a binormial distribution b(n,p) with p.d.f.

$$f(x) = \binom{n}{x} p^x (1-p)^{n-x} \quad \textbf{(22)}$$

The moment-generating function is given by:

$$M(t) = E(e^{tX}) = \sum_{x=0}^{n} e^{tX} \binom{n}{x} p^x (1-p)^{n-x} \tag{23}$$

$$M(t) = \sum_{x=0}^{n} \binom{n}{x} \left(pe^t\right)^x (1-p)^{n-x} = \left[(1-p) + pe^t\right]^n$$

$$M(t) = \left[(1-p) + pe^t\right]^n = (a+b)^n$$

where a = 1-p and b = pe^t

$$M'(t) = n\left[(1-p) + pe^t\right]^{n-1}\left(pe^t\right) \tag{24}$$

$$M''(t) = n(n-1)\left[(1-p) + pe^t\right]^{n-2}\left(pe^t\right)^2 + n\left[(1-p) + pe^t\right]^{n-1}\left(pe^t\right)$$

$$M'(0) = E(X) = \mu = np$$

$$\sigma^2 = E(X^2) - [E(X)]^2 = M''(0) - [M'(0)]^2 = Var(X) \tag{25}$$

$$Var(X) = \sigma^2 = n(n-1)p^2 + np - (np)^2 = np(1-p)$$

$$Var(X) = \sigma^2 = np(1-p)$$

When n = 1 in equation (23), X have a distribution called *Bernoulli distribution* and

$$M(t) = (1-p) + pe^t \tag{26}$$

is the moment-generating function M(t) for *Bernoulli distribution.*

Example 5: Poisson distribution: Let the number of changes occurring in a given continuous interval be countable. We would have an (approximate) Poisson process with intensity $\lambda > 0$ if the following conditions are satisfied:

a. The number of changes in non-overlapping intervals is independent.
b. The probability that exactly one change occurs in any λ h interval.
c. The probability that two or more changes occurs in an interval h is essentially zero.

If the interval is divided into n sub-interval, then h = 1/n and $p(X) = \lambda h = \lambda\ 1/n$ by condition (b). This is the approximate probability that exactly one change occurs in an interval 1/n. if $\lambda\left(\frac{1}{n}\right)$ is the probability of occurrence of a change, then $\left(1-\frac{\lambda}{n}\right)$ is the probability of non-occurrence of change.

Replacing p by λ/n in a binormial distribution $f(x)=\binom{n}{x}p^x(1-p)^{n-x}$ we have:

$$f(x)=\binom{n}{x}\left(\frac{\lambda}{n}\right)^x\left(1-\frac{\lambda}{n}\right)^{n-x} \quad \textbf{(27)}$$

$$f(x)=\frac{n!}{x!(n-x)!}\left(\frac{\lambda}{n}\right)^x\left(1-\frac{\lambda}{n}\right)^{n-x}$$

$$\lim_{n\to\infty}\left[\frac{n!}{x!(n-x)!}\left(\frac{\lambda}{n}\right)^x\left(1-\frac{\lambda}{n}\right)^{n-x}\right]=$$

$$\lim_{n\to\infty}\left[\frac{n(n-1)\ldots(n-x+1)}{n^x}\left(\frac{\lambda^x}{x!}\right)\left(1-\frac{\lambda}{n}\right)^{n-x}\right]$$

$$\lim_{n\to\infty}\left[\frac{n(n-1)\ldots(n-x+1)}{n^x}\right]=\lim_{n\to\infty}\left[1\left(1-\frac{1}{n}\right)\ldots\left(1-\frac{x-1}{n}\right)\right] \quad \textbf{(28)}$$

$$\lim_{n\to\infty}\left[1\left(1-\frac{1}{n}\right)\cdots\left(1-\frac{x-1}{n}\right)\right]=1 \quad (29)$$

$$\lim_{n\to\infty}\left(\left(1-\frac{\lambda}{n}\right)^{-x}\right)=1 \quad (30)$$

$$\text{Thus } \lim_{n\to\infty}\left[\frac{n!}{x!(n-x)!}\left(\frac{\lambda}{n}\right)^{x}\left(1-\frac{\lambda}{n}\right)^{n-x}\right]=\frac{\lambda^{x}e^{-\lambda}}{x!} \quad (31a)$$

$$f(x)=\frac{\lambda^{x}e^{-\lambda}}{x!};\ \text{[Poisson distribution]} \quad (31b)$$

Let X have a poisson distribution with p.d.f. $f(x)=\frac{\lambda^{x}e^{-\lambda}}{x!}$; then

$$M(t)=E(e^{tX})=\sum_{x=0}^{\infty}e^{tx}\frac{\lambda^{x}e^{-\lambda}}{x!}=e^{-\lambda}\sum_{x=0}^{\infty}\frac{\left(\lambda e^{t}\right)^{x}}{x!} \quad (32)$$

From series definition of an exponential function;

$$\sum_{x=0}^{\infty}\frac{\left(\lambda e^{t}\right)^{x}}{x!}=e^{\lambda e^{t}} \quad (33)$$

$$M(t)=e^{-\lambda}\sum_{x=0}^{\infty}\frac{\left(\lambda e^{t}\right)^{x}}{x!}=e^{-\lambda}e^{\lambda e^{t}}$$

$$M'(t)=\lambda e^{t}e^{\lambda(e^{t}-1)}$$

$$M''(t)=\left(\lambda e^{t}\right)^{2}e^{\lambda(e^{t}-1)}+\lambda e^{t}e^{\lambda(e^{t}-1)}$$

$$\text{The mean} \quad \mu=M'(0)=\lambda \quad (34)$$

The variance $Var(X) = M''(0) = \sigma^2 = (\lambda^2 + \lambda) - \lambda^2 = \lambda$ **(35)**

STEIN MODEL OF NEURON

An integrate-and-fire neuron is connected to many other neurons. Assuming some are inhibitory while others are excitatory and the integrate-and-fire neuron receives short pulses from these neurons following a Poisson process.

Suppose the excitatory synaptic strength [4] is denoted by w_E and inhibitory synaptic strength by w_I. We wish to know the voltage variation with respect to time of an integrated-and-fire neuron that accept spike generated by a Poisson distribution at a rate v_E (excitatory) and v_I (inhibitory) when the membrane potential V is applied. The stein neuron model is given by equation (36):

$$\frac{\partial V}{\partial t} = -\frac{V(t)}{\tau} + w_E \sum_k \delta\left(t - t_E^k\right) - w_I \sum_k \delta\left(t - t_I^k\right) \quad \textbf{(36)}$$

Making a change of variable Y(t)= $e^{t/\tau}$V(t) , equation (36) becomes;

$$\frac{\partial Y}{\partial t} = \frac{e^{t/\tau}}{\tau} V(t) + e^{t/\tau} \frac{\partial V}{\partial t} = e^{t/\tau}\left[w_E \sum_k \delta\left(t - t_E^k\right) - w_I \sum_k \delta\left(t - t_I^k\right)\right] \quad \textbf{(37)}$$

Integrating equation (37),

$$Y(t) = Y(0) + \int_0^t \left(e^{t/\tau}\left[w_E \sum_k \delta\left(t - t_E^k\right) - w_I \sum_k \delta\left(t - t_I^k\right)\right] dt \right) \quad \textbf{(38)}$$

The expected value of Y(t) is denoted by $\langle Y(t) \rangle$ and is given by equation (39).

$$\langle Y(t) \rangle = Y(0) + \int_0^t e^{t/\tau}\left(w_E v_E - w_I v_I\right) = Y(0) + \mu\left(e^{t/\tau} - 1\right) \quad \textbf{(39)}$$

Its steady-state-mean depolarisation is the mean

$$\mu = \tau \left(w_E v_E - w_I v_I \right) \tag{40}$$

Similarly, the variance of Y(t) is given by

$$\mathrm{var}(Y(t)) = \int_0^t e^{2t} \left(w_E^2 v_E - w_I^2 v_I \right) dt = \sigma^2 \left(e^{2t/\tau} - 1 \right) \tag{41}$$

Where the steady-state variance $\sigma^2 = (\frac{\tau}{2})\left(w_E^2 v_E - w_I^2 v_I \right)$ **(42)**

Equations (39) and (41) in terms of voltage V(t) required are

$$\langle V(t) \rangle = V(0)e^{t/\tau} + \mu\left(1 - e^{t/\tau}\right) \tag{43}$$

$$Var(V(t)) = \sigma^2 \left(1 - e^{2t/\tau}\right) \tag{44}$$

The stein model is an artificial neuromorphic neuron which is closer in behavior to a corresponding biological neuron than the normal integrate-and-fire neuron.

CONFLICT OF INTEREST

The author confirm that this chapter contents have no conflict of interest.

ACKNOWLEDGEMENTS

Cited works are appreciated.

REFERENCES

[1] Hodgkin AL, Huxley AF. The components of membrane conductance in the giant axon of loligo. J Physiol 1952; 116(4): 473-96. [http://dx.doi.org/10.1113/jphysiol.1952.sp004718] [PMID: 14946714]

[2] Hodgkin AL, Huxley AF. The dual effect of membrane potential on sodium conductance in the giant axon of loligo. J Physiol 1952; 116(4): 497-506. [http://dx.doi.org/10.1113/jphysiol.1952.sp004719] [PMID: 14946715]

[3] Hodgkin AL, Huxley AF. A quantitative description of membrane current and its application to conduction and excitation in nerve. J Physiol 1952; 117(4): 500-44. [http://dx.doi.org/10.1113/jphysiol.1952.sp004764] [PMID: 12991237]

[4] Stein RB. A theoretical analysis of neuronal variability. Biophys J 1965; 5: 173-94. [http://dx.doi.org/10.1016/S0006-3495(65)86709-1] [PMID: 14268952]

CHAPTER 3

Basic Fuzzy Neuron and Fundamentals of ANN

Abstract: The chapter's aim and objectives are to provide an artificial neural-based fuzzy-logic foundation, and a general framework for design and analysis of ANN systems. The first section therefore introduces membership functions, define and give a relatively full operational description of fuzzy-logic neuron. Subsequent section two introduces ANN design principles and analysis from which a general wave neural network is derived. A full understanding of this chapter may be sufficient to design and analyse any artificial neural network system.

Keywords: Aggregation operator, Bell-shaped, Composite, Delta-function, Experience, Fuzzy-set, Fuzziness, Gaussian, Hessian, Lower bound, Lagrange, Membership grade, Operator, Peak, Relation, Stimuli, Support set, Upper bound.

A FUZZY NEURON

Just as a probability value may be assigned to a random variable, so also is a grade of membership μ assigned to a fuzzy variable. Assigning a grade of membership μ to a fuzzy variable [1] x is often based on prior knowledge regarding measured values of x. The prior knowledge may have been formulated into an equation known as *membership function*. Evaluation of a membership function for a variable x gives a *membership grade* μ for that variable. Membership function is to fuzzy logic what probability distribution is to probability theory. Some notable types of membership function are now presented.

Delta-function: The delta function may be used as a membership function, given a threshold y_0, as follows.

Let F denote a fuzzy variable Y, then

$$\mu_F(y) = \delta(y - y_0) \tag{1}$$

Pierre Lorrentz

Where y = general datum $y \in F$. This is subject to:

$$\delta(y-y_0)=\begin{cases}1; & \text{when } y=y_0\\ 0; \text{otherwise}\end{cases} \quad \textbf{(2)}$$

This is a point-evaluation that has no spread. Assuming the fuzzy set F consist of Y_i; $i = 1,2,...,n$ fuzzy variables $y = y_i(y_i \in Y_i)$; $i = 1,2,...n$ then

$$\mu_F(y)=\mu_{Y_i}(y)\delta(y-y_0) \quad \textbf{(3)}$$

$$Y_i \in (\bigcup_{i=1}^{n} Y_i)$$

where each $y = y_i$ is subject to the constraint equation (2).

Triangular Membership Function: Here we would employ the equation of a triangle as a membership function as follows.

$$\mu_F = 1-\frac{|y-y_0|}{s}; \text{ when } |y-y_0| \le s \quad \textbf{(4)}$$

Where y_0 is the peak of the triangle, and s is the base of the triangle. The s is commonly referred to as the *support set* of the membership function. The y is a general point on the triangle. Assuming the fuzzy set F consist of Y_i; $i = 1,2,...,n$ fuzzy variable $y_i \in Y$ then

$$\mu_F(y)=\mu_{Y_i}(y_0)\mu_{A_i}(y) \quad \textbf{(5)}$$

$$\mu_{A_i}(y)=\begin{cases}1-\frac{|y-y_0|}{s_i}; & \text{when } |y-y_0| \le s_i\\ 0 & \text{otherwise}\end{cases} \quad \textbf{(6)}$$

For any y_i, the parameter s may be chosen to give different level of fuzziness to the fuzzy value.

Gaussian function: we have come across Gaussian (normal) distribution function in previous sections. To derive a membership function from a Gaussian distribution, express the exponential part of the normal distribution as a membership function.

$$\mu_{A_i}(y) = \exp\left(\frac{y - y_0}{s_i}\right)^2 \quad (7)$$

The Gaussian membership function (7) is a bell-shaped membership function. The equation (5) also hold for composite Gaussian membership function as long as (7) is employed in equation (5).

There are other possible special-purpose membership functions. But it suffices to describe the common ones because they are the more frequently encountered.

The Fuzzy-logic Neuron

We assume that fuzzy variables interact *via* the minimum ($\wedge$) and the maximum ($\vee$) operator [2]. *Fuzzy relations* are functions defined on fuzzy operators. For example, *R* ;*R*2;*R*3;... may be defined as:

$$\mathrm{R}_1 = \vee_i \{X_{1(i)} \wedge Y_{(i)}\}; R_2 = \vee_i \{X_{2(i)} \wedge Y_{(i)}\}; R_3 = \vee_i \{X_{3(i)} \wedge Y_{(i)}\} \quad (8)$$

where $i = 1, 2, 3, \ldots$ and $n = 0, 1, 2, \ldots$

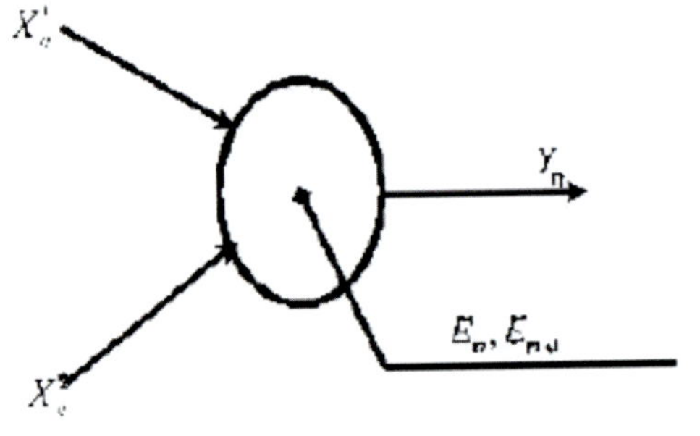

Fig. (1). A schematic of a dynamic fuzzy-logic neuron.

If E_n denote a past experience while E_{n+1} represents the next experience where n is a discrete time interval, then Fig. (**1**) shows that Y_n is the output and X_i is the input stimuli.

The behaviour of this neuron may be described as follows.

$$\begin{cases} E_{n+1} = E_n * R_1 \Delta X_n^1 * R_2 \Delta X_n^2 * R_3 \\ Y_n = X_n * R_4 \Delta X_n^1 * R_5 \Delta X_n^2 * R_6 \end{cases} \tag{9}$$

Initially when n = 0, E_1 may be calculated from (9) as given by equation (10).

$$E_1 = E_0 * R_1 \Delta X_0^1 * R_2 \Delta X_0^2 * R_3 \tag{10}$$

Then followed by E_2;

$$E_2 = E_1 * R_1 \Delta X_1^1 * R_2 \Delta X_1^2 * R_3 \tag{11}$$

Writing out in full,

$$E_2 = E_0 * R_1 * R_2 \Delta X_0^1 * R_2 * R_1 \Delta X_1^1 * R_2 \Delta X_0^2 * R_3 * R_1 \Delta X_1^2 * R_3 \tag{12}$$

Generally therefore,

$$E_n = E_0 * R_1^n \Delta \bigwedge_{i=0}^{n-1} X_i^1 * R_2 * R_1^{n-i-1} \Delta \bigwedge_{i=0}^{n-1} X_i^2 * R_3 * R_1^{n-i-1} \tag{13}$$

For an arbtrary k = n, the current experience of the fuzzy neuron may be given as:

$$E_k = E_0 * R_0^k \Delta \bigwedge_{i=1}^{k-1} X_1^1 * R_2 * R_1^{k-i-1} \Delta \bigwedge_{i=1}^{k-1} X_1^2 * R_3 * R_1^{n-i-1} \tag{14}$$

For an arbtrary k = n, the current output is

$$Y_k = E_0 * R_1^k * R_4 \Delta \left[\bigwedge_{i=1}^{k-1} \left[X_1^1 * R_2 * R_1^{k-i-1} * R_4 \right] \Delta X_k^1 * R_5 \right] \Delta \left[\bigwedge_{i=1}^{k-1} \left[X_1^2 * R_3 * R_1^{k-i-1} * R_4 \right] \Delta X_k^2 * R_6 \right] \tag{15}$$

where $k = 1,2,3,....$

There is a further chapter on fuzzy neural networks system, which employs a variant of this fuzzy neuron as building block.

PRINCIPLES OF ARTIFICIAL NEURAL NETWORK ANALYSIS AND DESIGN

This section contains fundamental principles which may govern ANN system design and analysis. Any ANN and Multi-expert system may be regarded as a special case of the generic and fundamental principle of this section, so also is part two this book. This may become apparent in due course.

Taylor's Theorem: Taylor's theorem is one of those important tool required in the design and analysis of neural network. The following is a version of the theorem limited to the third derivative, and d-by-d dimensions. Let Ω be a convex open set of $\mathbb{R}^d$ and let x* lie in its interior. Assume V(x):$\Omega \rightarrow \mathbb{R}^d$ is a function which is continuous on Ω and whose gradient g and Hessian H exist. Let $g^1 : \Omega \rightarrow \mathbb{R}^d$ denote the gradient of V and $g^2 = H : \Omega \rightarrow \mathbb{R}^d \times d$ denote the Hessian of V. Also suppose the third partial derivatives g^3 of V exists and is continuous. Let g^3 be:

$$g^3 = \frac{\partial^3}{\partial x_i \partial x_j \partial x_k}(q) \tag{16}$$

with respect to x_i, x_j, and x_k evaluated at $q \in \Omega$. Let $X = [x_1, x_2, \ldots z_d]$ and $X^* = [x^*_1, x^*_2, \ldots x^*_d]$. Then there exist a real-number $\Theta \in [0,1]$ such that for all $x \in \Omega$

$$V(x) = V(x^*) + g(x^*)^T (x - x^*) + \frac{(x - x^*) H(x^*)(x - x^*)}{2} + R_3 \tag{17}$$

where

$$R_3 = \frac{1}{6} \sum_{i=1}^{d} \sum_{j=1}^{d} \sum_{k=1}^{d} \frac{\partial^3 V(c)}{\partial x_i \partial x_j \partial x_k} (x_i - x_i^*)(x_j - x_j^*)(x_k - x_k^*) \tag{18}$$

$$\text{and } c = x^* + \theta(x - x^*) \tag{19}$$

It may happen in practice that one or more of g_1, g_2, g_3 evaluates to zero. As long as the equation V(x) and the corresponding R_3 satisfy either the small oh (*i.e.*; $R_3 = o(|x\text{-}x^*|3)$) or the big Oh (*i.e.*; $R_3 = O(|x - x^*|3)$), Taylor's theorem still hold.

Definition: Big "Oh" and Small "oh": Suppose that $h : \mathbb{R} \to \mathbb{R}$. There exist a finite non-negative number such that:

$$\frac{|h(x)|}{|x|} \le K;\ x \to 0 \tag{20}$$

Thus $R_3 = O(|x - x^*|3)$ in equation (18) above if g^3 is bounded. A special case exist when K = 0 – this is called the small "oh" (*i.e.*; $R_3 = o(|x\text{-}x^*|3)$). The h(x) is said to be a *big Oh function* when equation (20) above is satisfy. The *big Oh criteria* provide an *upper bound* for networks, functions and their resources. The same function or any function may be called Ω-function depending on the existence of an associated lower bound

Definition: A function h(x) is said to be Ω(|x|) if there exist a constant K and a number n_0 such that for all $n > n_0$;

$$|x|K \le h(x);\ \text{i.e.,}\ \frac{|x|}{|h(x)|} \le K;\ x \to 0 \tag{21}$$

The *Ω(|x|) criteria* (*i.e.*, equation (21)) provide a *lower bound* for networks, functions and their resources.

It may not often be possible to know the errors in a function or a network. But if it is known for sure that the network is stable or our function converges, then it is always possible to find K in equation (20), as this is most useful when the error cannot be calculated exactly. Fortunately, most networks and functions in nature (and also in this book) belong to the class of function or network whose errors converges *e.g.* the big "Oh" functions. There are many ways to estimate the errors R_i. One of the best method (if not the best) is *calculus of residue*. Another very good method is by estimating the remainder of the function after a sufficient number of accuracy has been achieved. *Lagrange remainder theorem* is an example of a remainder estimation method. *Lagrange remainder theorem* will be considered next.

Definition: Lagrange Semainder Theorem: Suppose that V has (n+1) continuous derivative on an open interval Ω containing 0. Let x ∈ Ω and $P_n(x)$ be the nth Taylor's polynomial for Ω. Then

$$R_{n+1}(x) = \frac{V^{n+1}(c)x^{n+1}}{(n+1)!} \quad \textbf{(22)}$$

where c is defined as in equation (22), and $V^{(n+1)}$ is the $(n+1)^{th}$ derivative of V.

Though *calculus of residue* is a superior method, *Lagrange formula, equation (22),* is more widely used because its accuracy satisfies many practical purposes; it is more resource-efficient, and more straightforward to calculate. It is usual to simply estimate $V^{(n+1)}$, $x^{(n+1)}$, and (n+1)! separately by any numerical method. Since $V^{(n+1)}$ exist and is continuous, $R_{n+1}(x)$ can always be found. A special circumstance is when $R_{n+1}(x)$ oscillate as $n \to \infty$, quite often in this case, the maximum value of $R_{n+1}(x)$ is taken from every value assumed by $R_{n+1}(x)$ and the experiment is stopped after a pre-defined number of cycle. It is noticeable that R3(.) of equation (18) is a special case of $R_{n+1}(x)$ (equation (22)). The V(x) of equation (17) may take many various form all of which may be written as a *hypergeometric function. Hypergeometric functions* express algebraic function of many variables and many dimensions. Two types of *hypergeometric functions* are *multinomial series* and *generalized factorial* introduced below

Definition: Multinomial Series: Let x be a small number less than 1, then

$$(1+a_1x+a_2x^2+\ldots+a_rx^r)^m = 1+\sum\frac{m(m-1)\ldots(m-\sum a_1+1)}{\alpha_1!\alpha_2!\ldots\alpha_r!}\alpha_1^{\alpha_1}\alpha_2^{\alpha_2}\ldots\alpha_r^{\alpha_r}x^n \quad \textbf{(23)}$$

The summation extends over all non-negative integral values of α_1, α_2, ...α_r such that

$$\alpha_1 + 2\alpha_2 + \ldots + r\alpha_r = n \quad \textbf{(24)}$$

Definition: Generalized Factorial: For any $a \in F$ and any non-negative integer n the *generalized factorial* is defined as:

$$(a)_n = \begin{vmatrix} 1;\ \text{if n} = 0 \\ a(a+1)(a+2)\ldots(a+n-1);\ \text{if n} = 1,2,\ldots \end{vmatrix} \quad \textbf{(25)}$$

Definition: Let p and q be non-negative integers. Let a_1, a_2,…, a_p; b_1, b_2,…, b_q be elements of F subject to the fact that n, $b_i + n \neq 0$ for all i;

$$F = \sum_{n=0}^{\infty} \frac{(a_1)_n (a_n)_n \ldots (a_p)_n}{(b_1)_n (b_2)_n \ldots (b_q)_n n!} x^n \quad \textbf{(26)}$$

is called a *generalized hypergeometric series*. Various special cases of equation (26) for one single variable have been introduced in probability section. Either equation (23) or (25) may be suitable both for the design and analysis of any system.

The O(|x|) and the Ω(|x|) criteria are sufficient to characterise any function or network. They also aid in estimating resource requirement. In attempting to measure the time required for a function to execute computationally, a *computational complexity theory* is introduced. This is because the O(|x|) and Ω (|x|) criteria is able to characterise most functions independent of the environment in which they execute. The *computational complexity theory (CCT)* considers the environment in which the network or function execute. In attempting to classify the level of difficulty of a network or function, the computational [3] complexity theory ascertains whether or not it is possible to solve a benchmark problem in a polynomial time. If a problem is un-solvable but a solution could be checked forvalidity if one is given, the computational complexity theory ascertain whether or not the solution provided is valid or not in a polynomial time. There are two main complexity classes; the **P**-class, and the **NP**-class

Definition: The **P**-class is the class of problem that can be *solved* in a polynomial time on a classical computer. The **NP**-class is the class of problem which have solutions that can be *checked* in a polynomial time on a classical computer.

The Wave Neural Networks

Consider a feed-forward kth layered $k = 0,1,...N-1$ neural network. The output of a neuron as a product and sum of the network is expressible as:

$$O_n = g\sum_{x_0} \cdots g_{N-1} \sum_{N-1} \prod_{K-1}^{N-1} w_{x_k x_{k-1}} v_{x_1 x_0}^{e} \tag{27}$$

The sum of product equation (27) is obtained from the multinomial series equation (23) by substituting the number of layers and other system parameters and expanding in sum of product.

The same procedure also applies to the generalized factorial equation (26). The neuron output O_n from equation (27) is a path through N layers in which the Kth vertex of a layer is at a neuron x_k in layer k given by:

$$O_n = g^N \prod_{K=1}^{N=1} w_{x_k x_{k-1}} \tag{28}$$

Neural network dynamics are dissipative [4] making it proper to employ the greedy variation of the Lagrangian formulation. The variable g_k represents the gain of the network at layer k. The product $\prod w_{x^k} w_{x^{k-1}}$ may be replaced by sum of exponent as follows.

$$g\prod w_{x_k x_{k-1}} \rightarrow \sum g \frac{\Delta x}{A} \exp\left(i w_{x_k x_{k-1}} \frac{(t_k - t_{k-1})}{h} \right) \tag{29}$$

Two time scales have been introduces. One $\frac{\Delta x}{A}$ is the gain gk function execution time, and the second $\frac{(t_k - t_{k-1})}{h}$ is the transportation time of signal from neurons of one layer to another. Substituting equation (29) into (27) gives equation (30).

$$O_n = \sum_{x_0} g \frac{\Delta x}{A} \ldots \sum_{x_{N-1}} g \frac{\Delta x}{A} \exp\left[i \sum_{K=1}^{N-1} w_{x_k x_{k-1}} \frac{(t_k - t_{k-1})}{h} \right] \quad \textbf{(30)}$$

Equation (30) is suitable for numerical integration but still may incur high computation overhead. In the limit as the network become denser we may replace equation (30) with a continuous version of the equation, that is, integral may replace the sums as follows:

$$O_n = \int_{-\infty}^{\infty} \ldots \int e^{(i/h)S} g \frac{\partial x_1}{A} \ldots g \frac{\partial x_{N-1}}{A} \quad \textbf{(31)}$$

$$\text{Where } S = \int_0^t w(\varepsilon) \partial \varepsilon \quad \textbf{(32)}$$

We take the limit in equation (30) as N→∞ to define a path integral [5, 6] with a functional measure μ_f (here μ_f = g/A). The path integral expresses information propagation in the neural network as given in equation (33).

$$O_n = \int_{path} e^{(i/h)S} \mu_f(\partial x) \quad \textbf{(33)}$$

Let a = (v_a,t_a) and b = (v_b,t_b) represent pairs of nodes in a neural network that connects, for h and a constant A(ε), define the kernel Γ(*b*,*a*) by means of an integral:

$$\Gamma(b,a) = \lim_{\varepsilon \to 0} \frac{1}{A} \int_{-\infty}^{\infty} \ldots \int_{-\infty}^{\infty} e^{(i/h)S[b,a]} \frac{dv_1}{A} \ldots \frac{dv_{N-1}}{A} \quad \textbf{(34)}$$

The mesh width $\varepsilon = \frac{v_a - v_b}{N}$ partitions the interval (v_a, v_b) uniformly into $v_1, v_2, \ldots v_{N-1}$. Also note that:

$$S[b,a] = \int L(\dot{v}, v)\, dt \quad \textbf{(35)}$$

Where $L(\dot{v}, v) = K(\dot{v}) - P(v)$ **(36)**

And $K(\dot{v}) =$ kinetic energy

$P(v)$ = potential energy

$\dot{v}$ = velocity term

So that equation (32) and (35) are equivalent by definition. Define a path integral on the kernel $\Gamma(b,a)$equation (34) with the functional measure μ_f(here $\mu_f = 1/A$)

(37)

as: $\Gamma(b, a) = \int_a^b e^{(i/\hbar)S} \mu_f(\partial v)$

Define a wave function $\Psi(v_2,t_2)$as:

(38)

$$\psi(v_2, t_2) = \int_{-\infty}^{\infty} \Gamma(v_2, t_2; v_1, t_1)\psi(v_1, t_1)dv_1$$

where the kernel $\Gamma(v_2,t_2;v_1,t_1)$ has the same property as that of (37) and the wave function has the probability amplitude given in equation (39).

(39)

$$\int_{-\infty}^{\infty} |\psi(v, 0)|^2 \, dv = 1$$

Equation (38) is the most general wave description of both biological and artificial neural network systems constraint on (39). From equation (38), both classical and quantum neural systems may be developed. We shall illustrate how a quantum neural network system may be developed from equation (38) constraint on (39) in other chapters.

CONFLICT OF INTEREST

The author confirm that this chapter contents have no conflict of interest.

ACKNOWLEDGEMENTS

Cited works are appreciated.

REFERENCES

[1] Karray FO, De Silva C. Soft computing and intelligent system design. Essex(England): Edinburgh Gate, Harlow, CM20 2JE: Pearson Educational Ltd. 2004.

[2] Gupta MM, Kiszka JB, Trojan GM. Multivariable structure of fuzzy control systems. IEEE Trans, SMC-16 No 5 1986.

[3] Hopfield JJ. Neural networks and physical systems with emergent collective computational abilities. Proc Natl Acad Sci USA 1982; 79(8): 2554-8.
[http://dx.doi.org/10.1073/pnas.79.8.2554] [PMID: 6953413]

[4] Mjolsness E, Miranker WL. A Lagrangian formulation of neural networks, Part I. Theory and analog dynamics; Part II. Clocked objective functions and applications. Neural Paral Sci Comp 1998; 6(8): 297-333. 334–372

[5] Feynman RP, Hibbs AR. Quantum mechanics and path integrals. New York: McGraw–Hill 1965.

[6] Dym H, McKean HP. Fourier series and integrals. New York: Academic Press 1972.

CHAPTER 4

Fundamental Algorithms and Methods

Abstract: An algorithm is a sequence of operations that is used to find a solution to a problem. The sequence of the operations are often well organised so that it may be representable as a flowchart or state-machine when possible. The first few sections of chapter 4 illustrate this by way of clustering algorithm and nature-inspired algorithms. Having laid the fundamental background of artificial neural networks (ANN) in previous chapters, in terms of definitions, theorems, and equations, it is now possible to organise one or more of these elements in such a way that it provide intelligent solution to some problems. The organisation of the elements has led to an attempt to give a formal definition of ANN in this chapter. Important and notable organisation of concepts and definitions may both help in reformulating problems as well as providing solution for them. The suitability of these solutions may be accessed by placing one or more performance metrics on the corresponding ANN as shown in the last section of this chapter. Such is the theme of this chapter.

Keywords: Allele, Chromosome, Covariance matrix, Cross-over, Deoxyribonucleic acid (DNA), Edges, Evolution, Fitness function, Flowchart, Genetic Algorithm (GA), Goodness-of-fit, Hypothesis testing, Mean-Square Error (MSE), Mutation, Nodes, Offspring, Principal Component Analysis (PCA), Ribonucleic acid (RNA), Selection, Walk.

INTRODUCTION

Chapter 4 begins with an introduction to density-based clustering algorithm.This is because density-based clustering algorithm is a clustering algorithm that may be developed from principle. The second section introduces evolution and nature-based algorithm like the genetic algorithm. The principle behind these algorithms lies in "survival-of-the-fittest" and "natural selection" from population genetics. A section on network method of analysis by using nodes and edges followed. Method of graphical analysis may be employed effectively to describe neural networks which are simple and completely tractable. Since it appears that sufficient introductions have been given in previous chapters, it is now adequate

Pierre Lorrentz

to formally define what an ANN system may be. So that the fifth section attempts to describe what intelligence may be and also formally define what an ANN system may be. Taking the definition of an ANN system for granted and designing an ANN system based on it, the performance of such an ANN system may be accessed as described in the last section of this chapter. Most sections of chapter three are completely introductory, and are meant to prepare the reader for subsequent chapters where they may be explained in detail and most definitely find use.

The methods of nodes and edges may find employment in explaining (away) most networks of other chapters *e.g.*; chapters 6, and 7. Most ANN systems are driven by their dynamics and so the definition of section four may apply to networks of chapter 6, 7, and 9 for example. Similarly, the performances of any ANN systems of subsequent chapters may be described by any of the concepts explained in the last section of chapter four.

Thus chapter 4 may have hopefully laid a fundamental background to ANN system design and analysis. And if not, it has nevertheless contributed, as one of the introductory chapters, to the principles on which lies the design and analysis of ANN systems in subsequent chapters.

DENSITY BASED ALGORITHMS: CLUSTERING ALGORITHMS

The concept of density modelling and mixtures of density modelling is hereby introduced. Density modelling is the usage of a probability density function (p.d.f.) in Bayes theorem [of chapter 2], this has very many implications and applications. If a p.d.f. is expressed as a linear combination of basis function in Bayes theorem, it is known as mixtures of density models or simply mixture models. In Bayes theorem, the unconditional probability $p(x)$, or the conditional probability $p(j|x)$, or both may be replaced by an equivalent expression which have been obtained from a given data. These equivalent expressions often represent a distribution over the given data. There are very many advantages derived from using a density model of given data, or a given problem in Bayes theorem as compared to any other alternatives. If in $p(x)p(j|x) = p(j)p(x|j)$, the $p(x)$ consist of M basis functions, then

$$p(x) = \sum_{j-1}^{M} p(j)p(x \mid j) \tag{1}$$

have introduced a mixture into Bayes theorem. The p(j) is known as the mixing coefficient. The p(j|x) is the density function. Since p(j) is the prior probability (a probability term), it follows that:

$$\sum_{j=1}^{M} p(j) = 1; \text{ and } 0 < p(j) \leq 1 \tag{2}$$

Recalling that by definition of a p.d.f.,

$$\int_{-\infty}^{\infty} p(x \mid j)dx = 1 \tag{3}$$

From Bayes theorem therefore;

$$p(j \mid x) = \frac{p(x \mid j)p(j)}{p(x)} = \frac{p(x \mid j)p(j)}{\sum_{j=1}^{M} p(x \mid j)p(j)} \tag{4}$$

One often seek p(x|j) from a given data, directly or indirectly. The next step is to ask what form of a density function does the given data satisfy, or what is the form of distribution over the data if any. This information may be obtained from the data by sampling and estimating both the mean μ and variance (or covariance) σ^2 of the data. The data mean μ and variance σ^2 are the main features of data, as the data can then be described by its distribution and its density function. A distribution or a density function is in turn described by its mean μ vector and its covariance σ^2 matrix. For a Gaussian distribution, there are three main density functions. Other possible density functions are mixture of these density functions in various degrees.

1. When the covariance matrix is a scalar multiple of identity matrix, then the density function is a "spherical" density function; *i.e.*,

$$\sigma^2 = \sigma_j^2 I \tag{5}$$

$$p(x \mid j) = \frac{1}{\left(2\pi\sigma_j^2\right)^{d/2}} \exp\left[-\sum_{i=1}^{d} \frac{\left\|\left(x_i - \mu_j\right)\right\|^2}{2\sigma_j^2}\right] \tag{6}$$

2. When a covariance matrix is obtained which is not simply a scalar multiple of the identity matrix but diagonal-dominant matrix, it is known as diagonal p.d.f. In this case, the equation (6) above becomes

$$p(x \mid j) = \frac{1}{\left(2\pi\Gamma_{i=1}^{d}\sigma_{ji}^2\right)^{d/2}} \exp\left[-\sum_{i=1}^{d} \frac{\left(x_i - mu_{ji}\right)^2}{2\sigma_{ji}^2}\right] \tag{7}$$

And

$$\sigma_j = \sum_i diag\left(\sigma_{j,1}, \sigma_{j,2} \ldots \sigma_{j,n}\right) \tag{8}$$

3. Otherwise, the covariance is a full (non-trivial) matrix and the p.d.f. is called a full Gaussian p.d.f. That is

$$p(x \mid j) = \frac{1}{\left(2\pi\right)^{d/2}\left\|\sigma^2\right\|^{1/2}} \exp\left[-\frac{1}{2}\left(x - \mu_j\right)^T \sigma^{-1}\left(x - \mu_j\right)\right] \tag{9}$$

$$\sigma = \sum_j \sum_i \sigma_{ji} \tag{10}$$

Most other p. d. f. occurring in nature can always be modelled by a mixture of one or more of the aforementioned density functions. For this reason, the Gaussian density function may be referred to as a universal approximator. For the same reason, the most widely used accurate error is the mean-squared-error (MSE), detail of which is given in subsequent section. The MSE underlies a popular algorithm called the Principal Component Analysis (PCA). Considering PCA on the basis of a corresponding density function enables a probabilistic density dependent mixture of PCA unit. It is referred to as mixture of component analysers by [1]. It corresponds to Probabilistic Principal Component Analysis (PPCA) [2]. Without a principled background offered by Gaussian density functions, a heuristic mixing of PCA may not be justified – it is often tedious in practice. A heuristic mixing of PCA is also not generative. It only follows that by the employment of any of these density functions in Bayes theorem to replace p(x|j), the underlining distribution can be modelled and thus PPCA is generative. Similarly, data representing most other distribution may be generated. For this reason, Gaussian mixture model is also known as a generative model.

Radial Basis Function (RBF) Network: The Gaussian distribution usually provides the Radial Basis Function of the RBF network. Structurally, the RBF network is an ANN which consist of input data layer, the RBF (Gaussian p.d.f) layer as hidden layer, and the output layer which is linear weighted sum of its input. The RBF network may be seen as a state-of-the-art full connected Artificial Neural Network System. More detail may be found in chapter 6.

NATURE-BASED ALGORITHMS

The nature-based intelligence refers to search-based and evolutionary-based intelligence in combination. Evolution gives account of life changes experienced by the offspring of a species due in part to the environment, food-source and the offspring themselves. The offspring inherits some characteristics of its parent to enhance its viability, coupled with his own intelligence and his adaptability to new surroundings. It is expected that some offspring may be fit for survival since it inherits the genes of its predecessor in addition to his positive adaptation to the new surroundings. Some offspring may go to extinction due to the inheritance of weak gene from its predecessor, and also due to their inability to be more adaptive to the new surroundings. Human thoughts conclude that these phenomena may be modelled for problem-solving techniques. The attempt at modelling the natural genetics and evolution give rise, therefore, to artificial nature-based algorithms known as evolutionary algorithms. Evolutionary algorithm comprises mappings from genetic processes (evolutionary process of DNA and RNA) within the organism, and also adaptation for survival. Evolutionary algorithms also include mappings from processes experienced by groups of the organism (species) across age-cycles (generations). The offspring of a species may increase its fitness or terminate after some generations (age-cycles) just like the corresponding algorithms may improve its fitness function or (prematurely) terminates after some cycles. The result of this mapping is loosely grouped as:

1. Genetic algorithm and programming
2. Evolutionary algorithm and programming
3. Natural behavioural algorithms.

The nature-based selection, searching, and mating of organisms have been partly successfully modelled and these models can be grouped loosely as above.

Evolutionary Algorithm and Programming

Nature-based algorithms represent a better method when problems are multi-objective or ill-defined. One of the reasons is because they are multi-point solution based. In a population, every individual is represented by a *chromosome.* Each chromosome is called *a gene* which has a value known as *allele.* An allele is a fitness value. The alleles of a chromosome are modified by a fitness function or an *objective function.* Before every fitness function evaluation, every chromosome is acted on by evolutionary operators. Evolutionary operators are:

1. Procreation: introduction of offspring
2. Mutation
3. Cross-over
4. Selection

A chromosome string is an encoded string on which the evolutionary operators and fitness functions act in alternation. A summary of the procedure assumed by an evolutionary algorithm in order to solve a problem is given below.

1. Chromosomes are encoded
2. Population initialized
3. Fitness function evaluation
4. Evolutionary operators
5. Generation of next population

These steps form a cycle of an evolutionary algorithm and genetic algorithms as shown in Fig. (**1**). The cycle of Fig. (**1**) repeats until a solution is found or the cycle repeats for a fixed number of times. The difference between evolutionary algorithm and genetic algorithm is that evolutionary algorithm does not use a crossover. On both methods, the mutation function is often a distribution (discussed in previous chapters) over the chromosomes. Many variants of evolutionary algorithm exist. Notable variants include evolutionary programming and evolutionary strategies. The difference between variants of evolutionary algorithms are mainly implementation differences, and of course mutation rate.

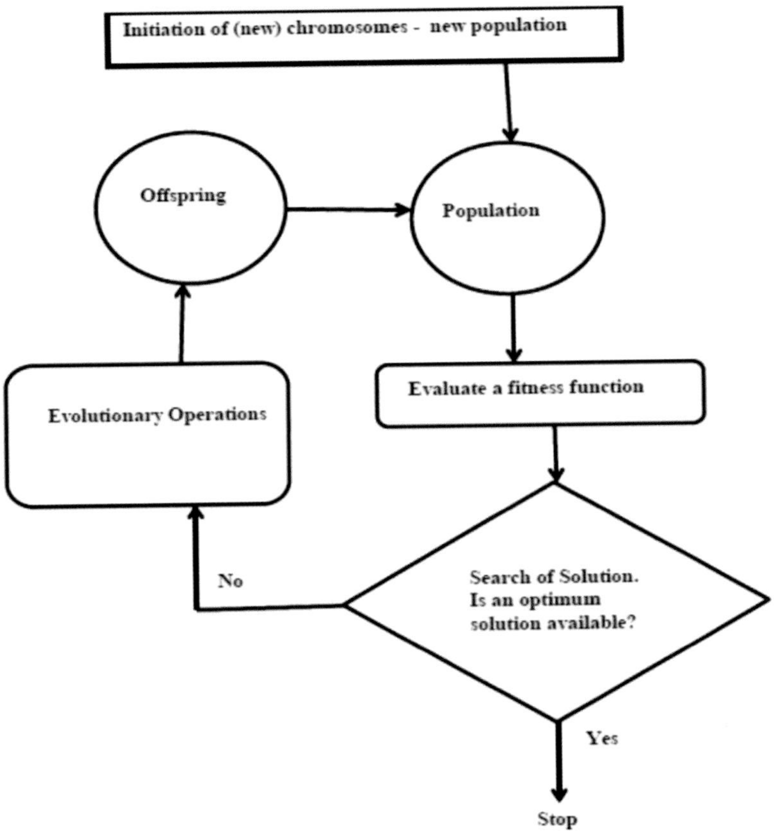

Fig. (1). Basic structure of evolutionary and genetic algorithms.

The GA is based, in principle, on biological evolution and "survival of the fittest" in solving an optimisation problem. The GA is said to evolve its solution by evaluation of functions given at some points that are chosen according to a distribution (see chapter 2), in the search space.

A random choice of points may serve to omit points of local optimum solution whereas in a derivative-based algorithm, a method of "climbing out" of a local optimum is required. However, the derivative-based algorithm does not suffer from premature death or extinction as does GA. Rather than evaluating a derivative, GA applies its operators to the populations of potential solution. Before explaining the genetic operators, there are two terminologies relevant to genetic algorithm which will be introduced now.

Genetic Algorithm

Genetic Algorithm (GA) is a multi-point stochastic search algorithm, using genetic and evolutionary modelling procedures, to reach a global optimum solution of a problem. It may not provide, however, an optimum solution or come very close to global optimum solution. The attractiveness of a GA is its simplicity, does not require derivatives, and is not resource intensive like many other alternatives.

Genotype: At initialization in GA, a set of potential solution are generated possibly by uniform distribution. A set of possible solution is referred to as a population, while a single solution out of this set is an individual. The term genotype describes the encoding of a potential solution represented by an individual. Since the encoding of a potential solution is a genotype, it is possible (as is often the case) for many individual in the population to posses the same genotype (*i.e.*; same solution code).

The genotype of an individual is also referred to as *chromosome*. The solution code (*i.e.*; the genotype) often exists as a string which, in turn, consists of elements called *gene*, the unit of genetic information. Each gene may assume more than one value.

A value assumed by a gene is called an *allele*. For example, when a genotype is a binary encoding, each gene has only two possible values "0" and "1". When a gene has "1" as a value, then the *allele* of that gene is 1.

Fitness Function: A fitness function is employed in the measurement of a performance, or goodness of a particular solution.When a fitness function is expressed as an optimisation problem, the objective function of the optimization problem is the fitness function. And a fitter individual gives a lower value of a minimization problem. The objective function accepts the genotype as input parameter, and return value(s) indicative of the fitness or performance of that solution string. Fitness functions are generally genotype dependent since input parameters and their relationship are encoded in the chromosome which expresses the genotype.

GA Operators

Schema theorem: The aim of a schema is to provide a template symbol for chromosome (population) generation. It states that if a chromosome is generated from a group of symbol (called an alphabet Ω) and some wildcard "*" (don't cares), then the corresponding schema comprises all those chromosomes whose symbols belong toΩU{ }. The type and number of schemata (plural of schema) that may be generated from an alphabet Ω and don't cares depend directly on the number of don't cares. For example, a schema with n number of don't cares will yield 2n chromosomes when coded in binary. It therefore follows that if the order of a schema is defined as the number of non-don't cares, then the smaller the order of a schema the larger the number of chromosome population generable from the schema. Furthermore, to characterise the compactness of a chromosome or the likelihood that any two genes may survive a crossover, the defining length (*i.e.*; the distance between the furthest two non-don't cares) is employed. Just as there are selection, mating, and mutation in evolution so are selection, crossover (in place of mating) and also mutation in the corresponding GA. These are known as GA operators.

Selection: To select fitter individuals, a distributive (*e.g.* using normal or uniform distribution) or stochastic function is applied to sample the population. Their fitness value (allele) determine if some chromosome move on to the next generation, while others with a lower fitness value (allele) die off. The actual number of individual that moves on to the next generation depends on the mechanism employed to select them; examples of the mechanism are elitism, and roulette wheel. The elitist model chooses the top fitter individuals while the roulette wheel method employs the probability assigned to the chromosomes.

Crossover: Crossover refers to the breaking of chromosomes of two parents, exchange of the genes, followed by recombination of genes to form a new chromosome of offspring. A random probability function is applied to select both the chromosomes required for crossover and the point along the chromosome where breaking and recombination is to occur. The outcome is an offspring consisting of the genotype that results from this recombination.

Mutation: Mutation describes changes in genetic constitution within a chromosome thereby resulting in a completely new genotype. In comparison with other operators, mutation produces a completely different and new offspring as a result of changes within the chromosome while crossover and selection result in a variant of an existing population of solutions. The mutation rate of chromosomes is mostly defined by a designer. The nature and position (in a chromosome) where mutation occur may follow a random distribution or be determined by the problem constraints.

APPLICATIONS OF GENETIC ALGORITHM

The architecture of a multi-layered perceptron (MLP) is normally pre-determined [3] before its application. The genetic algorithm (GA) may be applied in a *wrapper function* [4] to initialized the architecture of MLP, and to select optimal parameters and variables for the MLP as in [5, 6]. This method enables the MLP to learn incrementally and possess a dynamic architecture. The GA-MLP structure itself is an illustration of a hybrid multi-classifier.

NETWORK METHOD: EDGES AND NODES

A graph G comprises a finite set of points called nodes which include a prescribed set X of unordered pair of points (nodes). Note that the definition of a graph did not make mention of a line. In graphs, a line is defined as a pair of distinct nodes. Specifically, a line l is defined with respect to two distinct nodes "c" and "r" as l = [c, r]. The line l and node c are said to be *incident*, and the two nodes c and r are *adjacent*. Also note that a graph does not include any curve or loop. If a line joins a node with itself, it is *a loop*. When two or more lines join two nodes the lines (without direction indication) are said to be *parallel*. If a graph contains one or more parallel lines, it is called *a multi-graph*. In addition, if a graph contains one or more loop(s), it is known as a *general graph*. A subset of the general graph is a *directed graph*. A *directed graph* (also known as *digraph*) is defined as a finite collection of nodes and a prescribed collection of ordered pairs of nodes. Each such ordered pair of nodes [c, r] is known as a directed line $\vec{l} = \overrightarrow{[c, r]}$; the arrow indicating a direction.

Two graphs are said to be *isomorphic* if there exist a one-to-one map of nodes of one graph to nodes of the second graph, and the mapping preserves adjacency. The isomorphism condition applies both to a general graph and to a digraph. It should be of note that the word "graph" may be interchanged with "network" without ambiguity. Graphs form the structural basis of neural networks from which the name is derived. Though graphical methods may no longer be in use, it is nevertheless interesting as one of the earliest method of network design and analysis. It is a direct method of design and analysis but become intractable when problem dimensions exceed three. Also a slight change in design structure may prompt a re-analysis of the whole system. Graphs form the basis of stochastic network and may solve combinatorial problems. Two illustrations are given.

Taking a Walk: A walk is a sequence of nodes and lines in alternation, each line is incident on a node immediately before and after it, such that the walk starts and ends on (distinct) nodes. For example, a walk of c_0, r_1, c_1, …, c_n joins c_0 to c_n. The *length* of a walk is taken as the number of lines in it. A *trajectory* is a walk in which all lines are distinct while a *path* is a walk in which all nodes are distinct. A walk is said to be an *open walk* when the last node does not coincide with the first node, but when they coincide, it is a *closed walk*. A *cycle* is a closed walk that consist of distinct nodes, for which the first and the last nodes coincide. A graph is connected if each and every pair of nodes is joined by a trajectory. A *tree* is a connected graph which has no cycle. The *degree* of a node is number of lines incident on it. The sequence of the number of lines incident on a node (*i.e.*; sequence of degree) is called the partition of a graph. Now it is possible to take a random walk on a graph.

Assume a function f_i to be evaluated at every node, a *random walk* is a sequence [i, f_i]; i = 0, 1, 2.... of the number i of node visited and the function *fi* value at that node. The function f_i may be a distant function, a probability (density) function, or any function of interest. Random walk is a background to Markov chains and is also a background to many other interesting fields such as Poisson process, and other stochastic processes.

Grey Code: Graphical method defines an i-cube as a graph of 2^i (i = 0, 1, 2, ..., n) nodes, each of which is a binary sequence of i digits. In the i-cube, two nodes are adjacent only if they differ exactly in one digit. For example; a 2-cube gives $2^2 = 4$ nodes; a 3-cube gives $2^3 = 8$ nodes; *etc.*

Now let a line join two nodes that differ only in one digit; the Fig. (**2**) above is a typical result. Figs. (**3a**) and (**3b**) are grey codes. A grey code is a binary code in which a number differs from an adjacent number only in one digit. In form of the Fig. (**3**), a grey code is easily written as a state machine in which each node corresponds to a state, and the lines specify conditions on the state, input, and output. Grey code is a useful component often in sequential machines, pseudo-random number generator, and others.

MULTI-LAYERED PERCEPTRON

An MLP is represented by three types of layers. These are input layers, the hidden layers, and the output layers; the quantity of each layer in architecture is either data or designer dependent. All layers consist of nodes as active components. The units of active components at any node are the neuron. Many variants of neurons have been introduced in previous chapters, and all may be employed in MLP.

A default standard MLP may consist of one layer of input nodes, one layer of hidden nodes, and one layer of output nodes. When speed is preferred over accuracy, the hidden layer may be removed and input nodes become connected to output nodes linearly – the resulting network is normally much less accurate, and much faster, and termed Hybrid MLP. Such a case may be envisaged if in Fig. (**3a**) the nodes (00) and (01) are input nodes; the node (10) and (11) are output nodes. Then place full connections between the two layers. Another simple examples is from Fig. (**3b**); any face of the cube may act as an input layer, and the opposite may face act as the corresponding output layer, then followed by full connection between the layers without any hidden layer. This is the simplest possible MLP configuration.

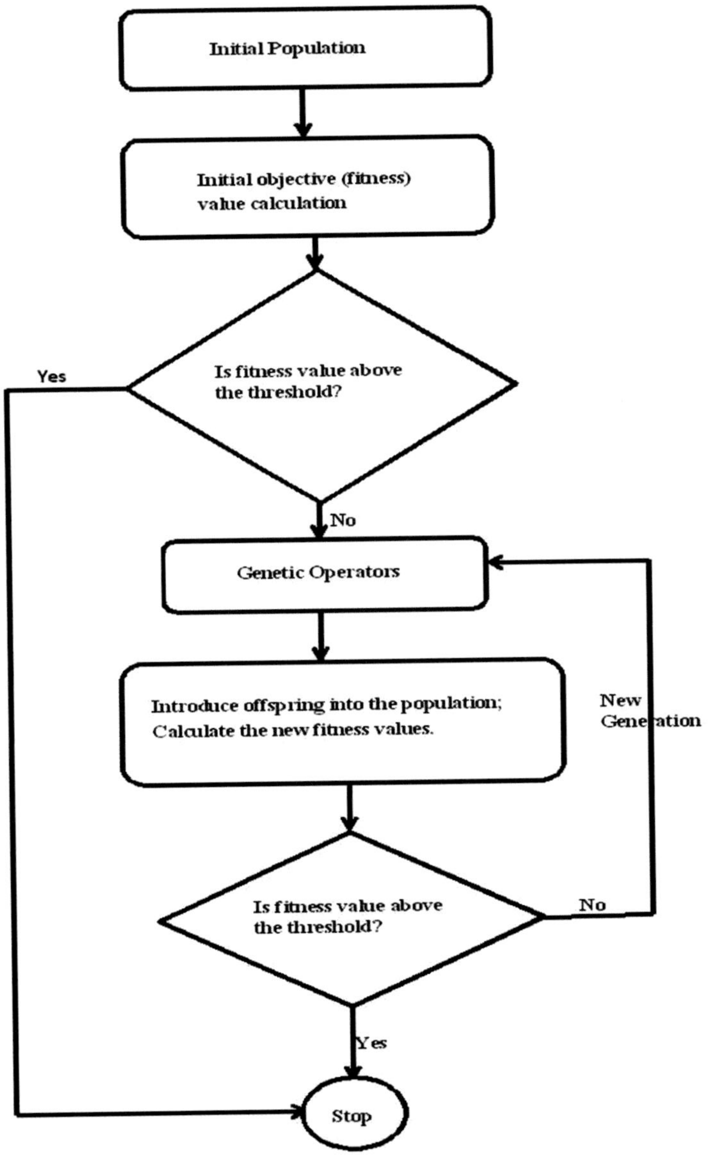

Fig. (2). Schematic of Genetic Algorithm (GA).

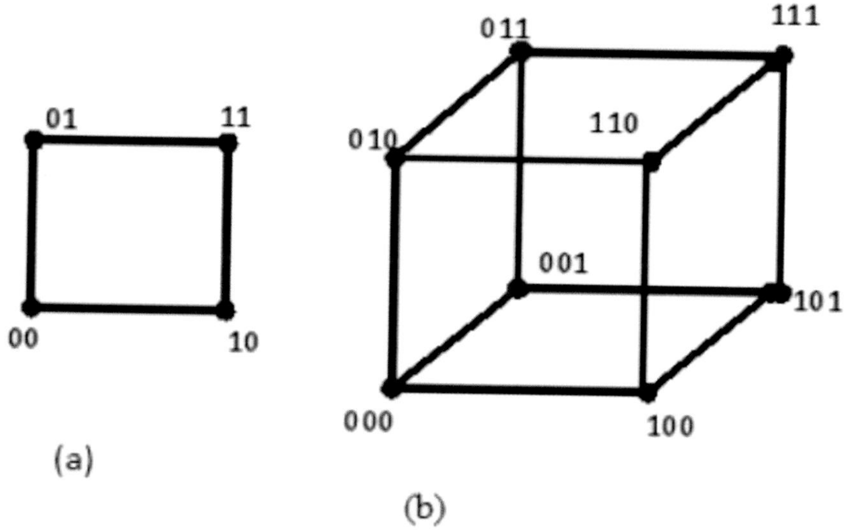

Fig. (3). The Schematics of common graphical networks.

REAL-TIME APPLICATIONS OF STATE-OF-THE-ART ANN SYSTEMS

In this section, state-of-the-art neural networks are presented in application. They may be used in conjunction with Genetic Algorithm (GA) in real-time applications. These applications are as follows.

1. In [7] Multi-Layered Perceptron (MLP) in employed in load forecasting for an Energy Power Station. The MLP is architecturally initialized and trained with either genetic algorithm or particle swarm optimisation (PSO) algorithm.Both MLP-GA and MLP-PSO are much faster than MLP trained using back-propagation algorithm which may not cope well with real-time load-forecasting.
2. The feed-forward and back-propagation learning algorithm of MLP is made linear in [8] and termed Hybrid (HMLP). Because linear MLP is much faster than higher order MLP, it is more suitable for real-time applications. Hybrid MLP is employed in [8] to design an adaptive Neuro-Controller for Dynamic Systems. The system parameters are initialized and adjusted by Recursive Least-Square (RLS) (chapter 6). The update of the controller parameters is recursive and often in order of milli-seconds in real-time. These make the adaptive neuro-controller based HMLP to function automatically, in real-time,

and response time is below milli-second.

3. The hierarchical genetic algorithm (HGA) is a special type of GA with the capability of initializing and adapting the structure of neural networks, and also adapting the system parameters of the ANN concerned. In [9], the HGA is applied to Radial Basis Function (RBF) network. The HGA employed in [9] is implemented as in [10, 11] to initialize and maintain both the structure and parameters of RBF. The RBF is used to model the lectrohydraulic system of a mine-sweeping plough. The detection of mines is immediately followed by the digging up of the mines by the same machine in this case. The RBF in the Hydraulic may not lag behind and should also not cause any lag – it should operate in real-time. Additional advantage of HGA over other alternative is that it enables self-growing and/or self-pruning of the HGA- RBF system.

DEFINITION OF ARTIFICIAL NEURAL NETWORKS (ANN)

Having had some familiarisation with neurons and ANN systems, this section describe, in general terms, what artificial neural network may be. Since the aim of ANN is to model intelligence, the discussion begins with what is described as intelligence.

Intelligence

Intelligent systems have a high propensity to acquire and apply knowledge. Intelligent systems also have the capability of perception, reasoning, learning, and making decisions based on incomplete information. They are able to correct and cope with disturbances and unexpected variations within the system and also around them. An intelligent system may achieve adaptability through (rapid) reconfiguration, partly of its parameters, partly of its structure, and also has the ability to change its environment. To varying extent, these are characteristics desirable from systems discussed in the book. To possess these characteristics, an ANN system must be capable of analysing and modelling information as part of its cognitive ability. Partly because intelligence is an ethic and complicated concept, a precise definition does not and may not exist. But there are some consensus on attributes of knowledge acquisition, making logical inferences, learning, processing incomplete and qualitative information, and uncertainties.

These attributes, plus intelligent reactions may only be characterized by outward behaviour since it enables and enhances adaptation to environment. Though a specific definition of intelligence may not be agreed upon, some characteristics exhibited by an intelligent system includes one or more of the following;

1. Perception
2. Pattern recognition
3. Learning and knowledge gained
4. Inferences from qualitative, estimated, and/or incomplete data (information)
5. Inference from knowledge and experience
6. Capability to adjust to abrupt or unfamiliar environment where possible.
7. Inductive reasoning

It is expected that most systems presented in this book have one or more of these characteristics. Putting ANN into the picture of intelligence, an ANN is presented with structured information, the ANN perceive and "study" this structured information to acquire knowledge – this is known as *learning*. Several instances of learning make the ANN an expert system in the area of that information which it has studied. The ANN is now said to have *specialized* in one area of profession.When the same ANN is presented with similar but a priori unseen data (information), the ANN should be capable of taking an expert decision – this is called *generalization*. Since the ANN is now an expert, it is expected of it to be capable of solving any problem in its area of expertise. The ANN is also capable of adaptation to changes in its environment and its profession by reconfiguration and parameter variation. Changes in its environment and its parameters (profession) are indicated by superscript "*" in equations (11) to (13).

An Artificial Neural Network (ANN) system

Basically, any system or device that is capable of experience, recollection, remembrance, and exhibit more than one characteristics of intelligence may be referred to as an ANN system. Artificial neural networks are sometimes called neural networks, connectionist system, neurocomputers, expert system, or parallel distribution processing (PDP) models.

Clinical and medical analyses of brain have revealed that it is a collective functioning of the neurons in the brain that is responsible for intelligent characteristics and not an individual neuron in isolation. Similarly, one should not expect much from a single component of an ANN system. As the outward characteristics living beings are termed intelligent, likewise are the outward characteristics of an ANN system termed intelligent when they are. ANN design often seeks to model the intelligent characteristics of a living object of interest. So that, structurally, an ANN system may, in general, be represented by a network graphs. In this graph, *the nodes represent the neurons while the lines represent connections (which may act as information channels, and/or weights*). Most processing activities occur in neurons which may be arranged in layers. Functionally, an ANN system may be described and analysed by graphs (see section entitled "Network Method" of this chapter) or as a dynamic system whereby an optimisation of a certain multi-parameter-valued function must be solved. The multi-parameter-valued function may also be multi-dimensional.

Modern day researches prefer the optimisation method because it is essentially independent of the structure. Hidden behind most of these optimisation methods are one or more distribution (density) functions so that knowing more about these distributions, as presented in other parts of this book, have two-fold advantages;

- The ANN system becomes much more tractable and easier to understand, describe, and analyse.
- It is possible to generate data structure typical to the expertise of an ANN system.

For these reasons, the book assumes mainly the stochastic dynamic system as ANN systems' functional description, while still assuming, tructurally, the network mode of description. An ANN system is often formally described first structurally, and then functionally, because this facilitates easier understanding. Most ANN system described in the book may follow the same method of description. Details of these two modes of description will follow.

An ANN Structure: A general description of an ANN system structure is given.An ANN system is divided into three main layers, the input layer, the hidden layer, and the output layer. Sometimes, hidden layer may be absent. Each layer consists of neurons which accept data from its external environment. When the input layer accepts input data and feedback data (which may consist of environmental information) the ANN is said to be a *recurrent network* as (shown in Fig. **4**). If the input layer accepts only data, is a *feedforward network*. In an ANN network, a neuron is connected to all other neurons in a subsequent layer but may not be connected to neurons in the same layer. A bias may also exist on the output layer.

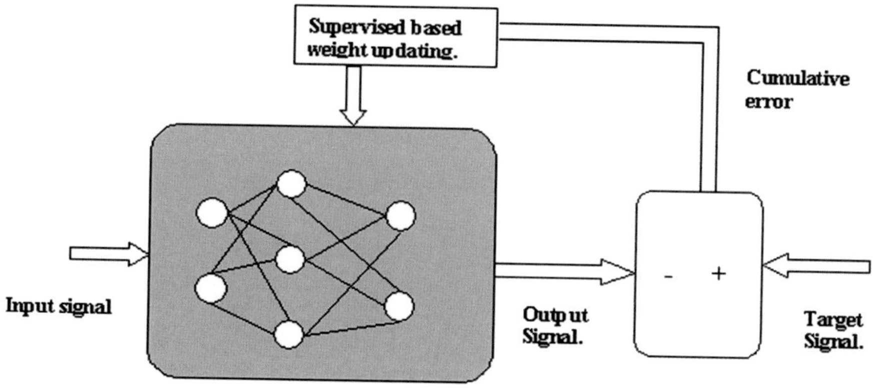

Fig. (4). A schematic of supervised learning rule.

The main functional unit of an ANN is the *neuron*. Apart from a specific learning and recognition algorithm which often varies, an *activation function* always applies to computation results at every neuron.

The activation function determines the weight connection of a neuron to the neurons of the next layer. A neuron is activated when it receive a weight greater than a pre-set threshold value. Depending on the problem and the type of ANN system employed, the computation at the input and output neurons may be the same or different from that which occur at the hidden layer. For a simple ANN system, it is possible to follow a network of neurons (nodes) and weights (lines), and analyse the system completely based on the graph. As the variables' dimension exceed three or the variables exceed two, the network (graphical) method of design and analysis become less tractable and tedious.

Functional ANN System Description: A state-and-space description of an ANN system is hereby given. A given problem is formulated for optimization. The variables are identified. The formulated optimization problem becomes part of (initial) input to the ANN system. The ANN system on the other hand is described by its learning and (subsequent) recognition algorithms. A supervised learning algorithm includes feedbacks from the environment and its output, as part of the input. An unsupervised learning algorithm attempts to discover patterns and features of its input without a feedback. One is interested in the behaviour of the ANN system over the learning and recognition cycles, and the role played by the activation function. The pattern of activation over time at a single neuron is called the system's state vector in a high-dimensional state-space. A unique activation pattern is a point in an activation state space that specifies the evolution of activation over time at that point. The activation pattern determines the tractability of the variables and so influences the behaviour of the ANN system. An intelligent ANN system (see Fig. **5**) may in general be defined as a dynamic system [12], that is:

<u>Definition: An Intelligent ANN System:</u> Let

$\Omega_s \subseteq \mathbb{R}^k$ be a set of input stimuli;

$\Omega_H \subseteq \mathbb{R}^m$ be a set hidden neuron memory;

$\Omega_R \subseteq \mathbb{R}^n$ be a set of output response;

$\Omega_O \subseteq \mathbb{R}^l$ be a set of feedbacks;

$W \subseteq \mathbb{R}^q$ be a set of weights (connection strenght);

$T \subseteq \mathbb{R}$ be a set of time indices ;

E_s the spatial environment with respect to Ω_s and T;

E_O the spatial environment with respect to Ω_O and T.

An intelligent ANN system is a system defined by the map Ø given by the dynamic equation (11):

$$\Psi : \Omega * T * T * E \rightarrow \Omega^* \qquad \textbf{(11)}$$

Superscripted "*" refers to new parameters, and the set of system states are given by vector equation (12):

$$\Omega = W * \Omega_H * \Omega_R;\ \Omega^* = W^* * \Omega_H^* * \Omega_R^* \tag{12}$$

And the environmental vectors E given by:

$$E = E_s * E_O;\ E^* = E_s^* * E_O^* \tag{13}$$

<u>Definition: A Stochastic Nonlinear System:</u> An intelligent ANN system that satisfies equations (11) to (13) and in addition updates its activation pattern in accordance to Bayes rule may be referred to as *stochastic nonlinear dynamic system.*

Formulating a given problem as optimization problem, and an intelligent ANN system as a dynamic system, has several advantages over other alternatives. These include;

1. Design and analysis of ANN is relatively independent of its network structure.

2. Error bounds are easier to estimate, on which resource utilisation may depend.

3. Dimension in excess of three and variables in excess of three are easily tractable.

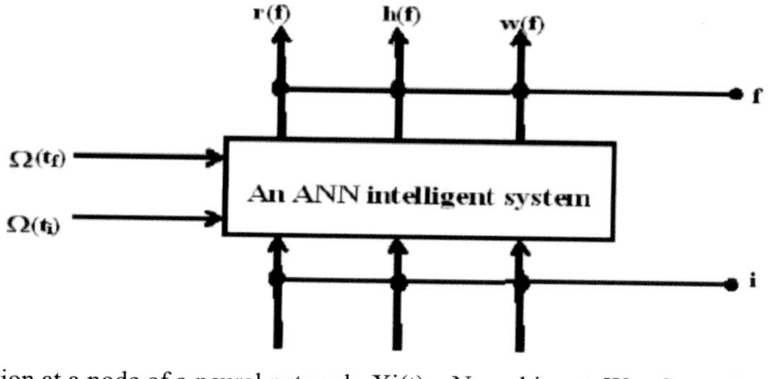

Fig. (5). The operation at a node of a neural network. Xi(t) – Neural input; W_i – Synaptic weights; i – 1,2,3.... y(t) = Nodal output.

PERFORMANCE MEASURES

Receiver's Operating Characteristics (ROC)

ROC originates from statistical decision theory. It is a tool used to evaluate discriminate effects among various methods. To plot ROC, it is ecessary first to obtain sensitivity and specificity values from data under consideration and transform (normalize) them into the same equal interval. To obtain sensitivity and specificity values, the following measurements are made:

1. True Positive (TP): Divide the number of TP in a sample by the sample size.
2. False Positive (FP): Divide the number of FP in a sample by the sample size.
3. False Negative (FN): Divide the number of FN in a sample by the sample size.
4. True Negative (TN): Divide the number of TN in a sample by the sample size.

Then, sensitivity (SE):

$$SE = \frac{TP}{TP + FN} = \frac{TP}{P} \quad \textbf{(14)}$$

Specificity (SP):

$$SP = \frac{TN}{FP + TN} = \frac{TN}{P'} \quad \textbf{(15)}$$

$$P' = (1 - P) \quad \textbf{(16)}$$

Some other parameters are defined and obtained from these measurements. To obtain standard error rate Serr(x) from the measurements, the calculation below is executed.

$$Serr(X) = \sqrt{\frac{X(1-X)}{N_0}} \quad \textbf{(17)}$$

where N_o is the population size and X is the measured variable. For example;

$$Serr(SE) = \left[\frac{SE(1-SE)}{N_0 P} \right]^{\frac{1}{2}} \quad (18)$$

$$Serr(SP) = \left[\frac{SP(1-SP)}{N_0 (1-P)} \right]^{\frac{1}{2}} \quad (19)$$

It is usual to suspect certain characteristics of a data, then process the data and perform tests on the data to check whether those characteristics are true. If p_i is the estimated probability of the presence of certain variable's characteristics X, and q_i is a test result to confirm the presence of that variable characteristics, then the mean of p_i (usually obtained from various experiments) is called prevalence pr; that is pr = mean (p_i). Similarly, the mean of q_i is called the level of test Q_l; that is Q_l = mean(q_i). It might be interesting to know if a certain test is fair, good, or not with respect to pre-set purposes and objectives. The chi-squared (see example 6 of chapter 2) test is used to compute test statistics and compare it to pre-set values (objectives and purposes). The chi-squared x^2 statistics is obtained as follows:

$$\chi^2 = N_0 \kappa(1,0) \kappa(0,0) \quad (20)$$

where N_o is as defined before, and are quality indices of the test.

$$\kappa(1,0) = \frac{SE(1-Q_l)}{Q_l^{'}} \quad (21)$$

$$\kappa(0,0) = \frac{SP - Q_l^{'}}{Q_l} \quad (22)$$

A ROC may have the sensitivity versus specificity plotted. The plot represents a graphical (chart) display of the system's performances. If several tests have been performed on data, the ROC curve can be used to compare their performances since the tests results have the same scale now. The area under the ROC measures the performances; the bigger the area the better the performances. A more detailed treatment of ROC may be found in specialized texts.

Hypothesis Testing

In case of replacing an existing ANN system with a new one, it might be interesting to know if the new system (device and/or procedure) brings certain specified improvements over the existing ANN system. The statistical test of hypothesis is a method used in this case. The hypothesis is whether the upcoming system is better than the present system or worse. The upcoming system may or may not be an ANN system. The hypothesis of the upcoming system being the same as the present system is known as a null hypothesis H_0 or simple hypothesis. A hypothesis of whether the upcoming system is different from the present system is called composite or alternate hypothesis H_1. Since the decision is to choose between two independent systems, it is governed by binomial distribution. An operational method is required between the two systems in order to decide which is better, or if they are the same. One of the most useful criteria is by counting the faults committed by the two systems at equal time interval. Now that there are three parameters to consider, namely two systems and time, the operational decision-making strategy may be modelled by Poisson distribution. In adopting the probability of faults made at equal time interval by the two systems, the decision made is prone to two types of errors:

Type-I Error: If the faults committed by upcoming system are statistically higher than the present system, but as a result of insufficient tests or otherwise, conclude that the faults committed by the upcoming system is lower than that of the present system, and adopt the upcoming system; it is called type-I error.

Type-II Error: If the faults committed by upcoming system are statistically lower than the present system, but as a result of insufficient tests or otherwise, conclude that the faults committed by the upcoming system is higher than that of the present system, and refuse to adopt the upcoming system; it is called type-II error.

Based on operational rule of accepting or not accepting the new system, these two types of errors can be calculated. Specifically, if p_0 = probability of the present system; p_I = estimated probability of the adopted system under type-I error; p_{II} = estimated probability of the adopted system under type-II error, then the two types of errors may be calculated. These probability values are obtainable if the two systems are in operation such that their faults may be measured. Note that the word "fault" is used with respect to the systems whereas the word "error" is used to qualify the human experts' error in making a decision. The human experts are now able to calculate their errors at a certain significant level. Specifically, the experts' error $>\alpha$, is calculated based on the faults of the systems and called significant level of the test; it is given by

$$\alpha_1 = p(p_I < p_0; p_0 = x_1) = \sum_{y=0}^{m} \binom{n}{y} x_1^y (1-x_1)^{n-y} \tag{23}$$

where n = number of products tested for faults; y = possible number of faults; x = probability of H_0; m = maximum number of possible faults. For the error to be accurately modelled by binomial distribution, n must be sufficiently large. For n sufficiently large, the distribution is also approximately modelled by Poisson distribution. The approximate equivalence follows because the two systems operate normally at equal time interval. The approximate equivalent Poisson distribution is given by:

$$\alpha_1 \approx \sum_{y=0}^{m} \frac{(nx)^y e^{-(nx)}}{y!} \tag{24}$$

Equations (23) and (24) are for the type-I error estimate. The equations for type-II error estimates is:

$$\alpha_2 = (p_{II} > p_0; p_0 = x_2) = \sum_{y=m}^{n} \binom{n}{y} x_2^y (1-x_2)^{n-y} \tag{25}$$

Note that the values x_2 may not equal x_1. The α_2 may similarly be approximated by Poisson distribution;

$$\alpha_2 \approx 1 - \sum_{y=0}^{m} \frac{(nx_2)^y e^{-(nx_2)}}{y!} \tag{26}$$

Hypothesis testing may be used to achieve an independent (independent of ANNs' error rate) comparison of a neural system with any other system which may be neural or not. There is a more general and frequently used testing procedure based on success of H_0: p = p_0 against other alternatives. The procedure adopts a normal distribution $N(p_0, \frac{p_0(1-p_0)}{n})$ of n independent Bernoulli trials that have approximately a probability of (*Y/n*) when n is large. The hypothesis considers the test of H_0: p = p_0 against H_1: p > p_0 (type-I error). The H_0 hypothesis is not accepted, and H_1 hypothesis accepted if and only if

(27)

$$z = \frac{\left(Y/n\right) - p_0}{\sqrt{p_0(1-p_0)/n}} \geq z_\alpha: \text{ for } H_1$$

That is H_0 hypothesis is not accepted, and H_1 hypothesis accepted if Y/n exceeds p_0 by *zα* standard deviation of Y/n. But for H_0 hypothesis accepted, and H_1 hypothesis not accepted H_0: p = p_0, the z is N(1,0) at significant α -level of test. If on the other hand Y/n is smaller than p_0 by *zα* standard deviation of Y/n, then the alternative hypothesis is $H_1 : p < p_0$ tested at α -level given by $z \leq z_\alpha$ (see equations above). The tests just illustrated are one-sided tests. A two-sided test occurs when testing $H_0 : p = p_0$ against $H_0 : p \neq p_0$. In a type-I error, the $H_0 : p = p_0$ hypothesis is rejected at a significant α -level of test and $H_0 : pp_0$ is accepted if and only if

(28)

$$|z| = \frac{\left|\left(Y/n\right) - p_0\right|}{\sqrt{p_0(1-p_0)/n}} \geq z_{\alpha/2}$$

The rejection region for H_0 is known as the *critical region* of the test. Rather than using normal distribution and its variance $(Y/n)^2$, if the mean μ is employed instead, the testing would be the null hypothesis H_0 :μ = μ_0 against H_0 :μ > μ0 and/or H_1 :μ ≤ μ_0 as one-sided alternative tests. The two-sided alternative is H_1 :μ ≠ μ_0 . An observed sample mean $\overline{X}$, close to μ, thereby supporting H_0, is usually measured in terms of standard deviation of $\overline{X}$; that is $Var(\overline{X}) = \sigma/\sqrt{n}$ and called *standard error of the mean*. The test statistics in terms of standard error of the mean then is defined by:

$$z = \frac{\overline{X} - \mu_0}{\left[\sigma^2/n\right]^{\frac{1}{2}}} = \frac{\overline{X} - \mu_0}{\sigma/\sqrt{n}} \tag{29}$$

The critical region at significant α -level for the three respective alternative hypotheses are (1) $z \geq z_\alpha$; (2) $z \leq -z_\alpha$; (3) $|z| \geq z_{\alpha/2}$. In terms of sample mean $\overline{x}$ these three regions may be expressed as

(1) $\overline{x} \geq \mu_0 + z_\alpha\left(\frac{\sigma}{\sqrt{n}}\right)$; (2) $\overline{x} \leq \mu_0 - z_\alpha\left(\frac{\sigma}{\sqrt{n}}\right)$; and (3) $\left|\overline{x} - \mu_0\right| \geq z_{\alpha/2}\left(\frac{\sigma}{\sqrt{n}}\right)$.

If the assumption of normal distribution N(0,1) is dropped and assumption of a general Gaussian distribution $N(\mu,\sigma^2)$ is adopted, the standard deviation σ should be replaced by sample standard deviation s; this is called a *t-test*, and the t is defined by:

$$t = \frac{\overline{x} - \mu}{\left(s^2/n\right)^{\frac{1}{2}}} = \frac{\overline{x} - \mu}{s/\sqrt{n}} \tag{30}$$

The main differences between an H-test and a t-test are:

a. A t-test is a more relevant test on experiments performed and results obtained as compared to H-test.
b. The replacement of $[\sigma^2/n]^{1/2}$ by an unbiased estimate $(s^2/n)^{1/2}$.
c. As pertain to critical region, the following equation (31) is employed; for two-sided t-tests.

$$|t| = \frac{\left|\overline{x} - \mu_0\right|}{s/\sqrt{n}} \geq t_{\alpha/2}(n-1) \tag{31}$$

Chi-squared (Goodness-of-fit) Test

The chi-squared test extends hypothesis testing by using the z^2 to test the suitability of various probability models. The z^2 is defined by:

$$z = \frac{Y/_n - p}{\sqrt{p(1-p)/_n}} = \left[\frac{Y/_n - p}{p(1-p)/_n}\right]\left(\frac{n}{n}\right) \quad \textbf{(32)}$$

$$z = \frac{Y - np}{n\sqrt{p(1-p)/_n}} = \frac{Y - np}{(np(1-p))^{\frac{1}{2}}} \quad \textbf{(33)}$$

$$z = \frac{Y - np}{(np(1-p))^{\frac{1}{2}}} \quad \textbf{(34)}$$

$$z^2 = \frac{(Y - np)^2}{np(1-p)} = Q_1 \quad \textbf{(35)}$$

The distribution of z^2 is chi-squared x^2 (1) with one degree of freedom. If $Y_2 = nY$ and $P_2 = 1\text{-}P$ then the z^2 may be re-written as:

$$Q_1 = \frac{(Y - np)^2}{np} + \frac{(Y_2 - np_2)^2}{np_2} = z^2 \quad \textbf{(36)}$$

If the systems tested are more than two, say k, then

$$Q_{k-1} = \sum_{i=1}^{k} \frac{(Y_i - np_i)^2}{np_i} \quad \textbf{(37)}$$

We may now show that Q_{k-1} is approximately $X^2(k\text{-}1)$ and use it to test the suitability of various probability models. Since the systems under consideration are independent of one another, then sampling from their data, and experiments on sampled data are independent. They are also mutually exclusive, and exhaustive. The joint probability may be omitted and Q_i of equation (36) becomes a suitable test subject. Let the experiment have k mutually exclusive and exhaustive outcome A_1, A_2… A_k when k systems are tested. The test of whether $p_i = p(A_i)$ is equal to a known probability value p_{i0}; i = 1,2, ..., k is formulated as $H_0 : p_i = p_{i0}$; i = 1, 2, ..., k. To test this H_0 hypothesis, n-times experiments are performed on each i system to obtain $p_i = p(A_i)$; and then H_0 would be accepted if: is small.

$$q_{k-1} = \sum_{i=1}^{k} \frac{(y_i - np_i)^2}{np_{i0}} \quad \textbf{(38)}$$

Since this implies $p_i \approx p_{i0}$ for n sufficiently large. The H_0 hypothesis will not be accepted if $q_{k-1} \geq X^2_\alpha(k\text{-}1)$ at significant α-level because Q_{k-1} is $X^2(k\text{-}1)$ in distribution. It should be observed that the chi-squared goodness-of-fit test is a multi-dimensional test in which Q_i also accommodates joint distribution when the experiments are not independent.

CONFLICT OF INTEREST

The author confirm that this chapter contents have no conflict of interest.

ACKNOWLEDGEMENTS

The definition of an ANN as a dynamic system in this chapter might have been influenced by [12]. Cited works are appreciated.

REFERENCES

[1] Michael T E, Christopher B M. Mixtures of principal component analyzers. Artifical Neural Networks. In: Conference Publication No. 440, *0* IEE; 7-9 July; 1997.

[2] Michael T E, Christopher B M. Probabilistic principal component analysis. J R Statist Soc, Ser, B, 61 1999; 611-22.

[3] David JM, Carey EP. The adaptive kernel Neural Network. 14 In: Proceeding 7th International Conference on Mathematical and Computer Modelling.; 1990; pp. : 328-33. [http://dx.doi.org/10.1016/0895-7177(90)90201-W]

[4] Kohavi R, John GH. Wrappers for feature subset selection. Artif Intell Arch 1997; 97(1-2): 273-324. [http://dx.doi.org/10.1016/S0004-3702(97)00043-X]

[5] Lac HC, tacey DA. Feature subset selection *via* multi-objective genetic algorithm. Int Joint Conf Neural Netw 2005; 3: 1349-54.

[6] Romero E, Sopena JM. Performing feature selection with multilayer perceptrons. IEEE Trans Neural Netw 2008; 19(3): 431-41.

[7] Mishra S, Patra S K. Short term load forecasting using neural network trained with genetic algorithm

& particle swarm optimization. In: First International Conference Emerging Trends in Engineering and Technology.; 16-18 July 2008; Nagpur, Maharashtra. IEEE. 2008; pp. 606-11. [http://dx.doi.org/10.1109/ICETET.2008.94]

[8] Sharun SM, Mashor MY, Wan Jaafar WNH, Mohd Nazid N, Yaacob S. Adaptive neuro-controller based on hybrid multi layered perceptron network for dynamic systems. Int J Control Sci Eng 2012; 2(3): 34-41. [http://dx.doi.org/10.5923/j.control.20120203.03]

[9] Xing Z, Yuan Z, Yong Q, Jia L. A Hierarchical Genetic Algorithm based RBF Neural Network Approach for Modelling of Electrohydraulic System. In: ICROS-SICE International Joint Conference 2009; August 18-21; Fukuoka International Congress Center, Japan. 2009.

[10] Tang KS, Man KF, Kwong S, Liu ZF. Minimal fuzzy memberships and rule using hierarchical genetic algorithms. IEEE Trans Ind Electron 1998; 45(1): 162-9. [http://dx.doi.org/10.1109/41.661317]

[11] Yen GG, Lu H. Hierarchical genetic algorithm based neural network design. In: Proceeding IEEE Symposium Combinations of Evolutionary Computation and Neural Networks; 11 May 2000; San Antonio, TX. 2000; pp. 168-75. [http://dx.doi.org/10.1109/ECNN.2000.886232]

[12] Richard Golden M. Mathematical Methods for Neural Network Analysis and Design. The MIT press, Massachusetts institute of Technology 1996. Massachusetts 02142

CHAPTER 5

Quantum Logic and Classical Connectivity

Abstract: The aim and objectives of this chapter is to introduce the principles and fundamental concepts of elements which are used as building block of new and emerging neural systems. The first section introduces quantum logic and quantum algebra. Only those concepts relevant to ANNs' gates production are introduced, and as such the mathematics involved has been kept to a minimum. The second section introduce a new non-volatile memory elements; the memristance. Since these phenomena are well known prior to their formal discovery (formulation), the fundamental concepts and the phenomena forms the subject of discussion in this chapter. The chapter has striven to be self-contained and brief in order to describe and impart information relevant to understanding of the ANNs' elements.

Keywords: Adjoint, Bell state, Cauchy-Schwarz inequality, C-NOT, Conjugate, Eigenvalue, Eigenvector, EPR pair, Flux linkage, Hadamard gate, Hermittian, Memristance, NAND, Orthonormal, Pauli matrices, Quantum gate, Qubit, Qu-NOT, Universal gate, XOR.

INTRODUCTION

The first section of chapter five describes quantum gates and quantum algebra. Both are described together so as to facilitate q-gates' production, in a CAD tool for example, and to promote understanding of the principle behind their functions. Instantiating the q-gates in an ANN circuitry may automatically render such an ANN system a quantum ANN system. The second section introduce memristance as the latest non-volatile memory element which is much more robust as compared to other alternatives in maintaining weights of an ANN system at desired values, with minimum drift.

Quantum gates and quantum algebra are related directly to chapter nine where quantum expert systems are described. They may also be related implicitly to other neural systems of other chapters when their equivalent quantum neural system is formulated and implemented. Similarly, memristance of the second

Pierre Lorrentz

section of this chapter is related to chapters 10 and 11 where a non-volatile memory element is essential. Memristance is also an advantage to other ANN systems of other chapters when weight drift is considered.

Looking into the future of ANNs' development, this chapter has achieved its aim by introducing these gates and primitives.

QUANTUM LOGIC AND QUANTUM MATHEMATICS

A quantum bit (also called *qubit*) is a mathematical unit of quantum information and quantum computation. A *qubit* has two stable and measurable state $|1\rangle$ and $|0\rangle$. The sign "$|\ \rangle$" is used to indicate that the state "1" and "0" are not permanent and many other states are also likely. Some of other possible state may be a linear combination of $|1\rangle$ and $|0\rangle$ thus:

$$|\psi\rangle = \alpha|0\rangle + \beta|1\rangle \tag{1}$$

Where α and β are real parts of a complex number of type: $z = xi + y$; (here $\alpha = x$ *and* $y = \beta$). By superposition of states $|1\rangle$ and $|0\rangle$ as in equation (1) above, an arbitrary $|\psi\rangle$ state may be derived by linear combination. The fundamental measurable states $|1\rangle$ and $|0\rangle$ forms an orthonormal basis of the vector space, and are known as computational *basic state*. However, in contrast to a classical bit, any particular state of a qubit cannot be determined accurately. That is, it is impossible to determine α and β accurately in equation (1). But a prolonged observation may reveal that only two states $|1\rangle$ and $|0\rangle$ can be determined with probabilities $|\alpha|^2$ and $|\beta|^2$ respectively such that

$$|\alpha|^2 + |\beta|^2 = 1 \tag{2}$$

Thus a qubit is a unit two-dimensional vector space.

Prolonged observations made on qubit by several researches have revealed that a qubit has the characteristics of probability theories and not that of laws of physics. For example, equation (2) is always true, and its validity is irrespective of how $|\alpha|^2$ and $|\beta|^2$ is determined. Equation (1) may also be expressed in a more useful form as:

$$|\psi\rangle = e^{i\gamma}\left(\cos(\frac{\theta}{2})|0\rangle + e^{i\varphi}\sin(\frac{\theta}{2})|1\rangle\right) \quad \textbf{(3)}$$

where θ, φ, γ are real numbers.

Equation (3) gives more explanation about the movement of qubit on a (unit) three-dimensional (3-D) sphere. The qubit $|\psi\rangle$ possesses certain probability of being in a continuum of states around the 3-D sphere. However, measurement attempts (of θ, φ, γ) is an interaction and cause changes in a state of qubit such that only two states are measurable, which are $|0\rangle$ with *probability amplitude* $|\alpha|^2$ and $|1\rangle$ with *probability amplitude* $|\beta|^2$. Thus it may be inferred that a single qubit is capable of expressing and representing connection weights between 0 and 1 in an ANN system irrespective of how complicated and large the ANN system might be. For multiple qubits, the number of possible state increase in respect of probability theory. As an example, two qubits have $2^2 = 4$ stable states 00,01,10,11. The linear combination of these four states by superposition gives

$$|\psi\rangle = \alpha_{00}|00\rangle + \alpha_{01}|01\rangle + \alpha_{10}|10\rangle + \alpha_{11}|11\rangle \quad \textbf{(4)}$$

Where $|\psi\rangle$= an arbitrary probable state. And

$$\sum_{i,j}|\alpha_{i,j}|^2 = 1;\ i,j \in [0,1]; \quad \textbf{(5)}$$

$|\alpha_{i,j}|^2$ are corresponding probabilities of the states i, j. The $|\alpha_{i,j}|$ is sometimes simply called amplitude. For an n-qubit, the computational basic states are $|x_1,x_2,...,x_n\rangle$, and require 2^n amplitudes to express a quantum state.

Quantum Gates (Primitives)

Similar to classical binary logic, operations of a quantum logic gate (qugate) may be expressed by truth table. Since a single qubit has two measurable states $|0\rangle$ and $|1\rangle$, a NOT qugate may perform: $X|0\rangle \rightarrow |0\rangle$ and *vice versa*. Recalling the corresponding probabilities $|\alpha|^2$ and $|\beta|^2$ of $|1\rangle$ and $|0\rangle$ respectively, an arbitrary state $|\psi\rangle$ may be taken to an opposite state by qu-NOT [1]. If X denote a qu-NOT matrix, then

$$X = \begin{bmatrix} 0 & 1 \\ 1 & 0 \end{bmatrix} \quad \textbf{(6)}$$

and $\begin{bmatrix} \alpha \\ \beta \end{bmatrix}$ denote the amplitudes of $|1\rangle$ and $|0\rangle$, then a qu-NOT performs:

$$\begin{bmatrix} \alpha \\ \beta \end{bmatrix}\begin{bmatrix} 0 & 1 \\ 1 & 0 \end{bmatrix} = X\begin{bmatrix} \alpha \\ \beta \end{bmatrix} = \begin{bmatrix} \beta \\ \alpha \end{bmatrix} \quad \textbf{(7)}$$

which is a 180° (π rad) rotation of amplitudes. Apart from qu-NOT gate used for π rad rotation of amplitudes, there are other possible forms of matrix X such that other rotations (as expressed by θ, φ, γ of equation (3) are possible on a qubit. A constraint on X is that it must be unitary, that is $X^2 = X^{\dagger}X = I$. The $X^{\dagger}$ is obtained from X by transposition followed by complex conjugating X^T.

<u>Example</u>

One value (matrix) of X = Z which is unitary is $Z = \begin{bmatrix} 1 & 0 \\ 0 & -1 \end{bmatrix}$. This value of X leaves $|0\rangle$ unchanged and change the sign of $|1\rangle$. This is known as *Z-gate*. Another value of X is called *Hadamard gate H*;

$$X = H = \frac{1}{\sqrt{2}}\begin{bmatrix} 1 & 1 \\ 1 & -1 \end{bmatrix} \quad \textbf{(8)}$$

It may be verified that $H^2 = H^{\dagger}H = I$

We have now produced three gate just by two-dimensional (2-D) rotation only; these are:

$$X : \begin{bmatrix} 1 & 0 \\ 0 & 1 \end{bmatrix}\begin{bmatrix} \alpha \\ \beta \end{bmatrix} \to \begin{bmatrix} \alpha \\ \beta \end{bmatrix} \quad \textbf{(9)}$$

$$Z:\begin{bmatrix}1 & 0\\ 0 & -1\end{bmatrix}\begin{bmatrix}\alpha\\ \beta\end{bmatrix}\rightarrow\begin{bmatrix}\alpha\\ -\beta\end{bmatrix}=\alpha|0\rangle-\beta|1\rangle \qquad \textbf{(10)}$$

$$H:\frac{1}{\sqrt{2}}\begin{bmatrix}1 & 1\\ 1 & -1\end{bmatrix}\begin{bmatrix}\alpha\\ \beta\end{bmatrix}\rightarrow\begin{bmatrix}\frac{\alpha}{\sqrt{2}}\\ \frac{\beta}{\sqrt{2}}\end{bmatrix}=\alpha\frac{|0\rangle+|1\rangle}{\sqrt{2}}+\beta\frac{|0\rangle-|1\rangle}{\sqrt{2}} \qquad \textbf{(11)}$$

X, Z, and H are symbolically represented as in Fig. (**1**). In fact, by simple rotations in an appropriate plane, almost all quantum computation may be performed. For a 2-by-2 matrix of a qubit, a corresponding arbitrary unitary matrix U may be decomposed thus:

$$U=e^{i\alpha}\begin{bmatrix}e^{-\frac{i\beta}{2}} & 0\\ 0 & e^{\frac{i\beta}{2}}\end{bmatrix}\begin{bmatrix}\cos(\frac{\gamma}{2}) & -\sin(\frac{\gamma}{2})\\ \sin(\frac{\gamma}{2}) & \cos(\frac{\gamma}{2})\end{bmatrix}\begin{bmatrix}e^{-\frac{i\delta}{2}} & 0\\ 0 & e^{\frac{i\delta}{2}}\end{bmatrix} \qquad \textbf{(12)}$$

Where β, δ, and γ are real-valued numbers. The U expresses most translational movements and rotations that an electron or a photon (as examples) may make about a unit sphere. An interesting situation occurs when a Hadamard gate (equation (11)) is applied to a two qubit, followed by observation of β only (or of α only, without βα combination). An example of such phenomena is an arbitrary state:

$$|\phi\rangle=\beta_{00}|00\rangle+\beta_{01}|01\rangle+\beta_{10}|10\rangle+\beta_{11}|11\rangle \qquad \textbf{(13)}$$

Take the right-hand-side (RHS) of equation (13) in pairs and apply Hadamard gate (equation (11));

$$|\beta_{00}\rangle=\frac{|00\rangle+|11\rangle}{\sqrt{2}} \qquad \textbf{(14)}$$

$$|\beta_{01}\rangle=\frac{|01\rangle+|10\rangle}{\sqrt{2}} \qquad \textbf{(15)}$$

$$|\beta_{10}\rangle=\frac{|00\rangle-|11\rangle}{\sqrt{2}} \qquad \textbf{(16)}$$

$$|\beta_{11}\rangle = \frac{|01\rangle - |10\rangle}{\sqrt{2}} \quad \textbf{(17)}$$

Equations (14) to (17) are known as *Bell state, EPR states,* or *EPR pair*. Note that equation (13) is only one (special) value of U, and Bell states are 4 states taken (by composition as stated above) out of very many probable states. An attempt to put equations (14) to (17) into a single closed form may be

$$|\beta_{xy}\rangle = \frac{|0,y\rangle + (-1)^{x}|1,\bar{y}\rangle}{\sqrt{2}} \quad \textbf{(18)}$$

in a general [x, y] 2-D vector space. In terms of symbols, one-input and one-output gates are:

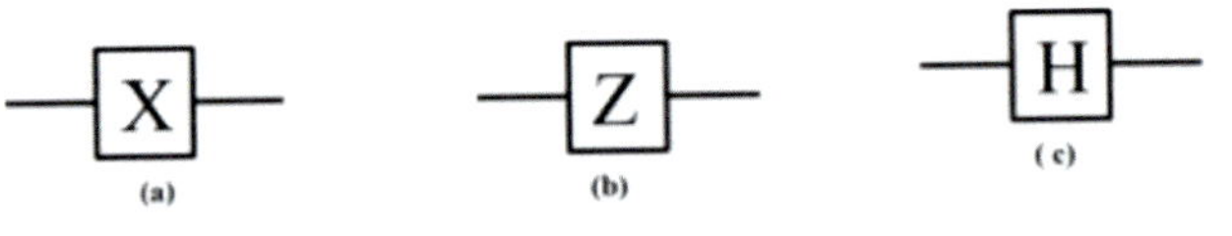

Fig. (1). Symbolic representation of (a) equation (9); (b) equation (10); (c) equation (11).

All symbols of classical binary logic of chapter 1 apply as well to quantum logic. There are additional basic gates that distinguish classical logic from quantum logic. For a two-input (or more) quantum gates and one (or more) quantum output gates, two additional basic gates are of importance. One of them is a *controlled-NOT* gate, sometimes written as C-NOT gate. The C-NOT gate results when U in equation (12) is evaluated for δ,β,γ, and α parameters to give:

$$U_{CN} = \begin{bmatrix} 1 & 0 & 0 & 0 \\ 0 & 1 & 0 & 0 \\ 0 & 0 & 0 & 1 \\ 0 & 0 & 1 & 0 \end{bmatrix} \quad \textbf{(19)}$$

Application of C-NOT gate to $\begin{bmatrix} x \\ y \end{bmatrix}$ may be symbolically represented by (Fig. **2**).

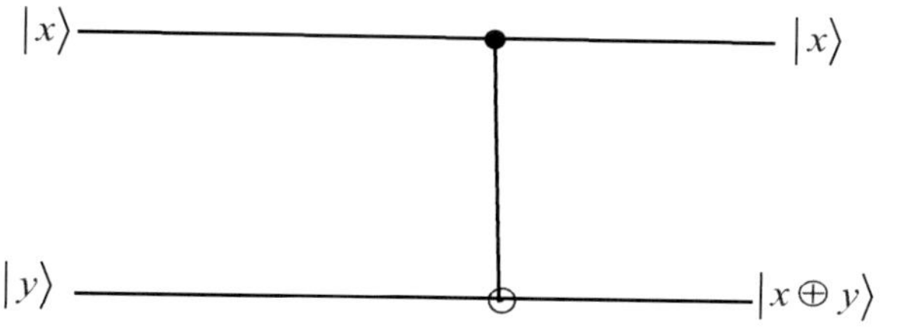

Fig. (2). Schematic representation of a C-NOT gate.

The x is called control qubit while y is the target (to be controlled) qubit. The C-NOT is a generalization of the classical XOR gate, often written as a map:

$$|x, y\rangle \rightarrow |x, x \oplus y\rangle; \quad x, y \in [0,1] \tag{20}$$

That is, the control qubit x and the target qubit y are eXORed and the result stored in the target qubit. The second important and basic quantum gate is the Hadamard gate, equation (11). Symbolically, it is represented by (Fig. **3**).

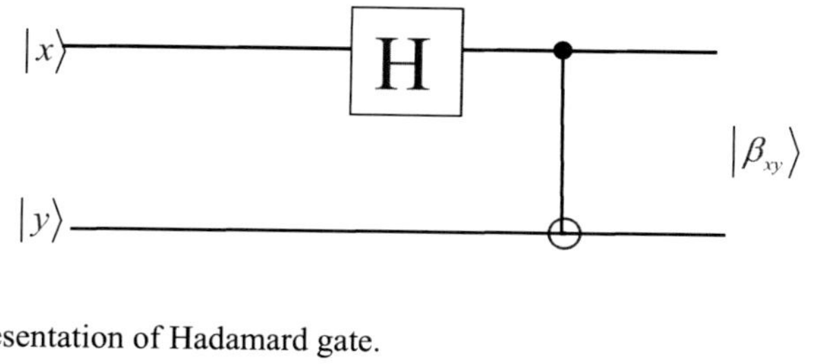

Fig. (3). Schematic representation of Hadamard gate.

Its functional operations are illustrated in equation (14) to (17) for a two qubit $|x, y\rangle \in [0,1]$ system.

The XOR and NAND gates are essentially irreversible and thus do not satisfy the unitary and invertible constraints that C-NOT satisfy. For these reasons, XOR and NAND gates cannot be regarded as a basic quantum gate. Because a unitary gate is essentially invertible, operations on it or with it are reversible. Thus all quantum (gate) processes are reversible. A C-NOT plus a single qubit satisfy the criterion. A C-NOT gate plus a qubit may be regarded as a unit of universal quantum gate.

Any arbitrary multiple qubit logic gate may be composed from a single qubit and a C-NOT gate.

A set of gates is said to be a universal quantum gate if any unitary operation may be approximated to any given accuracy by a quantum circuit involving only those gates. This set of gates are Hadamard gate, rotation (phase) gate, and C- NOT gate. The π/8 (radian) gate is a special type of a rotational (phase) gate. These gates are also referred to as *quantum universal primitives* for quantum circuits. When a quantum particle moves, equation (12) may be used to describe its movement. This includes any stochastic movements, harmonic movements, and movements toward an optimal solution. Luckily, equation (12) in quantum mechanics exists in simple forms very often. This probable simple form corresponds to stable states such as:

$$\sigma_0 = I = \begin{bmatrix} 1 & 0 \\ 0 & 1 \end{bmatrix}; \ \sigma_x = X = \begin{bmatrix} 0 & 1 \\ 1 & 0 \end{bmatrix} \tag{21}$$

$$\sigma_y = Y = \begin{bmatrix} 0 & -i \\ i & 0 \end{bmatrix}; \ \sigma_z = Z = \begin{bmatrix} 1 & 0 \\ 0 & -1 \end{bmatrix} \tag{22}$$

Where σ_0= the ground state or initial state; σ_x = bit flip; yσ= complex (phase) rotation; and σ_z = phase flip. The four matrices of equations (21) and (22) are known by various names, one of which is *Pauli matrices*.

Quantum Algebra

It is possible to perform some algebraic computation on or with a qubit. In multiplication, taking either the outer product, the inner product, or taking both are possible. The inner product space is often referred to as Hilbert space. Some notable results on Hilbert space are:

1. Quanta states $|w\rangle$ and $|v\rangle$ are orthogonal if their product is zero when none of them is a zero vector.
2. The norm of a vector $|v\rangle$ is defined as:

$$\| |v\rangle \| = \sqrt{\langle v | v \rangle} \tag{23}$$

3. To pize a quantum state vector $|v\rangle$, we calculate:

$$\frac{|v\rangle}{\||v\rangle\|} = I_v \quad \textbf{(24)}$$

4. **The Cauchy-Schwartz inequality**: for any two states $|w\rangle$ and $|v\rangle$,

$$|\langle v|w\rangle|^2 = \langle v|v\rangle\langle w|w\rangle \quad \textbf{(25)}$$

5. **Characteristic equation:** An eigenvector of a matrix X is a non-zero vector $|v\rangle$ such that:

$$X|v\rangle = \lambda|v\rangle \quad \textbf{(26)}$$

where λ is the eigenvalue of X corresponding to eigenvector $|v\rangle$. On a Hilbert space, the characteristic equation may be defined as:

$$c(\lambda) = \det\|X - \lambda I\| \quad \textbf{(27)}$$

The solution of a characteristic equation is the set of λ values such that:

$$\det\|X - \lambda I\| = 0 \quad \textbf{(28)}$$

A diagonal representation of matrix X on a Hilbert vector space H is defined by:

$$X = \sum_i \lambda_i |i\rangle\langle i| \quad \textbf{(29)}$$

Where $|i\rangle$ = orthopset of eigenvectors of X with a corresponding λ_i eigenvalues.

Suppose the matrix X represent a linear operator on a Hilbert space H, then there exist a conjugate-transpose matrix $X^\dagger$ of X such that:

$$(|v\rangle, X|w\rangle) = (X^\dagger|v\rangle, |w\rangle) \quad \textbf{(30)}$$

holds when $|v\rangle$ and $|w\rangle$ belong to the Hilbert space H. The set of linear operators (which are elements of) $X\dagger$ that satisfy the condition of equation (29) are called *Hermittian conjugate or adjoint*. They are unitary if they evaluate to the identity (matrix). In quantum vector notation, the vector $|v\rangle$ has a Hermittian conjugate $|v\rangle^{\dagger}$ that is:

$$|v\rangle^{\dagger} = \langle v|;\ \text{and}\ X|v\rangle^{\dagger} = \langle v|X \qquad (31)$$

Generally, Hermittian conjugation is achieved by taking a complex conjugate, followed by transposition;

$$X^{\dagger} = \left(X^{*}\right)^{T} \qquad (32)$$

If $(M^*)^T = M$ then the matrix M is said to be self-adjoint or M is simply called a Hermittian matrix. But if $(M^*)^T$ then $(M^*)^T = M\dagger$; we say that $(M^*)^T$ is a Hermittian conjugate of M, and denote $(M^*)^T$ by $M\dagger$.

Example:

$$\text{If } M = \begin{bmatrix} 1+2i & 3i \\ 1+i & 1-5i \end{bmatrix};\ \text{then } M^{*} = \begin{bmatrix} 1-2i & -3i \\ 1-i & 1+5i \end{bmatrix};\ \text{and } \left(M^{*}\right)^{T} = \begin{bmatrix} 1-2i & 1-i \\ -3i & 1+5i \end{bmatrix}.$$

This introduction to quantum algebra and gate is essential because it may enable the reader to produce a specific quantum gate for certain situations in a CAD tool. Producing the gates may become essential if they are not available. The gates may be employed in the next quantum neural network introduced.

QUANTUM NEURAL NETWORK

Assuming equation (34) of chapter 3 correspond to the kernel of communication between nodes i+1 and i (as indexed) in a neural network, and the speed v is identified by the time interval n, then the kernel may be approximated [2] by:

$$\Gamma(i+1,i) = \frac{1}{A}\exp\left[\frac{i}{h}\varepsilon L\left(\frac{v_{i+1}+v_i}{\varepsilon}, \frac{v_{i+1}+v_i}{2}\right)\right] \qquad (33)$$

Substituting (33) into equation (38) of chapter 3 gives:

$$\psi(v,t+\varepsilon)=\frac{1}{A}\int_{-\infty}^{\infty}\exp\left[\frac{i}{h}\varepsilon L\left(\frac{v_{i+1}+v_i}{\varepsilon},\frac{v_{i+1}+v_i}{2}\right)\right]\psi(v_1,t)dv_1 \quad \textbf{(34)}$$

The Lagrangian L required in equation (34) is given by equation (35).

$$L\left(\frac{v-v_1}{\varepsilon},\frac{v+v_1}{2}\right)=\frac{1}{2g'(u)}\left(\frac{v-v_1}{\varepsilon}\right)^2+E_v\left(\frac{v+v_1}{2}\right)\frac{v-v_1}{\varepsilon} \quad \textbf{(35)}$$

So that equation (34) becomes (36).

$$\psi(v,t+\varepsilon)=\int_{-\infty}^{\infty}\frac{1}{A}\left\{\exp\left[\frac{i}{2hg'(u)}\frac{(v-v_1)^2}{\varepsilon}\right]\right\}\times\left\{\exp\left[\frac{i}{h}(v-v_1)E_v\left(\frac{v+v_1}{2}\right)\right]\right\}\psi(v_1,t)dv_1 \quad \textbf{(36)}$$

Setting v1 = $v+\eta$ in equation (36)

$$\psi(v,t+\varepsilon)=\int_{-\infty}^{\infty}\frac{1}{A}\exp\left[\frac{i}{2hg'(u)}\frac{\eta^2}{\varepsilon}-\frac{i}{h}\eta E_v\left(\frac{2v+\eta}{2}\right)\right]\psi(v+\eta,t)d\eta \quad \textbf{(37)}$$

Equation (37) is a quantum (based) neural network system. By expanding (37) in a Taylor series about Ó, the 0th-order term gives the value of A *i.e.*:

$$A=\left(\frac{2\pi ih\varepsilon}{m(v)}\right)^{1/2} \quad \textbf{(38)}$$

$$\text{where } m(v)=\frac{1}{g'(g^{-1}(v))} \quad \textbf{(39)}$$

The first-order term of the expansion does not exist (vanishes identically). The second-order term gives a neural network of the Schrodinger type.

$$\frac{h}{i}\frac{\partial\psi}{\partial t}=\frac{h^2}{2m(v)}\frac{\partial^2\psi}{\partial v^2}+\frac{h}{i}E_v\frac{\partial\psi}{\partial v}-V\psi \quad \textbf{(40)}$$

The V in equation (40) is defined by:

$$V = V(v) = \frac{E_v^2(v)}{2m(v)} + \frac{ih}{2m(v)} E_{vv}(v) \quad \textbf{(41)}$$

Where E_v = energy

A specific implementation of quantum (mechanical) neural network of Schrodinger type is illustrate is subsequent chapters.

CLASSICAL PRIMITIVES AND WEIGHTS

It is part of a learning algorithm for weights to be updated, most especially during the learning and recognition stage. On a digital computer, weights can only be stored on permanent memory elements. Generally in this book, "weight storage" refers to temporary weight storage pending modification, except otherwise stated. For weights to be modified on PCs, they have to first be fetched, then modified, and then again stored. Thus making the learning (and subsequent recognition) time very long. Almost every aspect of ANNs' functionalities is hampered by noise and time (duration) when the memory elements of pPCs are used for weight storage. For these reasons dedicated devices and methods are required for ANNs' weight updates and storage. The main basic digital elements used by ANN systems are NAND and XOR which are described previously. In analogue circuits, the main basic elements used for weight updates and storage are filters, capacitance, and memristance. Capacitances are assumed well known. Filters are also well known, but few are closely related to specific learning algorithms. Filters which are related to learning algorithms include Least-Mean-Square (LM S), and Recursive-Least-Square (RLS). These filters are found suitable for weight management, and will be introduced in the other chapter. The new basic (primitive) classical element is the memristor, and will be introduced now.

Memristance

A memristive circuit update and store weights as conductance values. In a memristor, weights are stored and modified (update) *via* Ohm's law:

$$v(t) = M(q(t))i(t) \quad \textbf{(42)}$$

Where $M(q(t))$ is a charge dependent memristance. An off-the-shelf memristance does not exist at the time of writing, but two models of memristor exist. One is called window-based non-linear model, while the linear model [3] is called the Titanium dioxide $Ti0_2$ model.

Flux linkage φ is dependent on charge q. When flux linkage change with respect to charge q in motion, then

$$\varphi = \varphi(q); \quad \frac{d\varphi}{dt} = \frac{d\varphi}{dq}\frac{dq}{dt} \tag{43}$$

and

$$\frac{d\varphi}{dt} = v(t) = \frac{d\varphi}{dq} i(t)$$

Therefore,

$$v(t) = R(t)i(t) = \frac{d\varphi(t)}{dq(t)} i(t) \tag{44}$$

$$\text{Denote } M = \frac{d\varphi}{dq};\ i(t) = \frac{dq}{dt} \tag{45}$$

Equation (42) then follows. Memristance may be defined as the rate of change of flux-linkage per unit charge. It should be noted that equation (42) and (44) are equivalent. The memristance equation (45) may be manufactured by depositing a thin layer of Titanium dioxide $Ti0_2$ on one plate of a good electrical (charge) conductor, and an oxygen-deficient $Ti0_2$ on the second plate, both plates being made of the same material and physical extent. The two plates are sealed on the $Ti0_2$ side making good electrical (charge) contact, as shown schematically in (Fig. **4**).

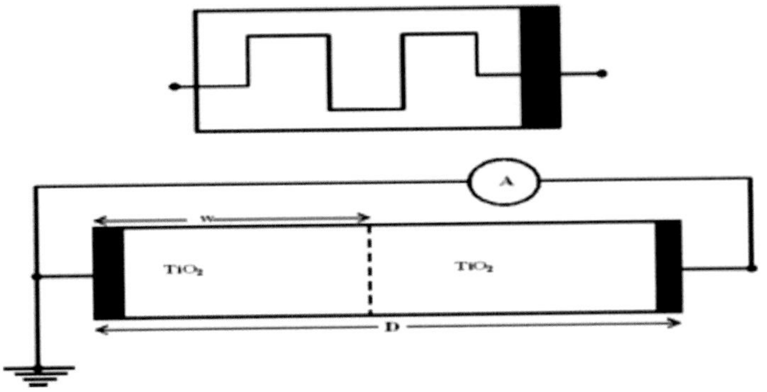

Fig. (4). Showing memristors; the upper figure is the symbol of memristor, while the lower circuit shows the variation in width w as current A passes though, and affects the concentration of Titanuim dioxide TiO_2; the TiO_2 concentration changes w due to their movement across the semi-permeable membrane (dotted line).

The memristance of TiO_2 depends on distances w and D (see Fig. (**4**)) of the memristor manufactured. In terms of w and D, the memristance of equation (45) may be represented by:

$$M(q) = R_{ON}\left(\frac{w}{D}\right) + R_{OFF}\left(1 - \frac{w}{D}\right) = R_{TOTAL} \quad \textbf{(46)}$$

Equation (37) means the "ON" resistance should be added to the "OFF" resistance as they are affected by w and D distances. Putting equation (45) into (41):

$$v(t) = \left(R_{ON}\left(\frac{w}{D}\right) + R_{OFF}\left(1 - \frac{w}{D}\right)\right) i(t) \quad \textbf{(47)}$$

The distance w changes with respect to charge mobility μ_v as given by:

$$w = kq;\; w = \mu_v\left(\frac{R_{ON}}{D}\right)q; \quad \textbf{(48)}$$

$$\text{where } k = \mu_v\left(\frac{R_{ON}}{D}\right)$$

And differentiating (47);

$$\frac{dw}{dt} = \mu_v \left(\frac{R_{ON}}{D}\right)\frac{dq}{dt} = \mu_v \left(\frac{R_{ON}}{D}\right) i(t) \tag{49}$$

By integration;

$$w(t) = \mu_v \left(\frac{R_{ON}}{D}\right)\int i(\tau)d\tau + w_0 \tag{50}$$

Substituting (50) into (46);

$$M(q(t)) = R_{OFF}\left(1 - \frac{\mu_v R_{ON}}{D^2}(1 - \frac{R_{On}}{R_{OFF}})\int_0^t i(\tau)d\tau\right) + \frac{w_0 R_{OFF}}{D}\left(\frac{R_{ON}}{R_{OFF}} - 1\right) \tag{51}$$

Substituting (51) into (42) and integrating;

$$v(t) = \left[R_{OFF}\left(1 - \frac{\mu_v R_{ON}}{D^2}(1 - \frac{R_{On}}{R_{OFF}})\int_0^t i(\tau)d\tau\right) + \frac{w_0 R_{OFF}}{D}\left(\frac{R_{ON}}{R_{OFF}} - 1\right)\right] i(t) \tag{52}$$

From $M(t) = \dfrac{d\varphi(t)}{dq(t)}$; $\varphi = \int M(\tau)dq(\tau)$ **(53)**

Substituting (51) into (53) and evaluating the right-hand-side;

$$\varphi(t) = R_{OFF}\left[q(t)\left(1 + \frac{w_0}{D}\left(\frac{R_{ON}}{R_{OFF}} - 1\right)\right) + \frac{\mu_v R_{ON}}{2D^2}\left(1 - \frac{R_{ON}}{R_{OFF}}\right)q^2(t)\right] + \varphi_0 \tag{54}$$

Equation (52) expresses the current i(t) controlled memristor and the detailed v-I relationship of a memristor. Equation (54) describes the flux-charge (φ-q) relationship. The basic principle of memristor has been described. The memristor may be utilised to set weights and maintain them. Some ways of doing this is given in subsequent chapters. Memrsitance is non-volatile memory elements which enables the direct design of artificial neuromorphic neural network that other electrical and/or electronic element do not have. The HH-cable equation (to be discussed next) is useful for HH-neuron analysis and study purposes; it may be unsuitable for a corresponding design and manufacturability.

HODGKIN-HUXLEY NEURON

Hodgkin and Huxley are the first scientists to perform a quantitative experiment directly on squid giant axon. They discovered that an active mechanism is responsible for the action potential. The ion-selective voltage-dependent gates, controlled by multiple gating particles play active role in it. Hodgkin and Huxley also establish three main types of current known as ionic current. These are Sodium current I_{Na}, Potassium current I_K, and leak current I_L mainly due to chlorine ions.

Fig. (**5**) shows an equivalent electrical circuit diagram whereby C_m is the axon membrane capacitance. They found that that the gating particles are related to currents in the following equations. The " R intra" models the resistance of the intracellular medium.

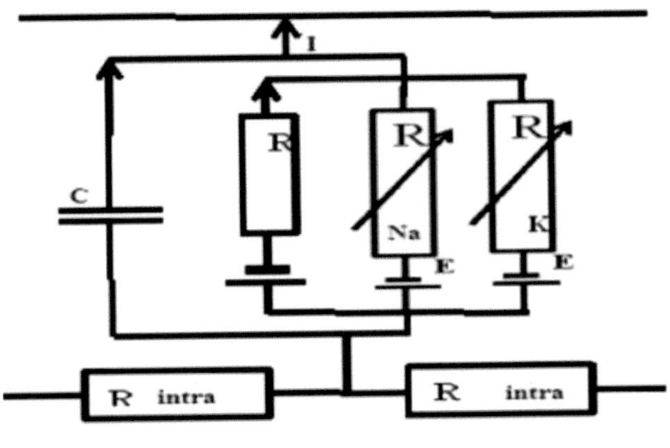

Fig. (5). Equivalent electrical circuit of an axon.

<u>Potassium:</u>

$$I_K = \bar{g}_K n^4 (V - E_K) \quad \textbf{(55)}$$

$$\frac{dn}{dt} = \alpha_n (1 - n) - \beta_n n \quad \textbf{(56)}$$

$\bar{g}_K$ = maximum potassium conductance per unit area of membrane n = potassium gating open particle

Sodium:

$$I_{Na} = \bar{g}_{Na} m^3 h (V - E_{Na}) \quad (57)$$

$$\frac{dm}{dt} = \alpha_m (1 - m) - \beta_m m \quad (58)$$

$$\frac{dh}{dt} = \alpha_h (1 - h) - \beta_h h \quad (59)$$

$\bar{g}_{Na}$ = maximum sodium conductance per unit area of membrane

m = sodium gating particle (for opening)

h = sodium gating particle (for closing)

An operational neuron is obtained by writing the sum of various currents to give:

$$C_m \frac{\partial V}{\partial t} = -\bar{g}_L (V - E_L) - \bar{g}_{Na} m^3 h (V^3 - E_{Na}) - \bar{g}_K n^4 (V - E_K) + \frac{d}{2R_a} \frac{\partial^2 V}{\partial x^2} \quad (60)$$

This equation (60) is a second-order (wave) equation. The discovery, manufacture of memristance, and its use in the production of ANN may enable a tentative industrial implementation of artificial neuromorphic neural network which may employ equation (60) as component neuron. This topic is addressed further in other chapters of the book.

CONFLICT OF INTEREST

The author confirm that this chapter contents have no conflict of interest.

ACKNOWLEDGEMENTS

Cited works are appreciated.

REFERENCES

[1] Micheal AN, Isaac LC. Quantum Computation and Quantum Information. New York, USA:

Cambridge University Press 2007.

[2] Richard Feynman P, Rober Leighton B. Matthew sands. The Feynman Lecture on Physics. Massachusetts, USA: Addson-Wesley Publishing Company 1966; 3.

[3] Kim H, Sah MP, Yang C, Roska T, Chua LO. Neural synaptic weighting with a pulse-based memristor circuit. IEEE Trans Circ Syst I Fundam Theory Appl 2012; 59(1): 148-58. [http://dx.doi.org/10.1109/TCSI.2011.2161360]

Part 2

Practices

CHAPTER 6

Learning Methods

Abstract: The first chapter of part II of this book introduces various common learning algorithms. The aim of chapter 6 is to acquaint the readers with the present-day knowledge in learning paradigms. Filters may be employed in implementation of learning algorithms, and *vice versa*. As such, the first few sections introduce Adaptive Linear Neuron (ADALINE) and recursive Least-Square (RLS) algorithms. Artificial intelligent systems may possess functional characteristics of living biological brain. The multi-agent network and neuromorphic network introduced in subsequent sections are examples of ANN systems with functional characteristics of living biological brain. The ability of the brain to process data is unparalleled; the human research efforts have however been able to discover a close match in Bayesian networks such that more than half of this chapter is devoted to presenting various types of probability-density-based learning algorithms. This is followed, in conclusion, by a hybrid neuro-fuzzy neural network section. By reading this chapter, one may fully understand the common ANN systems, and thus easily implement an ANN if required.

Keywords: Adaptive Linear Neuron (ADALINE), Adaptive Network-based Fuzzy Inference System (ANFIS), Agent, Capacitance, Efficacy, Expectation-Maximization (E-M) algorithm, Generative Topographic Mapping (GTM), Hodgkin-Huxley model, K-means, Knowledge base, Learning parameter, Membrane potential, Mixture models, Nodes, Radial Basis Function (RBF), Recursive Least-Square (RLS) algorithm, Sigmoid function, Sugeno-type Fuzzy system, Synaptic current, Weight matrix.

INTRODUCTION

The first section introduces one of the simplest types of neuron. These neuron exhibit main characteristics expected of a neuron. It is followed by the second section which illustrates also one of the simplest types of a learning algorithm. The Recursive Least-Square (RLS) algorithm possesses main characteristics of a learning algorithm. The third section describes the multi-agent network, an

Pierre Lorrentz

extended type of nature-inspired network. These three sections comprise a suitable start-off of ANN systems; for these reasons the three sections are on the first chapter of part II. The fourth section describes neuromorphic neural networks which closely mimic the functionality of a natural biological neuron. Because sufficient theory has been given in previous chapters, it is here suitable to introduce Bayesian neural networks in the fifth section. The last section presents the neuro-fuzzy system. This is because sufficient description of neuron and fuzzy logic has already been given in previous chapters.

Linear neuron may find use as a component of hierarchical neural networks of chapter 8. So also could RLS of the second section be employed in hierarchical architecture of chapter 8. Multi-agent networks of section three are better designed by using the graphical method (method of nodes and edges) of chapter 4. Genetic algorithm of chapter 4 could be an active agent at a node of a multi-agent network; so could a multi-layered perceptron of chapter 7. The best classical primitive (gate) suited to the implementation of the neuromorphic network of the fourth section of this chapter is the memristance of chapter 5. The neuromorphic network of chapter 6 is partially complete; it may be completed as discussed in chapter 11. The probability theory of chapters 2, form background studies to Bayesian networks of chapter 6. The Bayesian networks described here are standard networks which may be employed as components of a hierarchical mixture of experts that is described in chapters 8 and 9. Fuzzy logic introduced in chapters 3 are introductory texts to the neuro-fuzzy system described in the last section of this chapter.

As the first chapter of part II, chapter 6 has successfully describe various types of ANN systems and give standard neural network(s) for each type of ANN system mentioned.

THE ADAPTIVE LINEAR NEURON (ADALINE)

Filter is one of the standard means of weight initialisation and maintenance, but is not discussed in previous section. It is assumed that the reader is familiar with filters, but there are two exceptionally different filters that come in various disguises. These are Least-Mean-Square (LSM), and Recursive-Least-Square

(RLS) filters. The LSM and RLS filters will be discussed in this section in relation to learning algorithms.

A connectionist model of neuron called Adaptive Linear Neuron (ADALINE) was developed by Widrow [1] in 1962. The weights in this model are maintained according to LSM algorithm. The LSM algorithm is derived from a change in the gradient of a system's function. The change in the gradient is measured by a change in weight of ADALINE's function. The measurement is formal, methodical, and therefore given the name of its discoverer Widrow-Hoff learning rule [1]. The LSM algorithm adjusts the weight at every iteration step by an amount proportional to the gradient of the cumulative error E(x) of the network:

$$E(x) = \frac{1}{2}(t - o)^2 \tag{1}$$

where

t = target signal

O = output signal

E = expected error

$\Delta w = \eta(\Delta_w E(w))$

where η = learning parameter (or forgetting factor).

This weight adjustment constitutes the Widrow-Hoff leaning rule. The LSM that does the main weight adjustment is presented. Rather than an ad-hoc presentation, a slightly modified form of LSM which has been applied to human eye-iris recognition [2] is presented below.

The LSM Algorithm: An adaptive filter consists of two parts, namely; a digital filter with adjustable coefficient, and an adaptive algorithm which is employed in the adjustment and modification of the coefficient of the filter. In this report, an adaptive filter along with Widro-Hopf Least Mean Square (LMS) algorithm [1] provides a fan-in to a weightless classifier. The adaptive filter is produced from the input data **X**, which output a coefficient weight matrix **W**. Any system may be modelled *via* autoregressive model by sets of weight coefficients. The mean square error (MSE) e^2, that is the square of error ek signal (see Fig. (**1**)), is defined by

$$E = \frac{1}{N}\sum_{n=1}^{N} e^2(n) = \frac{1}{N}\sum_{n=1}^{N}(x(n) + \sum_{k=1}^{p} a(k)x(n-k))^2 \quad \textbf{(2)}$$

where $e(n)$ = error term, $x(n\text{-}k)$ = input data, and $a(k)$ = system parameter. Differentiating equation (2) and setting the differential to zero,

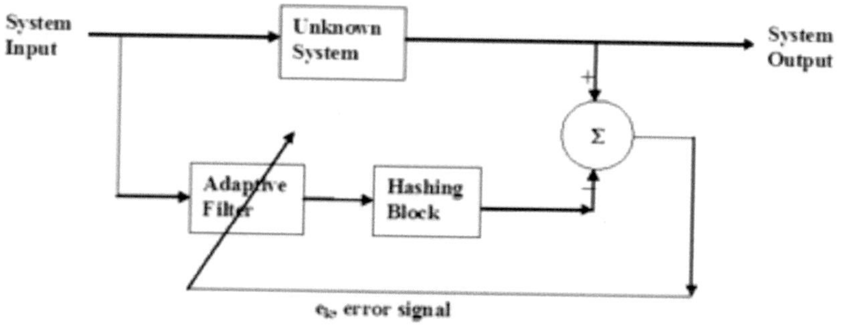

Fig. (1). System modelling by LMS.

$$R_{xx}(k-j)a(k) = -R_{xx}(k) \quad \textbf{(3)}$$

after some calculations. Equation (2) to (3) is schematized in (Fig. **1**). In equation (3), $\boldsymbol{R}_{xx}$ = correlation coefficient of input data. The weight matrix **W** is initialized to $\boldsymbol{R}_{xx}$ instead of arbitrary random value that characterise a normal LMS algorithm. This implies:

- It is a valid training set for the classifier, since each such matrix is a class correlation of input data.
- Where a learning algorithm of a classifier makes a one-pass over input data equation (3) produces an initial better training set rather than arbitrary random values.
- Initialization of weights to arbitrary random values may also access neurons at

random, illegal memory access to memory locations, and thus not advisable for weightless classifiers.

Differentiating e^2 and setting differentials to zero, after some calculations, the weight modification equation, W_{k+1} ,is given by;

$$W_{k+1} = W_k + 2\mu e_k X_k \qquad \textbf{(4)}$$

where $e_k = y_k - W_k^T X_k$; $\mu := 0\langle \mu \langle \frac{1}{\lambda_{max}}$; and $\lambda_{max} = W_k$ (maximum eigenvalue).

Equation (4) is known as Widro-Hopf LMS algorithm [1]. (See Fig. **2** for an illustration) The weight matrix **W** is afterwards modified according to equation (4). To the LMS algorithm's output may be attached a neural classifier.

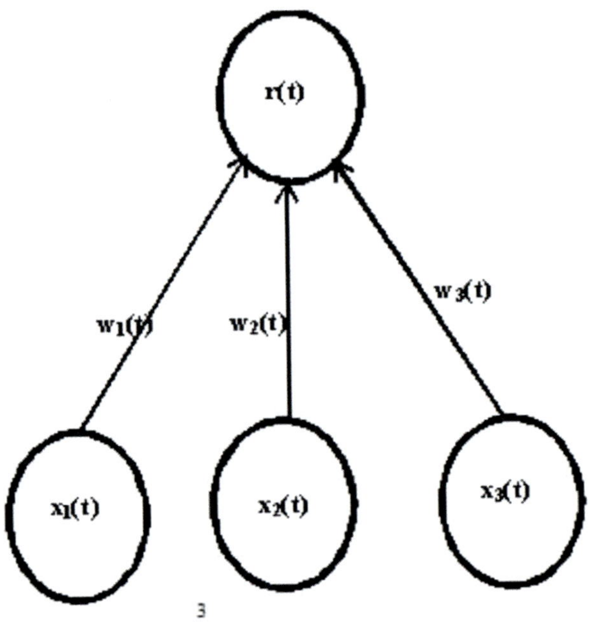

$$r(t) = \sum_{i=1}^{3} w_i(t) x_i(t)$$

$$w_i(t+1) = w_i(t) + \gamma[y_i - r(t)] x_i(t)$$

Fig. (2). Illustration of Widro-Hopf Learning rules. The y_i is the desired output, *r(t)* is an intermediate sum at time; and *y* is known as the forgetting factor.

THE RECURSIVE-LEAST-SQUARE (RLS) ALGORITHM

It is assumed that the reader is familiar with filters, but there is an exceptionally different filter that comes in various disguises. This is Recursive-Least-Square (RLS) filters. The RLS algorithm is discussed now in relation to a modified ADALINE. The presentation follows [3] closely where it is applied to prediction problem.

The Adaptive RADALINES: The adaptive Linear Neuron (ADALINE) [3] developed by Widro-Hoff is the raw material for external system/device identification and modelling for the RADALINES-EPCN (see chapter 7) system. Modifications made to ADALINE in order to generate RADALINES are:

1. The Boolean activation function is replaced by sigmoid activation function. For this reason an "S" is placed at the end of "ADALINE".
2. The Widro-Hoff learning rule is replaced by Recursive Least-mean Square (RLS) algorithm for learning. For this reason the letter "R" is placed at the beginning of "ADALINE" to give the RADALINES.

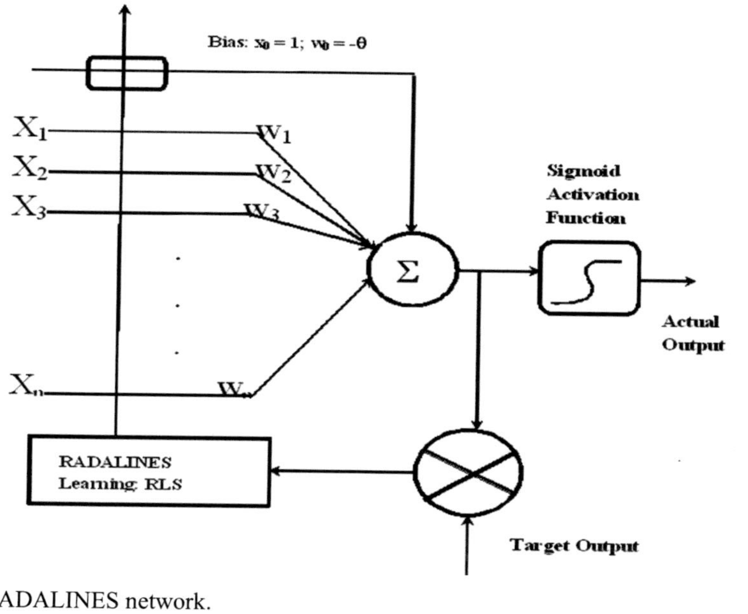

Fig. (3). The RADALINES network.

Fig. (3) is the diagrammatic representation of RADALINES. Learning in

RADALINES consists of search for sets of minimum weights to represent an external device (system) to which it is clamped.

The RADALINES output y_k is expressed as:

$$y_k = \sum_{i=0}^{n-1} w(i)x_k(i) + e_k \tag{5}$$

Where e_k = all immeasurable effects *i.e.* total errors with respect to k; w = filter weights; x = input signal; y = output signal. When written in uppercase bold letters, equation (5) represents matrices. The first set of weights, **W**, is initialized thus:

$$W_m = [X_m^T X_m]^{-1} X_m^T Y_m \tag{6}$$

Some features that further distinguish the RADALINES employed in RADALINES-EPCN fusion over other ADALINE employed elsewhere are:

- The weight matrix in the RADALINES-EPCN system is initialised to $\mathbf{W}_m$ of equation (6) instead of arbitrary random value as is customarily the case.
- It is a valid training set for the classifier, since each such matrix is a class property of input data.
- Where a learning algorithm of a classifier makes a one-pass over input data equation (6) produces an initial better training set rather than arbitrary random values.
- Initialisation of weights to arbitrary random values may also access neurons at random, illegal memory access to neurons' RAM-memory locations, and thus not advisable for weightless classifiers in general.

The weight matrix, $\mathbf{W}_m$, is thereafter updated by the following RADALINES algorithm for which matrix inversion is not required:

$$W_k = W_{k-1} + U_k e_k \tag{7}$$

$$e_k = Y_k - X_k^T W_{k-1} \tag{8}$$

where

$$U_k = \frac{V_{k-1}X_k}{\alpha_k} \tag{9}$$

$$\alpha_k = \gamma + X_k^T V_{k-1} X_k$$

$$V_k = \frac{1}{\gamma}[V_{k-1} - U_k X_k^T V_{k-1}] \tag{10}$$

and

γ = forgetting factor;

V_k= a factorization algorithm for [$X_k^T X_k$].

Fig. (**3**) shows a schematic of the RADALINES. The RADALINES is either connected to *data* input or an external *device* (system) input. It is further connected to EPCN *via* the Hashing block as output port. There are three constraints on **V**, these are:

- Most of its value must not be zero.
- Positive semi-definite; that is, the matrix should represent a stable system.
- The variables, *e.g.* device attributes, whose coefficients generate **V** should be linearly independent.

Note that the neural network EPCN to which RADALINES is attached may easily be replaced by any suitable neural network.

MULTI-AGENT NETWORK

Multi-Agent Network (M-AN) is an extended type of nature-inspired population based intelligent framework which is not overtly mathematical. Like other nature based computational intelligent system, it may typify flock of birds, school of fish, swarm of insects, and the like. The capability of M-AN may surpass that of Genetic Algorithm (GA), and fuzzy logic systems, since it may conveniently manage a very large distributive networks which may be difficult for GA or fuzzy system.

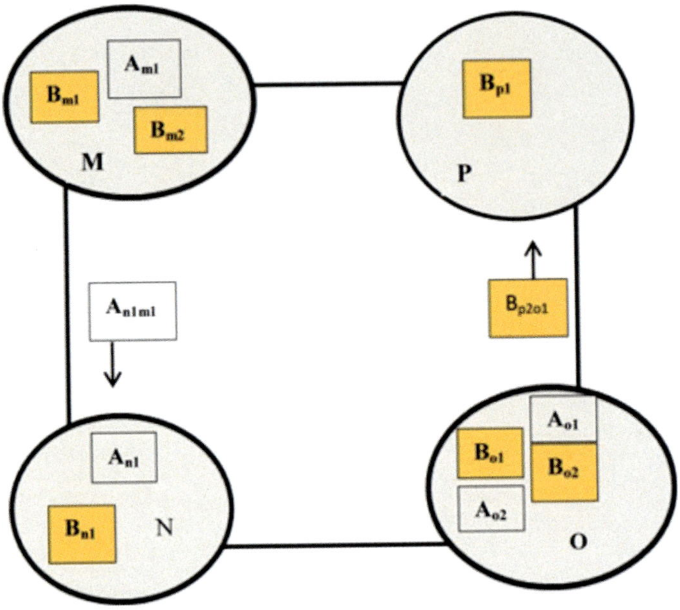

Fig. (4). A network of a hybrid M-AN that consist of 4 nodes M, N, O, and P. Associated with each node are agents A and B.

A multi-agent network may be defined as a system (a hardware/software structure), that consist of multiple interacting, autonomous, mobile, intelligent, and dynamic agents.This definition succinctly summarize M-ANs' behaviour. Depending on application, one or more of these characteristics: interacting; autonomous; mobile; intelligent; precede over M-ANs' behaviour.A distinctive characteristics of M-AN as compared to other nature inspired system is that an agent of M-AN is always an active agent. The brain of M-AN is a knowledge-base (similar to that of a fuzzy system), made up of a unit called *frame*. A *frame* in turn consists of *slots*.Movement of an agent within M-AN, and of M-AN, is according to a specific dynamics, and one or more qualitative, and/or quantitative rule(s)/law(s) with associated constraint(s). Irrespective of whether an agent is a communication agent or not, every agent communicates *via inter-variables* that connect an agent to its environment. *Intra-variables* are variables that may wholly be associated with a single agent. Network-graphical method (using nodes and edges; see chapter 4) is often employed to describe and analyse a M-AN. Fig. (**4**) shows a M-ANs' network. A M-AN may be a *homogeneous or heterogeneous (hybrid)* network. The Fig. (**4**) shows a hybrid M-AN whose agents are A and B with subscripts to denote their current location.Agents may also move like $_{An1m1}$ moving from node M to node N. A reachable node is known as an *adjacent node.* A node reachable from all other node is called a *globally reachable node.* The nodes are M, N, O, and P. The edges represent any means that facilitate movement and communication between nodes. Graphs topology may be either *fixed* or changeable.Changeable topology is sometimes referred to as *switch topology*. Generally, movement within node is called continuous movement while movement from node to another node is called discrete movement; just like Bp2o1 moving from O to P node in (Fig. **4**). Agents' movement is in response to resource requirement, optimization of its dynamic equation (*e.g.*; its error functio n), and constraints equations.

Constraint equations must be satisfied before movement/communication stops; this is known as hard constraints. It is not necessary to satisfy the optimization goal exactly before movement/communication stops; the optimization goal is a soft constraint.A solution close to the ideal solution, if not the ideal solution sought, of the optimization equation may have been reached after all hard constraints have been satisfied. This often serves as a stopping criterion.

Aggregate motion of M-AN may be guided by three main implicit rules [4] which are:

1. Alignment towards the average heading of the flock;
2. Movement to avoid overcrowding;
3. Movement toward the average position of the flock to achieve cohesion.

Using Fig. (**4**) for illustration, the four nodes possess various and different resources, and each agent may require different resources. The agent tends to spread in order to satisfy their requirement as offered by nodes' resources. The agents benefit from nodes' resources *via* continuous communication with the nodes.

The M-AN is a software/hardware networks structure suited to handling large distributed problems where GA and/or fuzzy network often fail to produce an optimal solution. The memory of a M-AN exist as a knowledge-base which consist of frame collections. Frames of a knowledge base may relate to one another as shown in Fig. (**5**) and (Fig. **6**). The agents work with an intelligent data structure of frames (their brain) by retrieving frames, manipulating frames, and storing frames in the relational database which is the knowledge base.

	Frame Name: Node Identifier	
	Variables	**Values**
SLOTS	**Name:**	Identifier of agent
	Type:	of node or Location of agent
	Task:	name of task group
	Fault:	Yes or No
	<slot a>:	[value]
	<slot b>:	[value]
	Environment:	[string; may include neighbours]
	message source:	last message received and its souce
	message:	last message sent and reciepent
	Condition:	fault condition: notice, warn, danger, or panic

Fig. (5). A frame of node (or substation).

When subsystems have interconnecting constraints, they are *neighbours*. The interconnection is achieved by agents having inter-variables which are substituted into the constraint equations. The constraint equation may express control, consensus, and/or stability. For control, any suitable control rule/law may be used, such as model predictive control. For stability condition, the M-AN may require satisfying a Lyapunov criteria, Hurwitz criteria, or any other stability criterion. When the dynamic equation is periodic or almost periodic, a regularization of the learning algorithm of the agents may be necessary to keep the M-AN in control.

Although an expert system shell of a M-AN may be implemented for general purposes, this is hardly ever done in practice. Instead, software packages exist tuned to the implementation of M-AN for specific purposes. A software package called JADE [5] is a M-ANs' dedicated package and conform to FIPA (Foundation of Intelligent Physical Agents) [6] standards. The JADE is suited for generation of a M-AN for any purpose. It is also usual to develop a M-AN from scratch. A M-AN may be developed from scratch by following the fundamental background explanation of this section. There are very many models of M-AN each of which targets a specific (group of) problem. Since each model is a problem (class) specific, a developer wishing to implement a M-AN (from scratch) may easily find a model that suits the purpose with associated algorithms.The section has avoided model description, and gives a direct, intuitive, and model-free description, which promotes understanding to enable the development of a possibly new models and new algorithms.

	Frame Name: Task Identifier	
	Variables	**Values**
SLOTS	**Name:**	Identifier of agent
	Type:	of task or Location of task
	Fault:	Yes or No
	<slot a>:	[value]
	Control:	status
	<slot b>:	[value]
	Environment:	[string]
	message source:	last message received and its souce
	message:	last message sent and reciepent
	Condition:	fault condition: notice, warn, danger, or panic

Fig. (6). A frame of task – the task is a slots' variable in Fig. (**5**) to which it establishes relationship.

NEUROMORPHIC NETWORK

The word Neuromorphic refers to circuitry designed which closely emulates biological neuron. The function ranges from classification to being used as sensor *e.g.* silicon retina, synaptic touchpad. The Pulse Coupled Neural Network (PCNN) is an example of a neuromorphic neural network. A common biological model of neuromorphic neural network is a model of the cortical column. This follows from the fact that the brains' cortical column is mainly responsible for information processing in the cerebral cortex. The cerebral cortex consists of neurons which vary slightly in anatomy. It is the interconnection between the neurons that plays a vital role in learning. A neuron model often used in Engineering is known as the Hodgkin and Huxley model [7]. The Hodgkin and Huxley model of a neuron is characterised by membrane potential V_{mem}, potassium ionic current i_k, sodium ionic current i_{Na}, leakage current i_{leak}, and a modulating current i_m. These currents are voltage V dependent. The time dependent equivalence of events at a synapse is described by a concept of spike timing-dependent plasticity (STDP). This describe the spike train (or the waveform against time) of an event at a synapse. A temporal model of a waveform at a synapse, the STDP, has been a subject of researches. The complex Hodgkin and Huxley model will now be presented.

The hardware neuromorphic equivalent of a neuron: This is given by the equation (11) which is an instantaneous value (snapshot at time t) of equation (60) of chapter 5.

$$C_{mem} \cdot \frac{d}{dt} V = g_m \cdot \left(V - E_l\right) + \sum_j p_j(t) \cdot g_j(t) \cdot \left(V - E_x\right) + \sum_k p_k(t) \cdot g_k(t) \cdot \left(V - E_i\right) \qquad \textbf{(11)}$$

where

$g_m\,(V-E_t)$ = model of ion channel current

$\sum_j p_j(t) \cdot g_j(t) \cdot \left(V - E_t\right)$ = excitatory synaptic current

$\sum_k p_k(t) \cdot g_k(t) \cdot \left(V - E_i\right)$ = Inhibitory synaptic current

c_{mem} = Total (constant) membrane capacitance

g_m = synaptic inductance

$p_{k\ or\ j}$ = synaptic open probability

E_l, E_x, E_i = Potentials

E_l = Final potential as time goes to infinity

E_x = Excitatory ion channel potential

E_i = Inhibitory ion channel potential

V(t) = The emulated membrane potential.

Hodgkin and Huxley Model: The membranous ionic current is proportional to the membrane's capacitance, and is given by

$$C_{mem} \cdot \frac{d}{dt} V_{mem} = - \sum_i i_{ion} + i_s \quad \textbf{(12)}$$

where

C_{mnem} = membrane capacitance

V_{mem} = membrane potential

i_s = synaptic current

i_{ion} = ionic channel current

The ionic current i_{ion} is given by

$$i_{ion} = g_{max} \cdot m^p \cdot h^q \cdot \left(V_{mem} - V_{equi}\right) \quad \textbf{(13)}$$

where

g_{max} = maximum conductance

m = activation term

h = inhibition term

V_{equi} = reverse potential

The permeability of the neuron membrane is given by the functional activities of $\tau_m \cdot \frac{d}{dt} m$ m and h terms. Their functional activity are govern by the differential equation

$$= \quad m_{\infty} - m \quad \textbf{(14)}$$

where

τ_m = time constant, since

$$m_\infty = \frac{1}{1+\exp\left[\frac{-(V_{mem}-V_{offset})}{V_{slope}}\right]} \quad \textbf{(15)}$$

is a solution.

m_∞ = steady-state value, and is a sigmoid function.

The activity of the ions at both sides of neuron membrane, inside the axon and across a synapse is electrical in nature, and gives a waveform (often called spikes) which is consistent with modulated (by convolution) Poisson distribution.

The interplay between the pre-synaptic cells and post-synaptic cells result in the concept commonly referred to as synaptic plasticity. This interplay, called synaptic plasticity, is believed to be mainly responsible for learning and memory of the brain. Synaptic plasticity is modelled in a weight update algorithm called spike timing-dependent plasticity (STDP). The weight update algorithm is given by:

$$\frac{d}{dt}w_{ij} = \quad \textbf{(16)}$$

$$\varepsilon_i \cdot \varepsilon_j \cdot \left[(w_{LTP}-w_{ij})\cdot\sum_{t_i} P\cdot\left[t-(t_j)^{last}\right]\cdot\delta\cdot(t-t_i) - (w_{ij}-w_{LTD})\cdot\sum_{t_j} Q\cdot\left[t-(t_i)^{last}\right]\cdot\delta\cdot(t-t_j)\right]$$

where

$$P(t) = A_+\exp\left(\frac{-t}{\tau_p}\right);$$

$$\varepsilon_i = 1-\exp\left[\frac{-\left[(t_i)^{last}-(t_i)^{last-1}\right]}{\tau_{post}}\right]$$; where P, Q = memory functions.

$$Q(t) = A\_exp(\frac{-t}{\tau_q})$$; ε_i = spike efficacy; τ = time constant.

$$\varepsilon_j = 1 - \exp\left[\frac{-\left[\left(t_j\right)^{last} - \left(t_j\right)^{last-1}\right]}{\tau_{pre}}\right];$$

Hardware *neuromorphic design* of neural networks in analogue implementation is very promising because this has the capability to mimic the biological neurons and synapses. This may be illustrated in an industrial application of Intel 8017 ETANN [8]. In [8], a proton-antiproton collider at Fermilab Tevatron, Intell ETANN chip is employed in the classification of energy deposited in a calorimeter as either from electron or from gamma rays.

BAYESIAN NETWORKS

Gaussian Mixture Model

For a Gaussian Mixrure Model (GMM), three different probabilities are required; the component likelihood (or prior probability) p(x|j) (also called activations), the data probability p(x), and the posterior probability p(j|x). The prior probability p(x|j) is also known as component's density function (see previous chapter).

To determine the GMM parameters μ,σ (called the mean, and standard deviation respectively) from a given data set, the data log likelihood is maximized. Maximizing the data log likelihood is the same as minimizing the negative log likelihood of the data. Thus we wish to solve:

$$E = -L = -\sum_{n-1}^{N} ln(p(x^n)) \qquad \textbf{(17)}$$

This may be treated as an error function. Equation (17) achieves a global minimum at a point x when $\mu_j = x$; and then the variance σ^2 tends to zero there. The value of this global minimum is $-\infty$ unfortunately. To avoid global minimum, very small value of σ^2 are often replaced algorithmically by a constant value.

To model large data, GMM require a reasonably large number of local minima. This large number of local minima corresponds to poor model of the density function of data to be modelled by GMM. The GMM would normally be initialised close to these local minima. The initialization of GMM is often multi-point and multi-dimensional, similar to genetic algorithms' population initialisation. To find the local minima of equation (17) requires differentiation. That is the storage of intermediate differentiation values may be an issue. Also the calculation of derivatives may be memory intensive. Luckily, an elegant procedure, called Expectation-Maximization (E-M) algorithm may replace differentiation. The E-M algorithm does not integrate nor differentiate, thus saving CPU and storage requirements. It does not require any parameter to be set either manually or by another algorithm. The E-M may fill in missing value for data-set that have missing values, provided the non-missing data is sufficiently large, as discussed in the previous chapter. Also for probabilistic graphical models, the E-M is able to provide upper bound on error E (equation (17)). This E-M algorithm is now presented.

The Expectation-Maximization Algorithm (E-M): Let I_j be the indices of the data point taken from component j. If N is the total number of data points, then the prior probability P(j) is given by;

$$P(j) = \frac{|I_j|}{N} \tag{18}$$

whereas the mean μ_j is given by

$$\mu_j = \frac{\sum_{i \in I_j} x_j^i}{|I_j|} \tag{19}$$

There are many forms in which the covariance may appear; for spherical covariance,

$$\sigma_j^2 = \frac{\sum_{i \in I_j} \left\| x^i - \mu_j \right\|^2}{d\left| I_j \right|} \quad \textbf{(20)}$$

For each data point x, there is a corresponding random variable z. Let y = (x,z), and w denote parameters (μ,σ^2) of the mixture model;

$$p((x, z = j) \mid w) = p(x \mid z = j, w)P(z = j \mid w) \quad \textbf{(21)}$$

$$p(x \mid z = j, w)P(z = j \mid w) = p(x \mid \theta_j)P(z = j \mid w)$$

$$p(x \mid w) = \sum_{j=1}^{M} p(x \mid \theta_j)P(z = j \mid w) \quad \textbf{(22)}$$

Where P(z=j|w) is the mixing coefficient in this case. If w^m is given, $y^m = (x^m, z^m)$, and equations (18) (19), and (20), may be used to estimate w^m+1. This is done by forming a function $Q(w|w^m)$ as shown:

$$Q(w \mid w^{(m)}) = E(\ln(p(y \mid w))p(z^n \mid x^n, w^{(m)}) \quad \textbf{(23)}$$

$$Q(w \mid w^{(m)}) = \sum_{j=1}^{M}\sum_{i=1}^{N} P(z^n = j \mid x^n, w^{(m)})[\ln(p(x^n, z^n \mid w))] \quad \textbf{(24)}$$

Take log of $p(x|\theta_j)P(z{=}j|w)$ *and set* $P(z{=}j|w) = P(j)$

$$Q(w \mid w^{(m)}) = \sum_{j=1}^{M}\sum_{i=1}^{N} [\ln(P(j)) + \ln(p(x^n \mid \theta_j))]P^m(j \mid x^n) \quad \textbf{(25)}$$

Apply Bayes Theorem to $P^m(j|x^n)$;

$$P^m(j \mid x^n) = P(z^n = j \mid x^n, w^{(m)}) = \frac{P^m(j)p(x^n \mid \theta_j^{(m)})}{\sum_{j=1}^{M} P^m(j)p(x^n \mid \theta_j^{(m)})} \quad \textbf{(26)}$$

Equation (17), when applied to (26) is the expected posterior distribution E(P^m (j

$| x^n$)) of the cluster considered in the observed data. This concludes the E- step of the E-M algorithm. In the M-step, we maximize Q as follows:

$$w^{(m+1)} = \arg(\max_w(Q(w \mid w^{(m)}))) \qquad \textbf{(27)}$$

Equation (26) is subjected to the constraint that $\sum_j P(j) = 1$.

The constraint may be re-written as

$$0 = \sum_j P(j) - 1$$

but by mulipying by Lagrange multiplier λ;

$$0 \leq \lambda\left(\sum_j P(j) - 1\right)$$

Adding to Q, we form

$$Q + \lambda\left(\sum_{j=1}^{M} P(j) - 1\right) \qquad \textbf{(28)}$$

Differentiate (28) with respect to P(j) and set the result to zero, it gives

$$P^{(m+1)}(j) = \frac{\sum_{n=1}^{N} P^m(j \mid x^n)}{N} \qquad \textbf{(29)}$$

Differentiate equation (28) with respect to μj and set the result to zero, which gives:

$$\mu_j^{(m+1)} = \frac{\sum_{n=1}^{N} P^m(j \mid x^n) x^n}{\sum_{n=1}^{N} P^m(j \mid x^n)} \qquad \textbf{(30)}$$

Thus the M-step updates the prior probability as in equation (29), the mean as in equation (30), and the covariance (matrices) as in equations (31 to 33) below. For the covariance matrices, Q is differentiated with respect to covariance matrix parameters and the result set to zero. Three different covariance cases are illustrated below:

a. Spherical covariance matrices:

$$\left(\sigma_j^{(m+1)}\right)^2 = \frac{1}{d}\frac{\sum_{n=1}^{N} P^m(j \mid x^n)\left\| x^n - \mu_j^{(m+1)} \right\|^2}{\sum_{n=1}^{N} P^m(j \mid x^n)} \quad \textbf{(31)}$$

b. Diagonal covariance matrices:

$$\left(\sigma_{j,i}^{(m+1)}\right)^2 = \frac{\sum_{n=1}^{N} P^m(j \mid x^n)\left(x_i^n - \mu_{j,i}^{(m+1)}\right)^2}{\sum_{n=1}^{N} P^m(j \mid x^n)} \quad \textbf{(32)}$$

c. Full covariance matrices:

$$\Sigma_j = \frac{\sum_{n=1}^{N} P^m(j \mid x^n)\left(x^n - \mu_j^{(m+1)}\right)\left(x^n - \mu_j^{(m+1)}\right)^T}{\sum_{n=1}^{N} P^m(j \mid x^n)} \quad \textbf{(33)}$$

The E-M algorithm iteratively modifies the GMM parameters such that E (equation (16)) decreases towards the local minimum.

K-means

The k-means algorithm find k vectors μj (j=1,2,…,k), called means, which represent an entire dataset. For a given data-set, μj means are calculated as:

$$\mu_j = \frac{\sum_{n \in S_j} x^n}{N_j}; \quad j = 1, 2, \ldots, K \quad \textbf{(34)}$$

where Sj is the j-th disjoint cluster, and N_j is the number of data points in cluster S_j. Then every data points x^n are arranged close to each μ_j means by minimizing the sum-of-square E_s error function;

$$E_s = \sum_{j=1}^{k} \sum_{n \in S_j} \left\| x^n - \mu_j \right\|^2 \tag{35}$$

When the k-means have been found, the dataset is said to be partitioned into k clusters. Since k-vectors are found and not a distribution, therefore the clusters does not constitute density models.

The k-means can be used to initialise means of data and thus partition data into k-clusters. The means μj and covariance σ^2 of each cluster can then be iteratively determined so that a GMM can be formed, or (at least) a Radial Basis Function (RBF) can be formed from them.

Radial Basis Function (RBF)

Suppose we have a classification problem consisting of c classes. We sought to obtain M density functions to represent the class-conditional densities. The density will be summed by j = 1, 2 ,..., Mover all density functions as given below. From Bayes theorem;

$$p(c_k \mid x)p(x) = p(x \mid c_k)p(c_k)$$

$$p(c_k \mid x) = \frac{p(x \mid c_k)p(c_k)}{p(x)} \tag{36}$$

The density will be summed by j = 1, 2 ,...,M over all density functions;

$$p(x \mid c_k) = \sum_{j=1}^{M} p(x \mid j)p(j \mid c_k) \tag{37}$$

The data (prior) probability is given by

$$p(x) = \sum_{k=1}^{c} p(x \mid c_k) p(c_k) \tag{38}$$

Followed by summation over all classes;

$$\sum_{j=1}^{M} p(x \mid c_k) p(c_k) = \sum_{k=1}^{c} \sum_{j=1}^{M} p(x \mid j) p(j \mid c_k) p(c_k) \tag{39}$$

$$\sum_{j=1}^{M} p(x \mid c_k) p(c_k) = \sum_{j=1}^{M} p(x \mid j) \left[\sum_{k=1}^{c} p(j \mid c_k) p(c_k) \right]$$

Similar to p(x), $p(j) = \left[\sum_{k=1}^{c} p(j \mid c_k) p(c_k) \right]$ **(40)**

Therefore $\sum_{j=1}^{M} p(x \mid c_k) p(c_k) = \sum_{j=1}^{M} p(x \mid j) p(j)$

and $p(x) = \sum_{j=1}^{M} p(x \mid c_k) p(c_k) = \sum_{j=1}^{M} p(x \mid j) p(j)$

From equation (35) and (36);

$$p(c_k \mid x) = \frac{p(x \mid c_k) p(c_k)}{p(x)} = \frac{\sum_{j=1}^{M} p(x \mid j) p(j \mid c_k) p(c_k)}{p(x)}$$

$$\frac{\sum_{j=1}^{M} p(x \mid j) p(j \mid c_k) p(c_k)}{p(x)} = \frac{\sum_{j=1}^{M} p(x \mid j) p(j \mid c_k) p(c_k)}{\sum_{j=1}^{M} p(x \mid j) p(j)}$$

Multiply by $\frac{p(j)}{p(j)}$

$$\frac{\sum_{j=1}^{M} p(x \mid j) p(j \mid c_k) p(c_k)}{\sum_{j=1}^{M} p(x \mid j) p(j)} = \frac{\sum_{j=1}^{M} p(x \mid j) p(j \mid c_k) p(c_k)}{\sum_{j=1}^{M} p(x \mid j) p(j)} \frac{p(j)}{p(j)}$$

$$\frac{\sum_{j=1}^{M} p(x \mid j) p(j \mid c_k) p(c_k)}{\sum_{j=1}^{M} p(x \mid j) p(j)} \frac{p(j)}{p(j)} = \frac{p(x \mid j) p(j)}{\sum_{j=1}^{M} p(x \mid j) p(j)} \left[\frac{p(j \mid c_k) p(c_k)}{p(j)} \right]$$

$$\text{denote } \phi_j(x) = \frac{p(x \mid j) p(j)}{\sum_{j=1}^{M} p(x \mid j) p(j)} = p(j \mid x) \quad \textbf{(41)}$$

$$\text{denote } w_{kj} = \left[\frac{p(j \mid c_k) p(c_k)}{p(j)} \right] = p(c_k \mid j) \quad \textbf{(42)}$$

$$\text{Then } p(c_k \mid x) = \sum_{j=1}^{M} \phi_j(x) w_{kj} \quad \textbf{(43)}$$

$$y_k(x) = p(c_k \mid x) = \sum_{j=1}^{M} \phi_j(x) w_{kj} + w_{k0} \quad \textbf{(44)}$$

Where w_{k0} is called the bias of $y_k(x) = p(c_k \mid x)$ and equation (44) can normally be re-written as:

$$y_k(x) = \sum_{j=0}^{M} \phi_j(x) w_{kj} \quad \textbf{(45)}$$

When $Ø_j(x)$ is a Gaussian p.d.f. (see chapter 3), the $y_k(x)$ is called Radial Basis Function (RBF). The RBF is a member of a general group of networks called Support Vector Machine (SVM). The SVM is as described by $y_k(x)$, where the function $Ø_j(x)$ is called the *support vector* of the space (data) considered. Several forms of $Ø_j(x)$ exist, and they are sometimes also referred to as *kernel functions*.The w_{kj} is known as the weight which connect the nodes of the network. Equations (36) to (45) represents SVM (RBF) algorithm which is developed from Bayes theorem. The function $Ø_j(x)$ may be expressed in various forms separately, depending on the features of the problem to be solved. Various types of $Ø_j(x)$ may be employed with the SVM (RBF) algorithm to achieve a desired solution. This is because the SVM (RBF) may be considered as a universal approximator.

Generative Topographic Mapping (GTM)

A computational tractable non-linear mapping from a latent space to data space by a mixture of Gaussian densities is called Generative Topographic mapping (GTM). By defining a probability density p(z) on the latent space, a corresponding probability density p(y|W) is induced on the data space. This is a situation whereby the data space $x = x_1, x_2, \ldots, x_n$ is a d-dimensional space, whereas the latent space data $z = z_1, z_2, \ldots, z_q$ is a q-dimensional latent space ($q < d$). The map y(z,W) maps every z in a latent space to a corresponding q-dimensional real(- numbered) space embedded in a d-dimensional space. The map y(z,W) may be written as:

$$y(z;W) = W\phi(z) \quad \textbf{(46)}$$

where the $\varnothing(z)$ represents the k fixed basis functions. The map is q-dimensional manifold parameterized by W, the network connection weights. Adjusting the weights W is equivalent to adjusting connections between nodes of a network. An important feature of GTM is that the kernel centres of the latent space is preserved by the map y(z;W) to data-space structurally. For data which are not complex-valued, spherical Gaussian with variance σ^2 is a suitable model, thereby casting the conditional data density $p(x|z,W,\sigma)$ into the form:

Equation (46) integrates to $p(x|W,\sigma) = \int p(x|\, z,W,\sigma)p(z)dz$ which is intractable even analytically. But if the probability density function p(z) of the latent variable z is given (it is $\varnothing(z)$ of equation (46)) by a sum of delta functions centred on the nodes $z_1, z_2, .., z_M$ of the network:

$$p(x\,|\,z,W,\sigma) = \frac{1}{(2\pi\sigma^2)^{d/2}} \exp\left(-\frac{\|y(z,W)-x\|^2}{2\sigma^2}\right) \quad \textbf{(47)}$$

$$p(z) = \frac{1}{M}\sum_{j=1}^{M}\delta(z - z_j) \quad \textbf{(48)}$$

a uniform Gaussian distribution may be feasible depending on whether the deltas are uniformly distributed or not. Even, an approximate distribution of the deltas suffices to facilitate a *sum of Gaussian representation* of the conditional data density as follows:

$$p(x\,|\,W,\sigma)=\frac{1}{M}\sum_{j=1}^{M}p(x\,|\,z_j,W,\sigma) \qquad \textbf{(49)}$$

Each of these M Gaussian has centres which is functionally represented by y(z,W), not independent of other centres, but constrained to lie in the manifold.Since a spherical Gaussian with variance σ^2 is suitable, modelling the real(- numbered) data with mixtures of Gaussian, and employing the RBF network for the mapping to lower space spanned by $Ø(z)$ basis function is suitable. The RBF may be trained either by a generalized E-M of the previous section, or a regularized E-M [9] algorithm. To employ the generalized E-M of the previous section for RBF's training, some notes to be take are as follows.

The log-likelihood $L(W,\sigma)$, of data is given by

$$L(W,\sigma)=\sum_{n=1}^{N}\log\left[\frac{1}{M}\sum_{j=1}^{M}p(x_n\,|\,z_j,W,\sigma)\right] \qquad \textbf{(50)}$$

The posterior probability (or responsibility) of the real data is

$$r_{jn}^{(m)}(W^{(m)},\sigma^{(m)})=p^{(m)}(j\,|\,x_n,W^{(m)},\sigma^{(m)})=\frac{p(x_n\,|\,z_j,W^{(m)},\sigma^{(m)})}{\sum_{j=1}^{M}p(x_n\,|\,z_j,W^{(m)},\sigma^{(m)})} \qquad \textbf{(51)}$$

For the M-step of the E-M algorithm, the complete (or maybe completed) data log likelihood $L_c(W,\sigma)$ is given by:

$$L_c(W,\sigma)=\sum_{n=1}^{N}\sum_{j=1}^{M}r_{jn}^{(m)}(W^{(m)},\sigma^{(m)})\log\left(p(x_n\,|\,z_j,W^{(m)},\sigma^{(m)})\right) \qquad \textbf{(52)}$$

Maximizing (51) with respect to weight W gives:

$$\sum_{n=1}^{N}\sum_{j=1}^{M}r_{jn}^{(m)}(W^{(m)},\sigma^{(m)})(W^{(m+1)}\phi(z_j)-x_n)\phi^{T}(z_j)=0 \qquad \textbf{(53)}$$

Maximizing (51) with respect to σ gives:

$$(\sigma^{(m+1)})^2=\frac{1}{Nd}\sum_{n=1}^{N}\sum_{j=1}^{M}r_{jn}(W^{(m)},\sigma^{(m)})\left\|W^{(m+1)}\phi(z_j)-x_n\right\|^2 \qquad \textbf{(54)}$$

The parameters of $\emptyset(z)$ is fixed to model the p. d. f of the latent space which is (approximately) Gaussian, and constitute the kernel whose structure is preserved by the map y(z, W) to real data space.

NEURO-FUZZY SYSTEM

Neuro-fuzzy system is the fusion between at least one neural network and multiple fuzzy-logic neurons of chapter 3. The fusion may be in any order, and any number of networks may participate in the fusion. The fusion is architecturally described as sequential, parallel, or hierarchical (modular) All other forms of combination of neural networks (the component neural networks should be independent) that is not either sequential, parallel nor hierarchical (modular) is hybrid. Various forms exist and could be grouped as follows:

1. Those that have the conventional topology but uses fuzzy neurons at their nodes.
2. The conventional fuzzy system that employs classical neural network for numerical computations either during derivation of membership function or during derivation of fuzzy rules. This is different from the sequential system, since the classical neural network could be located anywhere within the fuzzy system.
3. There exist a group of classical neural network that employs fuzzy methods to update their weights instead of a learning parameter and sensitivity function (*i.e.* differential of log-likelihood function with respect to weights).
4. A group consist of fuzzy systems and classical neural network, working independently, and synchronised.
5. A group involve one or more mixtures from the above-mentioned neural networks.

One example of Neuro-fuzzy hybrid NN was designed by Canuto [10, 11]. In this, a fuzzy neural network called RePART, a fuzzy multi-layer perceptron (F- MLP) and radial RAM was used. The RePART neural network is a normal ARTMAP but with reward/punishment process. The fuzzy MLP is a normal MLP but with fuzzy nodes at the output nodes. Radial RAM is a normal neuron but employs a radial region, defined by its Hamming distance from a reference point in its training and recall phase. The final output is then compared with a radial region defined by Gaussian distribution.

Another important example is the Adaptive-Network-based Fuzzy inference System shown in Fig. (7) (ANFIS), as proposed by Jang [12]. ANFIS is a Sugeno-type fuzzy system. The commonest ANFIS system is a first- or zero- order Sugeno system. A five-layered ANFIS would normally consist of a fuzzification layer as input (first) layer as shown in (Fig. 7). Fuzzification is done by application of bell shaped membership function μA(x)

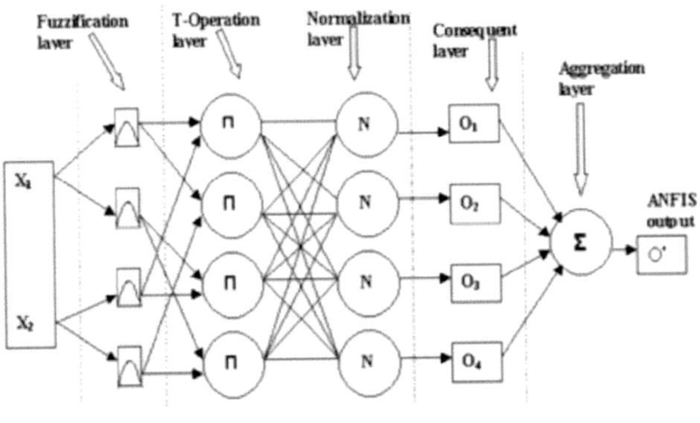

Fig. (7). An adaptive-network-based fuzzy inference system (ANFIS).

as defined in equation (54);

$$\mu_{(A_i)^p}(x_i) = \frac{1}{1+\left[\left(\frac{x_i - c_p}{a_p}\right)^2\right]^{b_p}} \quad \textbf{(55)}$$

where p_c, p_a, and p_b, are network parameters; x_i = input pattern (variable).

The fuzzification is employ in the definition of the linguist variable. The second layer nodes applies T-norm operator. Its output is normalised by the third layer. The fourth layer computes the "then" part of the fuzzy rule. The output of the fourth layer is summed by the output layer which is the fifth layer. Interested reader may consult [1] on ANFIS.

RESEARCH AND APPLICATIONS OF ANN SYSTEMS

Research publications on multi-classifier are increasing with notable methods of combinations. Breiman [13, 14] utilizes decision tree as base "classifiers" with boosting, and refers to decision tree multi-classifier system as the most significant development in classifier design in this decade. Refering to classifier diversity and biases, Gemam *et al.* [15], and Mitchell [16] maintained that different types of classifiers have different types of "inductive biases". The combination of base classifiers has witness sequences of development - from averaging [17], to majority voting by Bodgan [18], to using special techniques and/or function by Gunter [19]. The most advanced stage is the usage of other classifiers for combination [17]. Using classifier for classifier fusion is termed *intelligent combination*. In this section, sample industrial applications of ANN systems which have been described in other sections of this chapter are given.

Real-time machine health monitoring may be achieved by employment of GMM as in [20]. Also, machines may be diagnosed for faults as in [21] using GMM. Printers may be identified by GMM [22] depending on printed texts from printers. Tex independent identification using GMM may be achieved as in [23], in an automatic speaker recognition (ASR) framework.

On a dedicated circuit board called CogniBlox [24] featured a Radial Bases Function (RBF) and k-nearest neighbour. CogniBlok is stackable with each board in the stack having 4096 neurons. CogniMem [24] states that latency of recognition is independent of number of stacks, and also independent of numbers of chips that are daisy-chained. Buses on each board are 23-pins in parallel, and can be connected directly in the stack without connectivity and/or communication issues. Thus a hierarchical ANN system of many RBF and K-nearest neighbours may be constructed by simply stacking several CogniBlox boards. Sensors may then be attached to the stack in the usual way. The scalability offered by [24] may not degrade performances because of lack of increased latency, communication lag and/or connectivity issues.

Pertaining home appliances, cookers whose functionality depends on neuro-fuzzy ANN systems are manufactured by Zojirushi [25]. For safety purposes, a neuro-fuzzy ANN system may be constructed as in [26] for intrusion detection

CONFLICT OF INTEREST

The author confirm that this chapter contents have no conflict of interest.

ACKNOWLEDGEMENTS

Cited works are appreciated.

REFERENCES

[1] Karray F O, De Silva C. Soft computing and intelligent system design. Essex (England): Pearson Educational Ltd.: Edinburgh Gate, Harlow, CM20 2JE 2004.

[2] Lorrentz P, Howells WG, McDonald-Maier KD. FPGA-based enhanced probabilistic convergent network for human iris recognition. Proceedings of 17th Symp. On ANN, ESANN'2009..

[3] Aleksander , Thomas WV, Bowden PA. WISARD: A radical step forward in image recognition. Sensor Review 1984; 4(3): 120-4.
[http://dx.doi.org/10.1108/eb007637]

[4] Reynolds C. Flocks, herds, and schools: a distributed behavior model. Comput Graph 1987; 21(4): 25-34.
[http://dx.doi.org/10.1145/37402.37406]

[5] JADE - Java Agent Development Framework. TILab SpA, (C) 2000; TILab SpA, (C) 2001; TILab SpA, (C) 2002; and TILab SpA (C) 2003.

[6] FIPA. The Foundation for Intelligent Physical Agents, FIPA standards. Available from http://www.fipa.org. , [cited sept 2014];

[7] Hodgkin AL, Huxley AF. A quantitative description of membrane current and its application to conduction and excitation in nerve. J Physiol 1952; 117(4): 500-44.
[http://dx.doi.org/10.1113/jphysiol.1952.sp004764] [PMID: 12991237]

[8] Moerland P, Fiesler E. Neural Network adaptation to hardware implementations, IDIAP-RR 97-17. Handbook of Neural Computation. New York: Institute of Physics Publishing and Oxford University Publishing 1997.
[http://dx.doi.org/10.1887/0750303123/b365c78]

[9] Schneider Tapio. Analysis of Incomplete Climate Data. Estimation of Mean Values and Covariance Matrices and Imputation of Missing Values. Camridge: MIT Press Journals 2001. 55 Hayward Street, MA USA 02142-1315

[10] De Canuto AM. Combining Neural Networks and Fuzzy Logic for Application in Character Recognition. PhD Thesis. Kent (UK): University of Kent 2001.

[11] De Canuto AM, Howells WG, Fairhurst MC. The use of confidence measures to enhance combination strategies in multi-network neuro-fuzzy system. Connect Sci 2000; 12(3/4): 315-31.
[http://dx.doi.org/10.1080/09540090010014089]

[12] Jang JR. ANFIS: adaptive-network-based fuzzy inference system. IEEE Trans Syst Man Cybern 1992; 23(3): 665-85.
[http://dx.doi.org/10.1109/21.256541]

[13] Breiman L. Bagging predictors. Tech Report 421. Carlifornia: Dept of Statistics, University of California, Berkeley 1994.

[14] Breiman L. Combining predictors. In: Sharkey A, Ed. Combining Artificial Neural Nets. Springer-Verlag 1999; pp. 31-50.

[15] German S, Bienenstock E, Doursat R. Neural networks and the bias/variance dilemma. Neural Comput 1992; 4(1): 1-58.
[http://dx.doi.org/10.1162/neco.1992.4.1.1]

[16] Mitchell T. Machine Learning. California: Morgan Kaufmann San Mateo, CA, USA. 1997.

[17] Ranawana R, Palade V. Multi-classifier systems – review and a roadmap for developers. UK: Oxford: University of Oxford Computing Laboratory, 2006.

[18] Gabrys B, Ruta D. Genetic algorithm in classifier fusion. Appl Soft Comput 2006; 6: 337-47.
[http://dx.doi.org/10.1016/j.asoc.2005.11.001]

[19] Günter Simon, Bunke Horst. Feature Selection Algorithm for the Generation of Multiple Classifier Systems and their Application to Handwritten Word Recognition. Bern: Department of Computer Science, University of Bern, Switzerland 2004.

[20] Liu W, Xin Z, Jay L, Linxia L, Min Z. Application of a novel method for machine performance degradation assessment based on gaussian mixture model and logistic regression. Chin J Mech Eng 2011; 24(5): 879. N0. *

[21] Yu G, Li C, Sun J. Machine fault diagnosis based on Gaussian mixture model and its application. Int J Adv Manuf Technol 2010; 48(1-4): 205-12.
[http://dx.doi.org/10.1007/s00170-009-2283-5]

[22] Gazi Ali N, Pei-Ju Chiang, Aravind Mikkilineni K, George Chiu T, Edward Delp J, Jan Allebach P. Application of Principal Components Analysis and Gaussian Mixture Models to Printer Identification. Indiana, USA: School of Electrical and Computer Engineering, School of Mechanical Engineering, Purdue University, West Lafayette 2004.

[23] Maesa A, Garzia F, Scarpiniti M, Cusani R. Text independent automatic speaker recognition system using mel-frequency cepstrum coefficient and gaussian mixture models. J Info Secur Sci Res 2012; 3: 335-40.

[24] CogniMem™ Technologies. CognMem. 81 Blue Ravine Road, Suite 240; Folsom, CA 95630 USA.

[25] Casa.com. Cup Neuro Fuzzy Rice Cooker & Warmer. New Jersey: Zojirushi NS-ZCC10 5-1/2 . P.O. Box 483, Jersey City, NJ 07303, USA

[26] Chavan S, Shah K, Dave N, Mukherjee S. Adaptive Neuro-Fuzzy Intrusion Detection Systems. In: Proceedings of the International Conference on Information Technology: Coding and Computing (ITCC'04).; IEEE 2004; pp. 70-4.

CHAPTER 7

Neural Networks

Abstract: This chapter describe various types of ANN systems in relative detail. It is the aim of the chapter to give descriptions of advanced ANN system in such a detail as to facilitate easy implementation. The first few sections are dedicated to the recent weightless neural networks. This is followed by a weighted neural system section. Two advanced Bayesian network are introduced subsequently. The last section of the chapter explains the dynamics of ANN and how ANN nay be evaluated. The chapter has given a relatively extensive description of typical advanced neural networks from various categories of ANN systems.

Keywords: Adjustment, Back-propagation, Boltzmann distribution, Conditional probability, Division, Enhanced Probabilistic Convergent Network (EPCN), Generalized Likelihood Ration Test (GLRT), Helmholtz Machine, Kernel function, Kullback-Leibler divergence, Merging, Minimum Description Length, Mixture Density Network (MDN), Multi-classifier, Multi-expert System, Multi-Layered Perceptron (MLP), Probabilistic Convergent Network (PCN), Random Access Memory (RAM), Squared error, Wald test.

INTRODUCTION

In sections 1 and 2, some weightless neural networks are described in considerable detail. Weightless networks are presented here because they form a good alternative to weighted classical neural networks and also less prone to noise. A stereo-type weighted network, the Multi-Layered Perceptron (MLP), is described in the third section. The MLP is included because of its robustness and popularity; it represents a good example of weighted neural networks. Section four describes more advanced types of Bayesian classifier. They are suitably introduced here because the usual types of Bayesian classifiers have been described in chapter 6. The last section of chapter 7 presents the dynamics of an ANN system, and discussed the fusion mechanism of hierarchical network. This is followed by methods of independent evaluation of ANN systems.

Pierre Lorrentz

The first and second sections of chapter 7 show ANN systems whose learning and recognition algorithms are derived from Boolean logic.. The PCN and EPCN may be employed in selection mechanism described in chapter 8. Seeking minimal sets of weights by MLP may be synonymous to seeking a set of (minimal) basis functions. Whatever the structural architecture of MLP that has been determined may be implemented by using the classical primitives (gates) of chapter 5. The MLP can be used as a component neural network of neuro-fuzzy system of chapter 6. The probability theories of chapters 2 may have provided sufficient background principle to the Bayesian networks of the fourth section of chapter 7. Any of the Bayesian network may participate in the selection mechanism of chapter 8. The last section of this chapter may be regarded as a continuation of performance evaluation methods that has been introduced in chapter 4. The performance evaluation mechanism of the last section is algorithmic and in considerable detail, whereas that of chapter 4 is introductory. Most ANN systems of other chapters may be evaluated for performance by using the methods of the last section of chapter 7.

Chapter 7 has described large number of standard ANN systems in considerable detail.

WEIGHTLESS NETWORKS

This section introduces a neural network whose functionality depends essentially on Boolean logic.

Probabilistic Convergent Network (PCN)

Many prediction problems and pattern recognition problems can be solved by performing Boolean logic on them. In situations whereby prediction or recognition problems can be interpreted in terms of Boolean logic, a type of random access memory (RAM) based network called Probabilistic Convergent Network (PCN) becomes suitable. An added advantage of PCN over existing RAM-based network is the inclusion of confidence measure.

To carry out a logic representing, it is anticipated that all inputs be condensed to threshold image. Due to the complexity of architecture and function of PCN, some terminologies are worth introducing which will be used throughout this section. They are explained below

Binary inputs:- The Probabilistic Convergent Neuron (PCN) accepts as input, binary images only. Any input data is threshold-binarized and appropriately resized so that PCN may make sense of the data.

Compound Symbol:- Symbols are used to denote the neuron output of PCN. The architecture of PCN is shown in (Fig. **1**). Neuron outputs are inherently restricted to a small set of symbols often only "1" and "0". These are set of symbols often called base symbols. To extend the size of symbols which a neuron may employ, other symbols may be presented. For instance, if classes are labelled with numbers 0 – 9, the same set of characters 0 to 9 may be used also as additional symbol. This permit the storage and recall of those symbols which correspond with input class label. The RAM-based ANN concern is said to have used a compound symbol. As an illustration, a compound symbol that consist of class "5" and "6" may be "56" that is classes "5" and "6" might have been learned to the RAM-based ANN. The main difference in neuron output of PCN, as compared to other weightless nets, is the indication of frequency. The rate at which one class queries a certain memory is designated in PCN and Enhanced PCN (EPCN). For instance, if two classes querying a memory, if class "1" query the memory 75 times and class "2" query the same memory 25 times, the output of the RAM-neuron will be [75, 25]. If class "2" queries the memory 25 times and class "1" queries the memory 75 times, the result is: [25, 75]. Thus PCN and EPCN give the "probability" of incidence of every pattern class in a database.

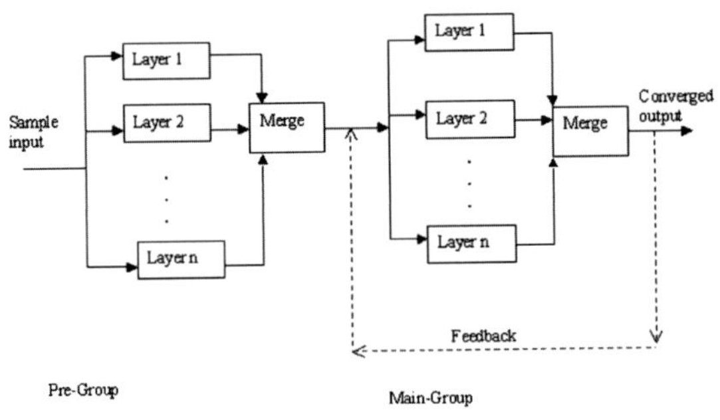

Fig. (1). A schematic representation of Probabilistic Convergent Network (PCN). This is an example of a RAM-based Neural Networks (NNs) [1].

Adjustment:- For N training pattern and x division, a number "a" occurring in a memory location will be adjusted as:

$$\hat{a} = a\frac{x}{N} \text{ , followed by } \tilde{a} = round\left(\hat{a}\right) \quad \textbf{(1)}$$

where ã=the new value replacing a in that location. This adjustment is essential to limit the probability measure of every class to the number-of-division (a constant value) which is chosen a priori. If the quantity per class of learning pattern differs, classes having enormous learning set may also have big probability during classification, even if the quantity of their test or validation set is small. Adjustment minimizes this big probability to the true value present during classification. Adjustment is also employed in extermination of rounding errors and truncation errors.

Division:- This is an integer that denotes the total of all the weighted probability of the classes. The probability of existence of each class is related to division. As an illustration, assuming we have 3 classes and the division is set to 100, then if the result of PCN is say [50 25 25], the total of this would be 100. This output may be construed to mean: The pattern trained to the ANN pertain to class "1" with probability 0.5, to class "2" with probability 0.25, and to class "3" with probability 0.25. It is noteworthy that the length of the array [50 25 25] output of PCN is often identical to the sum of classes being considered.

Merging:- For a given class, the memory locations of all layers may be called, and adjusted (as explained previously) using the constant *division*, a single compound symbol will then be formed as a result of this – it is repeated for all classes. It may also lead to collapsing of all layers into one layer called the *merge layer*; this process is known as *merging*.

Neuron:- The smallest complete activity maintenance unit in the PCN and EPCN is known as a neuron.

PCN Network Architecture

The PCN consist of a pre-group, a merge layer for the pre-group, the main- group, and merge-layer for the main-group. A response from the main-group merge-layer to the main-group layers themselves is explicitly implemented as shown in Fig. (**1**). Each group is arranged in layers. Each layer consists of neurons. Each neuron consists of storage locations called the N-tuple locations. An alternative view is to regard each layer as a look-up table (LUT). The neurons are arranged in (x * y)-matrices where (x* y) represents image dimension. Every element in an input image is associated, *via* connectivity and multiplexing, with a neuron in each layer.

Learning or Training

Learning starts when a new pattern is presented to the NN. It is assumed that the pattern is thresholded (*i.e.*; binarised). The procedures are as follows:

- Addresses are formed from input pattern. These addresses (also called connectivity) are used to access neurons within a layer and location within neuron.
- The locations within a neuron are relative to number of classes.
- The size of a layer is relative to the size of pattern.
- Depending on which pattern class an address is formed from, a corresponding location will have its value incremented.
- A normalisation phase followed. This consists of dividing the value in each neuron location by the number of corresponding training pattern followed by multiplication by the number of division. The result is rounded to the nearest whole number as in equation (1).
- These whole numbers will be stored back in neuron locations of the pre-group.

Recognition or Classification

A recognition procedure is as follows:

- The pre-group layers will be merged into a single layer; this is called pre-group merge-layer.
- Values in the neuron location of the merge layer will be adjusted to make the "sum-of probabilities" [1] equal to the number of division.
- The connectivity and pre-group merge-layer will be employed in the formation

of the main-group layers.

- Adjustment of values in the RAM-location follows.
- Merging of main-group layers gives main-group merge-layer.
- Values in the merge layer will be summed and adjusted to become neural networks' output. The output may be feedback iteratively into the main-group layers.

THE ENHANCED PROBABILISTIC CONVERGENT NETWORK (EPCN)

The EPCN is a classifier which gives a confidence measure to all classes, based on supervised learning, when a pattern is presented to it for classification. Two types of EPCNs are implemented; one is called rand-EPCN and the other termed fix-EPCN. The major differences between an EPCN and the customary PCN [2] are:-

- The EPCN offers the possibility of adjusting and rescaling any input pattern.
- Formation of connectivity by EPCN may be by using consecutive bits within input pattern coupled with rejection criteria.
- Random selection method of address formation: This method is the customary method of connectivity formation but with the exception in rand- EPCN that coordinates are functionally initialized and dynamic.
- Improved system interfacing: For example, EPCN can learn/recognize
- pattern of moving objects, while PCN cannot.

Because of these enhancements (modifications), the PCNs with these characteristics are known as EPCN – Enhanced Probabilistic Convergent Networks.

THE EPCN

Weighted Neural Network is the ANN system whose performance depends on connection strength and modification of connection strength. The ANN system that first minimize a problem to obtain a logic equivalent, solve the problem in the logic domain, then present the result in a simple (algebraic) form is known as Weightless Neural Network or RAM-based Neural Network [3]. One of the advantages of a weightless Neural Network is its fast learning algorithm, of which the EPCN is an example. The EPCN consist of neurons which are organized into sheets. The structure of EPCN comprises of two sets of sheets. The set of sheets employed in the course of the learning procedure is called the pre-group layer. The set of sheets used mainly in the course of the classification procedure is known as main-group layers. The structure of EPCN comprises essentially of these four constituent sheets known as pre-group layer, pre-group-merge layer, main-group layer, and main-group-merge layer. There is an external feedback from the main-group-merge layer to the main-group layer. Every group of layer consists of certain quantity of sheets with each sheet containing neurons (defined in previous chapters) which themselves consist of a number of memory sites called RAM-locations, depicted in Fig. (**2**).

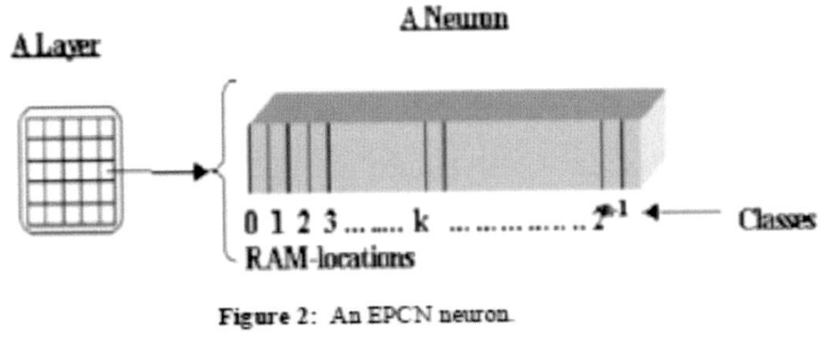

Fig. (2). An EPCN neuron.

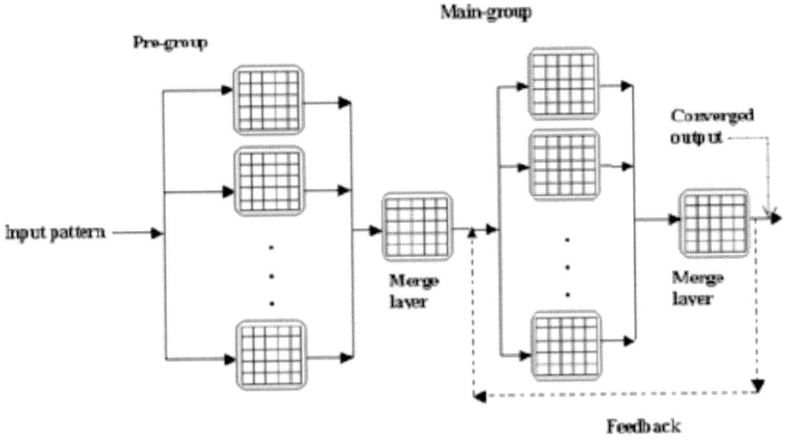

Fig. (3). A schematic representation of EPCN.

Each neuron storing site is distributed among pattern classes. An alternative view is to regard each layer as a look-up table (LUT). The neurons are arranged in (x * y)-matrices where (x* y) represents the input image dimensions. Every constituent of an input pattern allied with a neuron in each layer. The EPCN has a training algorithm that utilizes the pre-group layers, ending the learning with a pre-group-merge layer. Similarly, the classification algorithm utilizes the main- group layer, and ends the classification in the main-group-merge layer. Both algorithms go through adjustment using division and merging (discussed previously) in order to produce their corresponding merge layers. Two types of EPCN are implemented; one is called rand-EPCN and the other termed fix-EPCN. A comparison of the two types of EPCN is presented in Table **1**. The functionality of the architecture depicted in Fig. **(3)** is divided into two procedures called *Learning* and *Recognition* procedure. Both learning and recognition algorithms are now presented.

Table 1. Differences between fix-EPCN and rand-EPCN.

fix-EPCN	**rand-EPCN**
During connectivity formation, random number generator is not used.	During connectivity formation, random number generator is used. Hence the name rand-EPCN.
Successive bits from input image (quantity of bits is subject to type of image) are employed in the composition of connectivity.	Random sampling of bits within image may be employed in the course of connectivity composition.
Precisely same address can be replicated; that is, for the same pattern and the same system parameters, the connectivity is fixed. For this reason, it is known as fix-EPCN.	For the same image and system parameter, different connectivity can be produced. Formation of same connectivity is probable.

Training Process

The EPCN is a weightless supervised ANN. For EPCN to be functional, it uses samples items and images in a training process.

The training process is as follows:-

1. All layers within the network are trained independently.
2. Essentially the pre-group layers only are learned for a specified image class.
3. For each and every neuron in the pre-group layer, connectivity is produced

from threshold image relative to specified connectivity configuration for the layer.

4. Each location in a neuron consists of an array of numbers, each member of this array representing a class. Depending on which pattern class an address is formed from, a corresponding number within the neuron location will be incremented. Otherwise the previous value in that location will be maintained.
5. Following this is an adjustment phase described previously. Adjustment consists of dividing each memory location count by its corresponding number of training pattern and multiplying by the number of division. The result is rounded to the nearest whole number.

After the Learning procedures terminates, EPCN is able to recognise similar objects and patterns. This is done by employing Recognition procedures. Other views about the training procedure may be found in [1].

Recognition procedure

The Recognition procedures for EPCN are as follows:-

1. Connectivity is produced for every neuron in the pre-group similar to the learning algorithm for training. Input data produce connectivity which may correspond to the connectivity patterns of various layers.
2. The main-group layers will be combined to make a single sheet *by the process of merging*. The RAMs inside the neurons of the main-group merge-layer consist of autonomously estimated means (compound symbol!) from analogous RAMs of the main-group layers.
3. After the second step, an adjustment is necessary to ensure that the "sum of probabilities" [1] is identical to the quantity known as division.
4. The result from the main-group merge-layer is fed back in iteration, a fix amount of times, or iterates pending when the result stabilizes, whichever occurs first.

The EPCN Software Implementation

This sub-section gives a short description of the software implementation of EPCN by using Matlab as an example software platform. The software modeling of EPCN chooses Matlab because of its availability, custom functions (*e.g.* sin, cos, plot, *etc.* functions) exist already, and because it is more suitable for engineering prototyping. As compared to alternative modelling software, matlab require less effort in order to produce simulations. In Matlab, help about an EPCN functions is obtainable for individual function by typing:

```
>>help function_name
```

on the command-line. Here, "function_name" is the name of an EPCN function under inquisition. These functions are written in Matlab, with the usual Matlab's function naming method *i.e.*

```
function ans = function_name(variables)
```

as the first line in the M-file. After that, important constants are specified, which is followed by the algorithm which the function implements when called. It is often the case that one function calls another. This maintains interrelationship between PCN functions, analogous to the synapse between neurons.

A WEIGHTED NETWORK

Multi-Layer Perceptron (MLP)

The Multi-layer perceptron (MLP) is the neural network most used for practical applications. Generically, it consists of layers of adaptive weights with full connectivity between the layers. The layers are known as input layer, hidden layer, and output layer. The MLP is capable of approximating, to arbitrary accuracy, any continuous function from a compact region of input space. For this reason it is called a universal approximator. The degree of accuracy depends on the number of hidden layer, the weights, and biases. If the input data to the MLP network is denoted by xi where i = 1, 2, 3, ..., d. The first layer of MLP forms M linear combinations of these input data to give a set of intermediate activation variable $a_j^{(1)}$;

$$a_j^{(1)} = \sum_{i=1}^{d}\left[(w_{ji})^{(1)} x_i + (b_j)^{(1)}\right] j = 1, 2, 3, \ldots, M \qquad (2)$$

Where w_{ji} is an element of the first layer weight matrix, and $b_j^{(1)}$ are the bias parameters.

To begin training, the weight elements w_{ij} are initialized to small random values while the biases are initialized to a constant value (usually +1 or -1). The input layer uses linear combination of weights and biases (equation (2)), the hidden layer normally utilises hyperbolic tangent for activation function, given by equation (3)

$$z_j = tahn\left(a_j\right)^{(1)} \quad \textbf{(3)}$$

which has the property that

$$\frac{d^{(1)}}{d_j^{(1)}} z_j = 1 - z_j^2 \quad \textbf{(4)}$$

Collection of equation (2) forms a fan-in to the second layer, which is also a linear combination given by equation (5).

$$a_k^{(2)} = \sum_{j=1}^{M} w_{ji}^{(2)} z_j + b_k \quad \textbf{(5)}$$

The activation function of the output layer is always different from that of the hidden layers. There are various possible activation functions for the output layer; the common ones are:-

1. **Linear function:-** A linear function of the form

$$y_k = a_k^{(2)} \quad \textbf{(6)}$$

This is the output activation function used for regression problems.

2. **Sigmoid activation function:-** This is also called logistic activation function, it is given by

$$\frac{d}{da_k^{(2n)}} E^n = \left(y_k^n\right) - \left(t_k^n\right) \quad \textbf{(7)}$$

This type of activation curve is used for classification problems involving independent attributes. Sigmoid activation function was discovered by many researchers as the best function that describes the electrical activity of a natural biological neuron (Read the section on neuromorphic neuron of chapter 6 for more detail). For this reason, the sigmoid equation has been since then adopted in most ANN as the activation function of choice.

3. For a set of c mutually exclusive classes, the *softmax activation function* given by

$$y_k = \frac{e^{-\left(a_k^{(2)}\right)}}{\sum_k e^{-\left(a_k^{(2)}\right)}} \quad \textbf{(8)}$$

is often employed in a classification problems.

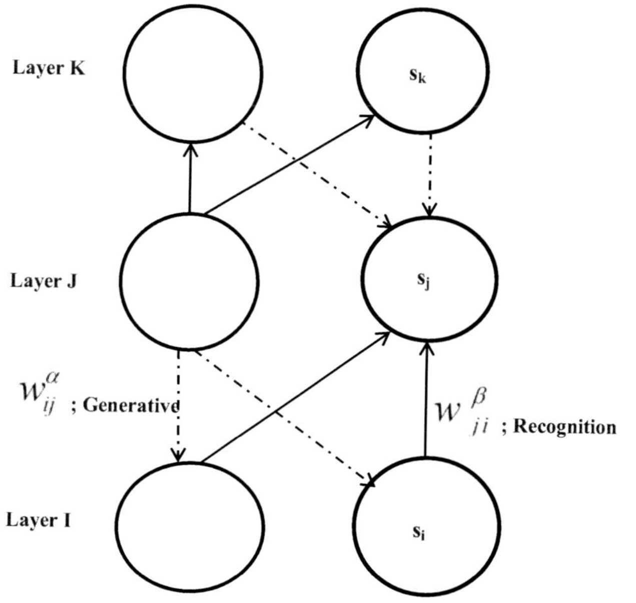

Fig. (4). Schematic representation of SHM showing the input I, hidden J, and output K layers.

Each of the activation function corresponds to a specific error function which is used in the back-propagation algorithm. Fig. (**4**) of chapter 4 schematize the occurrence of events at a node in any layer of MLP.

The explanation of MLP given here is to be regarded as simplistic and generic. There is several variation of multi-layer perceptron, and the variation depends on area of application. Back-propagation involves the evaluation of derivatives of an error function with respect to network weights and biases. The evaluation involves successive application of the chain rule of partial derivatives which are then propagated backward through the network, starting from the output units.

Back-propagation learning is based on gradient descent technique. Gradient descent technique involves minimisation of a cost function. With MLP, the cost function is the sum of squared error E(k) between the target output t(k) and network output y_k *i.e.*

$$E_k = \frac{1}{2}\sum_{k=1}^{n}\sum_{i=1}^{q}\left[\left(y_k^{(i)}\right)-\left(t_k^{(i)}\right)\right] \tag{9}$$

Evaluation of the partial derivative of E_k with respect to output activation a_k is the same for all error functions, and is given by

$$\frac{d}{da_k^{(2n)}}E^n = \left(y_k^n\right)-\left(t_k^n\right) \tag{10}$$

If $\delta^{2n}{}_k = (y_k{}^n)-(t_k{}^n)$ then the derivatives of E_k with respect to weights are given by

$$\frac{dE}{dw_{kj}^{(2)}} = \sum_{n=1}^{N}\left(\delta_k^{2n}\right)\left(z_j^n\right) \tag{11}$$

While the derivatives with respect to output biases are given by

$$\frac{dE}{db_k^{(2)}} = \sum_{n=1}^{N}\left(\delta_k^{(2n)}\right) \tag{12}$$

To propagate the derivatives backward from the second (denoted by superscript "2") to the first layer (denoted by the superscript "1"), the backpropagation learning equation assumes the form

$$\delta_j^{(1n)} = g'\left(a_j^{(1n)}\right)\sum_{k=1}^{c}\left(w_{kj}^{(2n)}\right)\left(\delta_k^{(2n)}\right) \quad (13)$$

$$\delta_j^{(1n)} = 1-\left(z_j^{(n)}\right)^2\sum_{k=1}^{c}\left(w_{kj}^{(2n)}\right)\left(\delta_k^{(2n)}\right)$$

The assumptions made here are:

1. z(a) = g(a) = tanh(a)
2. g'(a) = 1- $\tanh^2$(a) = 1 - z^2(a)

Variations of backpropagation learning has additional parameters like learning rate, momentum term *etc*. Cases of usage of learning rate and momentum term may be found in applications of MLP.

Industrial Applications of MLP

Sample industrial applications of MLP may be illustrated as follows. Designing, developing, and implementing a production activity scheduling system may be accomplished, on industrial scale, as in [4]. To predict stock market prices, Multilayer Networks with dynamic back propagation may be employed as in [5]. In [6] a two-step of (1) selecting input variables and delays, and (2) selecting MLP network structure are solved using a multilayer perceptron model (MLP) in a co- evolutionary scheme.

BAYESIAN NETWORKS

Mixture Density Network (MDN)

The conventional approach of neural networks to learning involves the minimization of sum-of-squares error. The sum-of-squares errors have been applied in LSM and RLS algorithm of previous chapter. The finite sum-of-squares over errors may be replaced by infinite sum as:

$$E^s = \lim_{n\to\infty}\frac{1}{2n}\sum_{q=1}^{n}\sum_{k=1}^{c}\left[f_k\left(x^q,w\right)-t_k^q\right]^2 \quad (14)$$

$$E' = \frac{1}{2}\sum_{k=1}^{c}\int\int\left[f_k(x^q,w)-t_k^q\right]^2 p(t,x)dtdx \qquad \textbf{(15)}$$

The minimization of this sum involves the calculation of least squares from which the means and (co-)variance of input data may be calculated (or estimated) without knowledge of the probability distribution over data.

An alternative method involves the assumption of a distribution of the type:

$$p(t_k\,|\,x) = \frac{1}{\sigma(2\pi)^{1/2}}\exp\left(-\frac{[F_k(x)-t_k]^2}{2\sigma^2}\right) \qquad \textbf{(16)}$$

The distribution of type (16) specifies the conditional probability $p(t_k|x)$ over target data t_k; where σ^2 represents the variance. The complete conditional probability is a product of equation (16);

$$p(t\,|\,x) = \prod_{k=1}^{c} p(t_k\,|\,x) = \frac{1}{\sigma^c(2\pi)^{c/2}}\exp\left(-\frac{\sum_{k=1}^{c}[F_k(x)-t_k]^2}{2\sigma^2}\right) \qquad \textbf{(17)}$$

The assumption of (16) may be verified by obtaining data parameters (*i.e.*; the mean μ, and variance σ^2) *via* a different method, which enables (16) to be generalized. The MDN may be designed to perform this role. It involves taking the negative logarithm of (17) and "recovering" the sum-of–squares from the result. But first we need to sample the given data independently, and measure (16) for each sample, the product of which is called the likelihood L of data, given by: This may be given to a clustering algorithm or a neural network to produce the data variance σ^2 , given by:

$$L = \prod_{q=1}^{n} p(t^q, x^q) = \prod_{q=1}^{n} p(t^q\,|\,x^q)p(x^q) \qquad \textbf{(18)}$$

The negative logarithm of (18) gives:

$$-\ln(L)=E=-nc\ln(\sigma)+\frac{2}{nc}\ln(2\pi)+\frac{1}{2\sigma^2}\sum_{q=1}^{n}\sum_{k=1}^{c}\left[f_k\left(x^q,w\right)-t_k^q\right]^2+\sum_{q=1}^{n}\ln\left[p(x^q)\right] \quad \textbf{(19)}$$

"Recovering" the error function gives:

$$E'=\frac{1}{2\sigma^2}\sum_{q=1}^{n}\sum_{k=1}^{c}\left[f_k\left(x^q,w\right)-t_k^q\right]^2 \quad \textbf{(20)}$$

This may be given to a clustering algorithm or a neural network to produce the data variance σ^2, given by:

$$\sigma^2=\frac{1}{cn}\sum_{q=1}^{n}\sum_{k=1}^{c}\left[f_k\left(x^q,w\right)-t_k^q\right]^2 \quad \textbf{(21)}$$

Apart from computation overhead, there are two main added advantages of employing either a clustering algorithm or a neural network. These are:

1. Missing data (points) can easily be completed.
2. Principled regularization of learning algorithm to match data distribution is possible.

Since the target data distribution is unknown, but the mean μ and variance σ^2 are now know (or estimated), the conditional probability $p(t \mid x)$ may be calculated (or estimated). To begin, the $p(t \mid x)$ may be expressed as:

$$p(t\mid x)=\sum_{i=1}^{m}\alpha_i(x)\phi_i(t\mid x) \quad \textbf{(22)}$$

Subject to constraint:

$$\sum_{i=1}^{\infty}\alpha_i(x)=1 \quad \textbf{(23)}$$

The equation (22) may now replace (17) since the assumption of (17) is no longer required. What is now required is to express data parameters in terms of outputs from the neural network or the clustering algorithm's output. Denote this output by z_k. The α_i of equation (22) is known as the *mixing coefficient* while Φ_i is called the *kernel function, probability density function (p.d.f.), basis function,* or simply *basis*. The previous assumption of a Gaussian distribution has now been relaxed. The relaxation enables the formal introduction of the Mixture Density Network (MDN) symbolically represented by equation (22). Thus, instead of a Gaussian distribution, the conditional probability now consists of mixtures of p.d.f.; a more general perspective which may be adapted both for one-to-one mapping and one-to-many mapping. Data parameter may be expressed as a function of z as follows:

$$\sigma_i = \exp(z_i^{\sigma}); \tag{24}$$

$$\mu_{ik} = z_{ik}^{\mu}; \tag{25}$$

$$\alpha_i = \frac{\exp(z_i^{\alpha})}{\sum_{j=1}^{M} \exp(z_j^{\alpha})} \tag{26}$$

Observation of the "softmax" equation (26) reveals that the constraint (23) is met. The exponentiation of z_i keeps us away from zero value.

The total error is the sum of individual errors:

$$E = \sum_{q} E^q \tag{27}$$

Where each error E^q is given by the negative log-likelihood function:

$$E^q = -\ln\left[\sum_{i=1}^{m} \alpha_i(x^q)\phi_i(t^q \mid x^q)\right] \tag{28}$$

Equations (24) through to (28) may now go to the second level of MDN which is a mixture of components represented by (22). For these components, there are varieties of choices. Our choice of components should be able to solve the *inverse problems* associated with 1-to-N mappings (*i.e.*; that of finding the inverse of a multi-valued function). Secondly, high computational overhead, associated with derivatives of (28), should be avoided. These two problems present us two good choices; one is the E-M algorithm that has been explained in the previous chapter.

Another is the back-propagation algorithm. The same back-propagation employed by MLP of previous section. Good components that make a suitable mixture are:

1. The RBF using E-M learning algorithms. For E-M, the regularisation of Tapio Schneider [8] is recommended, should it be required. The RBF may also require the basis function Φ_i $(t \mid x)$ given by:

$$\phi_i(t \mid x) = \frac{1}{(2\pi)^{c/2}\sigma_i^c(x)} \exp\left(-\frac{\|t-\mu(x)\|^2}{2\sigma_i^2(x)}\right) \quad \textbf{(29)}$$

2. The MLP using back-propagation algorithm.
3. Any other suitable neural networks.

The components require expressions which are equivalent of derivatives of equation (28). Minimization of (28) entails the setting of its derivatives to zero:

$$\frac{\delta E^q}{\delta f_k(x,w)} = 0 \quad \textbf{(30)}$$

From this, the components of MDN may obtain the posterior probability of data using Bayes theorem [7 - 9]. The posterior probability π_i (x_i,t) may be expressed as:

$$\pi_i(x_i,t) = \frac{\alpha_i \phi_i}{\sum_{j=1}^{M} \alpha_i \phi_i} \quad \textbf{(31)}$$

Observation of (31) reveals that it sums as follows:

$$\sum_{i=1}^{\infty} \pi_i(x) = 1; \quad \textbf{(32)}$$

Suppose $\frac{\delta E^q}{\delta z_k} = \delta_k^q$; and $t^q_k = \delta_{kl}$ then from (28), (29), and (30);

$$\frac{E^q}{\pi_i} = -\frac{\ln\left[\sum_{i=1}^{m}\alpha_i(x^q)\phi_i(t^q\,|\,x^q)\right]}{\alpha_i\phi_i \Big/ \sum_{j=1}^{M}\alpha_i\phi_i} = -\frac{\left(\sum_{j=1}^{M}\alpha_i\phi_i\right)\ln\left[\sum_{i=1}^{m}\alpha_i(x^q)\phi_i(t^q\,|\,x^q)\right]}{\alpha_i\phi_i}$$

$$\frac{E^q}{\pi_i} = -\frac{\ln\left[\sum_{i=1}^{m}\alpha_i(x^q)\phi_i(t^q\,|\,x^q)\right]}{\alpha_i\phi_i \Big/ \sum_{j=1}^{M}\alpha_i\phi_i} = -\frac{\left(\sum_{j=1}^{M}\alpha_i\phi_i\right)\ln\left[\sum_{i=1}^{m}\alpha_i(x^q)\phi_i(t^q\,|\,x^q)\right]}{\alpha_i\phi_i}$$

$$\frac{E^q}{\pi_i} = -\frac{\left(\sum_{j=1}^{M}\alpha_i\phi_i\right)}{\alpha_i\phi_i}\int\frac{1}{\left[\sum_{i=1}^{m}\alpha_i(x^q)\phi_i(t^q\,|\,x^q)\right]}d\alpha = -\frac{\left(\sum_{j=1}^{M}\alpha_i\phi_i\right)}{\left[\sum_{i=1}^{m}\alpha_i(x^q)\phi_i(t^q\,|\,x^q)\right]}\int\frac{1}{\alpha_i\phi_i}d\alpha$$

$$\frac{E^q}{\pi_i} = -\frac{\left(\sum_{j=1}^{M}\alpha_i\phi_i\right)}{\sum_{q=1}^{n}\left[\sum_{i=1}^{m}\alpha_i(x^q)\phi_i^2(t^q\,|\,x^q)\right]}\int\frac{1}{\alpha_i}d\alpha$$

$$\frac{E^q}{\pi_i} = -\int\frac{1}{\alpha_i}d\alpha$$

$$E^q = -\pi_i\int\frac{1}{\alpha_i}d\alpha$$

$$\frac{\partial E^q}{\partial \alpha_i} = -\frac{\pi_i}{\alpha_i}$$

$$\frac{\partial E^q}{\partial \alpha_i} = -\frac{\pi_i}{\alpha_i} \qquad \textbf{(33)}$$

Similarly, differentiate $\alpha_i = \frac{\exp(z_i^a)}{\sum_{j=1}^{M}\exp(z_i^a)}$, then substitute α_i and δ_{kl}

$$\frac{\delta\alpha_i}{\delta z_k^a} = \delta_{ik}\alpha_i - \alpha_i\alpha_k \tag{34}$$

By chain rule, $\frac{\partial E^q}{\partial z_k^a} = \sum_i \frac{\partial E^q}{\partial \alpha_i}\frac{\delta\alpha_i}{\delta z_k^a}$; therefore;

$$\frac{\partial E^q}{\partial z_k^a} = \alpha_k - \pi_k \tag{35}$$

Substitute (29) into (28), differentiate with respect to σ_i, then use (30).

$$\frac{\partial E^q}{\partial \sigma_i} = -\pi\left[\frac{\|t-\mu_i\|^2}{\sigma_i^3} - \frac{c}{\sigma_i}\right] \tag{36}$$

From equation (24) by differentiation;

$$\frac{\partial \sigma_i}{\partial z_i^\sigma} = \sigma_i \tag{37}$$

Similarly, substituting (37), (24) into the chain rule;

$$\frac{\partial E^q}{\partial \sigma_i} = -\pi_i\left[\frac{\|t-\mu_i\|^2}{\sigma_i^2} - c\right] \tag{38}$$

From equations (25), (28), (26), and (29);

$$\frac{\partial E^q}{\partial z_{ik}^\mu} = \pi_i\left[\frac{\|\mu_{ik}-t_k\|^2}{\sigma_i^2}\right] \tag{39}$$

This completes the MDN algorithm. The MDN is the first example of a hierarchical neural network. Hierarchical neural networks, whether parallel, serial, or modular, are known as Multi-Expert System (MES) or Multi-Classifier System (MCS).

Helmholtz Machine

Methods of previous sections can be utilized to obtain the data mean and co-variances. Other methods such as Principal Component Analysis (PCA), Vector Quantization (VQ) may also be employed as components of a system which require the means and co-variances as system parameters.

Previous sections have also presented NNs which uses supervised learning algorithms. A learning algorithm which requires part of neural networks' output to be explicitly feedback to the input is called supervised learning algorithm [10, 11]. A learning algorithm in which an external environmental variable is explicitly feedback to the input as an environmental response of the external surrounding is called reinforcement learning algorithm. That part which is explicitly feedback to the input, for weight update, is usually the error function, or a control function. A learning algorithm which does not require any explicit feedback mechanism in order to achieve a set performance is known as unsupervised learning. The Minimum Description Length algorithm which is presented in this section is a good example of unsupervised learning algorithm. The Minimum Description Length algorithm when implemented on a bi-directed net (bi-graph) gives that net the name Helmholtz Machine (HM). The Minimum Description Length builds on Shannon's coding theorem which states that it requires -log(p(x)) bits to communicate an event that has probability p(x); where p(x) is calculated from a distribution agreed upon by both the sender and the receiver. In Minimum Description Length, this agreement may not be necessary, because the probability is drawn from an adaptable factorial distribution which may be reconstructed by the receiver. Being factorial means there are large number of possible distribution to choose from. Being adaptable means having chosen the closest possible distribution, the chosen distribution can be adjusted to reconstruct the input pattern. One possible choice of the distribution is:

$$p(s_v) = \frac{1}{1 + \exp(-b_v - \sum_u s_u w_{uv})} \quad \textbf{(40)}$$

The probability $p(s_v)$ that a node v is on (s_v=1), where sv is the activity on the v node, is given by the right-hand-side of equation (40). In equation (40), b_v is a bias on node v, s_u is an activity on node u, and w_{uv} is the weight w connecting node u to node v.

From our knowledge of simple binary logic, let a random variable s assumes only one possible outcome out of two possible outcomes, in an event. If one outcome is denoted by zero 0, and the other by one 1, then the probability density function (p.d.f.) of such event may be written as:

$$f(s) = p^s(1-p)^{(1-s)} \quad \textbf{(41)}$$

We say that s has a Bernoulli distribution (see chapter 2). Taking the negative logarithm of equation (41);

$$-\log(f(s)) = C(s) = -s\log(p) - ((1-s)\log(1-p)) \quad \textbf{(42)}$$

Equation (42) is known as the *description length* of the binary state *s* (=1 or 0) of a node.

When a pattern is presented to HM, a representation of this pattern is created at the input layer. A representation of the representation at the input layer is created at the first hidden layer. The representation creation is repeated throughout all layers. Denote an arbitrary representation by α ; the activity state *s* of a hidden unit i having a representation α is denoted by s^{α}_{i} $i = 1,2,3,\ldots$. When equation (40) acts on node i sending it to state s_i, the description length is given by;

$$C(s_i) = -s_i\log(p_i) - ((1-s_i)\log(1-p_i)) \quad \textbf{(43)}$$

The minimum of equation (43) is called *Minimum Description Length (MDL). The aim of a Helmholtz machine is to minimize the MDL with respect to system parameters and connection weights.* If the state sv assume only 1 and 0, it is called binary stochastic. The equation (41) represents a single event occurring at a single node. A network may consist of more than two layers, each layer in turn consist of many nodes. Let an activity s be observed at many nodes n, and p to represent the probability that s = 1, while (1-p) the probability that s = 0. If x nodes out of n nodes (x < n) are turned on, then n-x nodes are turned off. Assuming the activities occur independently, the number of events for which s = 1 may be expressed generally as:

$$\binom{n}{x} = \frac{n!}{x!(n-x)!} \tag{44}$$

The probabilities with respect to equation (44) are given by:

$$f(x) = \binom{n}{x} p^x (1-p)^{(n-x)} \tag{45}$$

Substituting (44) into (45) reveals that the number of nodes x turned on is factorial, and x is said to have a binomial distribution. If the value of s is allowed to be any value between -1 and +1, also the dimension of x is greater than 2, then the nodes are said to be stochastic and the distribution is known simply as a factorial distribution. In a Helmholtz Machine, the nodes are usually simply stochastic nodes – called *stochastic neurons*.

For a component x_i; $x_i \in X$; of input vector X to be encoded, using a coding scheme, to within a quantization width t, the Gaussian probability distribution may be assumed. Assuming X has a Gaussian probability distribution $p(x_i)$ with a mean zero and standard deviation σ , the $p(x_i)$ is given by

$$p(x_i) = \frac{t}{\sqrt{2\pi\sigma^2}} \exp\left(-\frac{1}{2}\left(\frac{x_i}{\sigma}\right)^2 \right) \tag{46}$$

Provided σ is large with respect to width t, the cost of coding xi is defined as – log($p(x_i)$) and is obtained by taking the negative logarithm of $p(x_i)$; equation (46) given by:

$$-\log(p(x_i)) = -\log(t) + \frac{1}{2}\log(2\pi\sigma^2) + \frac{1}{2}\left(\frac{x_i}{\sigma}\right)^2$$

$$C_{si} = -\log(t) + \frac{1}{2}\log(2\pi\sigma^2) + \frac{1}{2}\left(\frac{x_i}{\sigma}\right)^2 \tag{47}$$

Given an input vector X, the energy of a code is defined as the sum of code cost and the reconstruction cost. If a Helmholtz machine picks a code i with probability p_i , the cost C_{st} of the code is given by;

$$C_{st} = \sum_i p_i E_i \tag{48}$$

Comparing equation (47) with (48), the energy E_i may be described in terms of the distribution over input data vector. If the prior probability of a code i is $p(x_i)$ and the squared reconstruction error is ε^2 the energy E_i of the code is given by taking the negative logarithm of:

$$e^{E_i} = \frac{p_i t^k}{(2\pi\sigma^2)^{k/2}} \exp\left(-\frac{1}{2}\left(\frac{\varepsilon}{\sigma}\right)^2\right) \tag{49}$$

This follows since there are exponentially many ways of picking a code i with energy E_i when assuming a Gaussian distribution over data vector X. Taking the negative logarithm of equation (49);

$$-\log\left(e^{-E_i}\right) = -\log(p_i) - k\log(t) + \frac{k}{2}\log\left(2\pi\sigma^2\right) + \frac{\varepsilon^2}{2\sigma^2}$$

$$E_i = -\log(p_i) - k\log(t) + \frac{k}{2}\log\left(2\pi\sigma^2\right) + \frac{1}{2}\left(\frac{\varepsilon}{\sigma}\right)^2 \tag{50}$$

where k = dimension of input vector X, and σ^2= the variance

The description length of xi input vector is the total cost of the hidden states at all hidden layers plus the cost of describing the x_i input pattern given the hidden states *i.e.*;

$$C(\alpha, x) = C(\alpha) + C(x \mid \alpha) = \sum_{l \in L} \sum_{j \in l} C(s_j^\alpha) + \sum_i C(s_i^\alpha \mid \alpha) \tag{51}$$

When there are many other alternative descriptions Q of x_i, a stochastic coding scheme may be designed to benefit from the entropy of these alternative descriptions. Under this condition, the cost of describing x_i is:

$$C(x_i) \stackrel{?}{=} \sum_{\alpha} Q(\alpha \mid x_i) C(\alpha, x_i) - \left(-\sum_{\alpha} Q(\alpha \mid x_i) \log Q(\alpha \mid x_i) \right) \tag{52}$$

The $Q(\alpha \mid x_i)$ is the conditional distribution over the total representation á by the recognition weights. The question mark (?) signifies checking on the right- hand-side (RHS) to see if it equals the left-hand-side (LHS). When the LHS equals the RHS, $C(x_i)$ could be minimize by Boltzmann distribution defined as:

$$P(\alpha \mid x_i) = \frac{\exp(-C(\alpha \mid x_i))}{\sum_{\alpha} \exp(-C(\beta, x_i))} \tag{53}$$

This is done by differentiating (52), setting the result to zero, and substituting (53). The differentiation may be effected by using Monte Carlo approximation [12] method. Setting the derivatives to zero is computationally attractive but may not have physical analogy. This becomes apparent when equation (52) is re- written as:

$$C(x) = \sum_{s} P(\alpha \mid x) C(\alpha, x) - (-\sum_{s} P(\alpha \mid x) \ln(P(\alpha \mid x))) + \sum_{s} Q(\alpha \mid x) \ln\left[\frac{Q(\alpha \mid x)}{P(\alpha \mid x)}\right] \tag{54}$$

The Helmholtz Machine uses the recognition weights to produce a factorial distribution in the minimum description length algorithm [13, 14]. The total description length is obtained by summing equation (43) over all neurons. Summing (43) over all x neurons is equivalent to summing (45) then taking the negative logarithm of the sum. When the dimension of x is greater than or equal to 2 (*i.e.*; $\dim(x) \geq 2$), the sum should comprise three terms, symbolically written as equation (54). Equation (54) is the dynamic equation (the driving force) of a Helmholtz machine. The dynamic equation (54) accepts various input parameters depending on layers and neurons. This is the total description length which HM aims to minimize.

Comparing equations (52) with (54) is synonymous to comparing two models of which their main difference is the third term on the RHS of (54):

$$KL[P,Q] = \sum_{s} Q(\alpha \mid x) \ln \left[\frac{Q(\alpha \mid x)}{P(\alpha \mid x)} \right] \tag{55}$$

called Kullback-Leibler (KL) divergence. The KL is always positive and is expected to approach zero – this justifies the setting of derivatives to zero. Though the KL does not always approach zero, the KL nevertheless is minimal when $P(.|x_i)$ achieves a Boltzmann distribution as given by (53).

The MDL Algorithm: The MDL consists of two phases, each phase in turn consist of two steps. The phase/step divisions are for ease of explanation and understanding. The Stochastic Helmholtz Machine (SHM), of Fig. (**4**), internally initializes two types of models, the generative models enumerated by generative weights G, and the recognition models which are enumerated by reconstruction weights R. For the generative model, the activation on each neuron is given by equation (56):

$$p(s_i^{\alpha} = 1) = \frac{1}{1 + \exp(-(\sum_{j} s_j^{\alpha} w_{ij}^{\alpha} + b_i))} \tag{56}$$

i,j=0,1,2,...; $w_{ij}^{\alpha} \in G$; b_i=biases

considering two typical neurons i and j. For the reconstruction model weights R, the activation on each neuron is given by equation (57):

$$p(s_i^{\beta} = 1) = \frac{1}{1 + \exp(-(\sum_{j} s_j^{\beta} w_{ij}^{\beta} + b_i))} \tag{57}$$

The wake-phase consists of two steps:

1. The recognition model calculates a probability distribution using equation (57) in order to effect a representation.

2. The generative model computes the activation of equation (56) in order to effect a representation. The recognition weights are fixed and the activation from step 2 is used to adapt the generative weight. The difference between the input data and the reconstructed data vector from generative weight are used to adjust the generative weights as given by equation (58):

$$\Delta w_{ij}^{\alpha} = \gamma s_i^{\alpha}(s_j^{\alpha} - p_j^{\alpha}) \quad \textbf{(58)}$$

γ = learning parameter; $p_j^{\alpha} \in P$

The biases may be absorbed into the weight vectors by allowing indices to start from zero.

The sleep-phase consists also of two steps:

1. The input data vectors may be the unbiased samples from the network's generative model which is employed in evaluating equation (56) in order to determine the activation of each neuron.
2. The recognition model weights are used to determine the neuron activation as in equation (57) so as to modify the reconstruction weights. The generative model is unmodified but the recognition model weights changes as in equation (59):

$$\Delta w_{ij}^{\beta} = \gamma s_i^{\beta}(s_j^{\beta} - q_j^{\beta}) \quad \textbf{(59)}$$

γ = learning parameter; $q^{\beta}_{j} \in Q$

Thus in the sleep-phase, the generative model drives the recognition weights R so as to improve the estimation of input pattern. Whereas in the wake-phase, the reconstruction model drives the generative weights G in order to (re-) construct an accurate input pattern internally.

THE DYNAMICS AND EVALUATION OF ANN SYSTEMS

Introduction: Chi-Squared Probability Density Function

In a Poisson distribution with mean λ number of changes in the unit interval, let

W denote the waiting time until the α -th change occurs. The distribution of W when w (an element of W) ≥ 0 is given by:

$$F(W) = p(W \le w) = 1 - p(W \ge w) \tag{60}$$

$F(W)=1-p$ (fewer than α changes occur in $[0,w]$)

$$F(W) = 1 - \sum_{k=0}^{\infty} \frac{(\lambda w)^k}{k!} e^{-\lambda w} \tag{61}$$

Where the mean $\mu = \lambda w$ is the total mean in the interval 0,w. If W is a continuous-type random variable, then F'(W) is equal to the p.d.f. of W whenever the derivative exist. Provided that w > 0.

$$F'(W) = \lambda e^{-\lambda w} - e^{-\lambda w} \sum_{k=1}^{\alpha-1} \left[\frac{k(\lambda w)^{k-1} \lambda}{k!} - \frac{(\lambda w)^k \lambda}{k!} \right]$$

$$F'(W) = \lambda e^{-\lambda w} - e^{-\lambda w} \left[\lambda - \frac{\lambda(\lambda w)^{\alpha-1}}{(\alpha-1)!} \right]$$

$$F'(W) = \frac{\lambda(\lambda w)^{\alpha-1}}{(\alpha-1)!} e^{-\lambda w} = \frac{\lambda(\lambda w)^{\alpha-1} e^{-\lambda w}}{(\alpha-1)!} \tag{62}$$

Substitute $u = \lambda w$; $\frac{\partial u}{\partial w} \lambda; \partial u = \lambda \partial w$ into

$$\frac{\partial F(W)}{\partial W} = \frac{\lambda(\lambda w)^{\alpha-1} e^{-\lambda w}}{(\alpha-1)!} = \frac{\lambda(u)^{\alpha-1} e^{-u}}{(\alpha-1)!}$$

$$F(w) = \frac{1}{(\alpha-1)!} \int u^{\alpha-1} e^{-u} \partial u = \frac{1}{(\alpha-1)!} \int \lambda(\lambda w)^{\alpha-1} e^{-\lambda w} \partial w \tag{63}$$

$$\Gamma(u) = \int u^{\alpha-1} e^{-u} \partial u = \int \lambda(\lambda w)^{\alpha-1} e^{-\lambda w} \partial w \tag{64}$$

A p.d.f. in the form of equation (63) is called a *gamma p.d.f*, and w is said to have *a gamma distribution*. Equation (64) is the *gamma function*. Another p.d.f. may be formed from equation (64) by:

$$f(w) = \frac{\lambda(\lambda w)^{\alpha-1} e^{-\lambda w}}{\Gamma(u)} = \frac{u^{\alpha-1} e^{-u}}{\Gamma(u)} \tag{65}$$

Substituting $\lambda = \frac{1}{2}$; and $\alpha = \frac{n}{2}$ into equation above:

$$f(x) = \frac{\lambda^{\frac{n}{2}} (x)^{\frac{n}{2}-1} e^{-\frac{x}{2}}}{\Gamma(\frac{n}{2})} \tag{66}$$

$$\chi^2(n) = \frac{\lambda^{\frac{n}{2}} (x)^{\frac{n}{2}-1} e^{-\frac{x}{2}}}{\Gamma(\frac{n}{2})} \tag{67}$$

The f(x) of equation (38) is known as $X^2(n)$ *chi-square (probability density function)* with n-degree of freedom.

The Dynamics

Assuming a maximum a prior (MAP) classification dynamic possesses a probability model;

$$F_w = \{p(.|w) : S \to [0, \infty); w \in W\} \tag{68}$$

where braces {} denote sequences, $s \in \mathbb{R}^d$, and $w \in \mathbb{R}^q$.

Let a set of x (i); i = 0.1.2…. be a sample path of $\bar{x}\,(i)$ stochastic process which comprises of independent and identically distributed vector, but with one common probability density function (p.d.f.) p_e;

$$p_e : s \to [0, \infty) \tag{69}$$

A function that maps a connection weight into the likelihood of the observed learning data x(i) with respect to the probability model F_w is known as a *negative log likelihood objective function*. This type of log likelihood function is always a suitable objective function of ANNs because, an ANN that minimize the negative log likelihood objective function, is looking for connection weights w that make the observed data x(i) most likely under the probability model F_w. Under the probability model F_w, a single input x(i) data vector with a connection weight w produces a conditional probability p(x(1)|w). Similarly, for two input vectors x(1), and x(2) under the same probability distribution model F_w gives the likelihood $p(x(1),x(2)|\ w) = p(x(1)|\ w)p(x(2)|\ w)$. Generally therefore, under the same F_w distribution model:

$$p(\underset{i=1,2,\ldots,n}{x(i)} \mid w) = \prod_{i=1}^{n} p(x(i) \mid w) \tag{70}$$

If the negative $\frac{1}{n}Log$ is denoted by L_n, then taking the negative logarithm of equation (70);

$$-\frac{1}{n}Log\left[p(\underset{i=1,2,\ldots,n}{x(i)} \mid w)\right] = -\frac{1}{n}\sum_{i=1}^{n}\log p(x(i) \mid w) = L_n \tag{71}$$

Since equation (71) is a measure of the likelihood of data x(i) given the connection weight w, the equation (71) is called negative log likelihood function. The expression (71) allows one to propose a learning objective function L_n from a probability model F_w such that a global minimum of L_n consist of connection weights w which makes the observed data x(i) most likely. Denote these global minimum weight vectors by w_{min} ; $w_{min} \in W$. A global minimum $w_{\min}$ of L_n on W with respect to F_w, if $p_e \in F_w$, is known as maximum likelihood estimate of W with respect to F_w .

Normally, the negative log likelihood function will converge with probability 1 to some deterministic objective function L. If equation (69) holds when $L_n \rightarrow L{:}W \rightarrow [0,\infty)$; where L accepts connection weights $w_{\min}$ corresponding to pe distribution at convergence, then the deterministic function L which is the limit of L_n is called *Kullback-Leibler information criterion (KLIC) risk function*. KLIC is defined on

$w_{min} \in W$ as in equation

$$KLIC = \sum_{x \in S} p_e \log[p(x \mid w_{min})] \tag{72}$$

Example of KLIC is (69) for Helmholtz machine. The expression (72) is also referred to as *KLIC sample risk function* because data samples are often processed. The KLIC also has many other names such as cross-entropy, divergence, information gain, *etc.* between $p_e(.)$ and p(.|w). The minimum of KLIC itself is obtained if and only if the environmental probability p_e and the probability p(.|w) from F_w are equal with respect to a sample data space.

To express the ANNs' objective function in terms of KLIC, an ANN should seek a probability density function $p(.|\, w) \in F_w$ that best matches pe of the environment.

Fusion

An ANN learns from data so as to gain full knowledge of the data and its generator (source), thus becoming an expert. An ANN may not memorize data, because memorizing data produces poor generalization performance. Under this condition, an ANN may be referred to as an expert system. Before the ANN study this data, it is empty and thus regarded as a shell – an expert shell. The ANN merits the name "expert" so long as the generalization performance with respect to a learning objective is acceptable.

When many expert systems are linked in parallel, serially, modular or hierarchical, they are regarded as one system called a Multi-Expert System (MES), because they have one objective function to solve. A MES is also sometimes called a Multi-Classifier (MCS). There are two types of MES:

1. Heterogeneous MES: This consists of ANNs which utilizes more than one type of learning algorithm. A good example is the mixture density network of Bayesian networks' section. Under the Bayesian networks' section, the MLP used its own learning algorithm and RBF its own learning algorithm.
2. Homogenous MES: This consists of more than one ANN of the same kind, all ANNs utilizing the same learning algorithm. A good example of this is the

Helmholtz machine of previous section.

Generalized Likelihood Ratio Test (GLRT)

a. Let

$$p(.|.): S \times Y \rightarrow [0, \infty) \tag{73}$$

where $S \in \mathbb{R}^d; Y \in \mathbb{R}^q$

Define $G_Y = \{p(. \mid y) : y \in Y\}$ as a full probability model.

b. Let F_w be a subset of G_Y called a reduced probability model nested in G_Y, and defined as:

$$F_w = \{p(. \mid w_r, y^{(2)}); y^{(2)} \in \mathbb{R}^{q-r}\}; r \leq q \tag{74}$$

where ; $w_r = y^{(1)} \in \mathbb{R}^r$, $y^{(2)} \in \mathbb{R}^{q-r}$, and $\left[y^{(1)} y^{(2)}\right] \in Y \subseteq \mathbb{R}^q$

c. Let x(1),x(2),...,x(n) be a sampled path of a stochastic process $\bar{x}(1), \bar{x}(2),..., \bar{x}(n)$ which are independent and identical distributed random variable with a common p. d. f. pe as defined in equation (69).

The null hypothesis H_0 for the GLRT is to test

$$H_0 : y^{(1)} = w_r \tag{75}$$

The functions L_n and L are KLIC functions as defined in previous sub-sections. The basic procedure of GLRT is to compute the log likelihood ratio test statistic:

$$\bar{\delta}_n = -2n\left[L_n(\bar{y}_n; x(1), x(2), ..., x(n)) - L_n([w_r, y^{(2)}]; x(1), x(2), ..., x(n))\right] \tag{76}$$

The $\bar{\delta}_n$ is observed by GLRT and expresses a random variable that has a chi-squared distribution with r degree of freedom, given that H_0 is true. But $\bar{\delta}_n \rightarrow \infty$ with probability 1 as $n \rightarrow \infty$ if H_0 is false.

Basically, assume the first term of equation (68) is a KLIC of a large network, and the second term of equation (68) represents the KLIC of a hypothetical small network nested within the large network. The GLRT watches the large networks $\bar{\delta}_n$, prune the large network until $\bar{\delta}_n$ describe a chi-squared distribution. By then, the small network structure must have been achieved whose F_w probability distribution matches the data distribution most likely. The situation is similar if the large network G_Y is a hypothetical network and the small network F_w is a real network. When this is the case, the structure of the F_w network is increased gradually (invers pruning – growing network) until $\bar{\delta}_n$ describe a chi-squared distribution. For comparing two separate ANN systems, the GLRT is a reliable statistical test to check if the probability model G_Y fits the observed data more likely than the probability model F_w or *vice versa*.

GLRT Procedure:

Step 1: Inspect $-\log[p(.|.)]$ to see if it is regular;

Step 2: Calculate the maximum likelihood estimate of $\bar{y}_n : \bar{y}_n \in \mathbb{R}^q$ of the full model G_Y;

Step 3: Inspect KLIC L_n to see if the distribution G_Y fits the observed data and that $\bar{y}_n$ is a strict local minimum.

Step 4: Calculate the maximum likelihood estimate $y_n^{(2)} \in \mathbb{R}^{q-r}$ such that the r-dimensional vector $y^{(1)} = w_r$.

Step 5: Compute the $X_\alpha^2(r)$ chi-squared statistics such that the chi-squared variable with r-degree of freedom will exceed $X_\alpha^2(r)$ at a significant α level.

Step 6: Do not accept the null hypothesis $H_0 : y^{(1)} = w_r$ if $\bar{\delta}_n > X_\alpha^2(r)$, where $\bar{\delta}_n$ is given by equation (76).

Wald Test

a. Let W be a closed, convex, and bounded subset of $\mathbb{R}^q$;

b. Let w_r be a minimum of W;

c. Let $w_1, w_2, \ldots, w_n$ be a stochastic sequence of connection weights converging to w_r such that as $n \to \infty$, $\sqrt{n}(w_n - w_r)$ converges in distribution to a Gaussian random variable with mean zero and real symmetric positive definite covariance matrix Cm.

d. Let the null hypothesis H_0 be defined as:

$$H_0 : Rw_r = r \tag{77}$$

Where R = matrix of rank m and (m x q)-dimension; and r = m-dimensional column vector.

e. Define a Wald function Wn such that:

$$W_n = n[Rw_n - r]^T [RC_m R^T]^{-1} [Rw_n - r] \tag{78}$$

If the null hypothesis H0 is true, equation (78) converges in distribution, as $n \to \infty$, to a chi-squared X_α^2 (m) random variable with m-degree of freedom. If the null hypothesis is not true, then $Wn \to \infty$ as $n \to \infty$. To see this, define a function as:

$$f_n = \sqrt{n}[RC_m R^T]^{-\frac{1}{2}} [Rw_r - r] \tag{79}$$

Assuming H_0 $:Rw_r = r$is true, then $|f_n|^2$ converges in distribution, because f_n is a continuous linear function of w_r, to a sum of square of m normal Gaussian variable which are independent with zero means and unit variance, as $n \to \infty$. The $\left|\underset{n\to\infty}{f_n}\right|^2$ has X_α^2 (m) chi-squared distribution with m-degree of freedom. Assuming H_0 is not true, then $Rw_r \neq r$. Given that $w_n \to w_r$ with probability one as $n \to \infty$ then:

$$\frac{W_n}{n} \to K; \quad K \in [0, \infty) \tag{80}$$

Because $[RC_mT^T]$is a positive definite real number. Therefore $\underset{n\to\infty}{W_n} \to nK$ with probability one as $n \to \infty$.

Wald Test Procedure:

1. Inspect $\sqrt{n}(w_n - w_r)$ to ensure the q-dimensional random variable converges in distribution to a Gaussian random variable with mean zero and covariance matrix C_m.
   Compute the Wald statistic equation (78) with respect to the null hypothesis H_0 $:Rw_r = r$; where R is an (m x q)-dimensional matrix of rank m (see equation (7 7)).
3. Accept that H_0 is true if $W_n > X_\alpha^2$ (m), otherwise do not accept H_0 at α

significant level.

Wald test is often applied to prune any homogenous MCS by removing those neurons whose connection weights are redundant or impede the system's generalization performance.

CONFLICT OF INTEREST

The author confirm that this chapter contents have no conflict of interest.

ACKNOWLEDGEMENTS

Cited works are appreciated.

REFERENCES

[1] Howells WG, Fairhurst MC, Rahman F. An exploration of a new paradigm for weightless RAM-based neural networks. Elec Connect Sci 2000; 12(1): 65-9.

[2] Howells WGJ, Fairhurst MC, Bisset DL. PCN: The Probabilistic Convergent Network. CT2 7NT, U.K: Kent: Electronics Engineering Laboratories: University of Kent, Canterbury 1995.

[3] Austin J, Ed. RAM-based neural networks New Jersey. River Edge, NJ: World Scientific Publishing Co. Inc. 1998. ISBN: 9810232535

[4] Shan Fenga, Ling Li, Ling Cen, Jingping Huang. Using MLP networks to design a production scheduling system. Comput Oper Res 2003; 30: 821-32. [http://dx.doi.org/10.1016/S0305-0548(02)00044-8]

[5] Victor Devadoss A, Alphonnse Ligori TA. Forecasting of Stock Prices Using Multi-Layer Perceptron. Int J Comput Algorithms 2013; 02: 440-9.

[6] Souza Francisco, Matias Tiago, Ara´ujo Rui. Co-evolutionary Genetic Multilayer Perceptron for Feature Selection and Model Design. P´olo II, PT-3030-290 [http://dx.doi.org/10.1109/ETFA.2011.6059084]

[7] Schneider Tapio. Analysis of Incomplete Climate Data. Estimation of Mean Values and Covariance Matrices and Imputation of Missing Values. Massachusset: MIT Press Journals 2001. 55 Hayward Street Cambridge, MA USA 02142-1315

[8] Christopher Bishop M. Markus Svensen, The Generative Topographic Mapping. Neural Comput 1998; 10(1): 215-34. Copyright © MIT Press [http://dx.doi.org/10.1162/089976698300017953] ; 1998.

[9] Bishop CM. Novelty detection and neural network validation: Special issue on applications of neural networks. IEE Proc Vis Image Signal Process 1994; 141(4): 17-222. [http://dx.doi.org/10.1049/ip-vis:19941330]

[10] Bishop CM. Neural Networks for Pattern Recognition. Oxford University Press: Great Claredon Street,

Oxford, UK 1995.

[11] Bishop CM. Mixture Density Network. Neural Computing Research Group. Birmingham: Dept. of Computer Science and Applied Mathematics, Aston University, 1994.

[12] Ian Nabney T. Netlab: Algorithms for Pattern Recognition. Springer 2004. ISBN 1-85233-440-1

[13] Dayan P, Hinton GE, Neal RM, Zemel RS. The Helmholtz machine. Neural Comput 1995; 7(5): 889-904.
[http://dx.doi.org/10.1162/neco.1995.7.5.889] [PMID: 7584891]

[14] Geoffrey Hinton E, Dayan Peter, Brendan Frey J, Neal RM. The wake-sleep algorithm for unsupervised neural networks. Toronto: Department of Computer Science: University of Toronto, 6 King's College Road, M5S 1A4 1995.

CHAPTER 8

Selection and Combination Strategy of ANN Systems

Abstract: It is often required to select and combine two or more neural networks in order to process a given data. The aim and objectives of this chapter is to describe the selection and combination strategy of ANN systems. Two methods of ANNs' selection and combination that are derived from principle are described in detail. Manual selection and combination which is possible only if it involve few networks are not considered. Also not considered are heuristically determined set of networks, because of additional large experimentation that must be performed to select a suitable number and configuration of ANNs. These hindrances are relieved by the selection and combination strategy described in this chapter. The chapter has described two methods of selection and combination of ANNs which may be applied to minimize ANN's network errors. The selection and combination strategies descried in this chapter are principled, more robust, and of wider applicability than other alternatives.

Keywords: Classifier selection, Combiner configuration, Combiner engine, Combiner unit, Converter, Error – independent, Factorial selection, Fusion, Fuzzy – neuron, Group method, Interpreter, Kolmogorov-Gabor Polynomial, Main-group, Minimum complexity, Pool of networks, Pre-group, Statistical selection, Topology, Volterra series.

INTRODUCTION

The first section of chapter 8 describes the factorial selection of component classifier in an ensemble. Factorial selection solves class-dependent classification problems. The second section describes the group methods of selecting component classifier in an ensemble. Both methods may be developed from principle.

The probability theories of chapter 2 are fundamental to factorial selection strategy of the first section. The classifiers of chapter 6 and 7 may be component classifiers of the factorial selection strategy. Similar to the factorial selection, the

Pierre Lorrentz

group method accepts any classifier from chapter 5 and 6 provided the classifier achieves a performance beyond a set threshold. The threshold may be ascertained by one or more of the performances of chapter 4 and 7.

The selection and combination strategies of this chapter may be developed from principle and thus superior to those developed heuristically which are less tractable and may not be reproducible exactly.

The decision to include a Neural Networks (NN) in a Multi-Classifier System (MCS) is commonly referred to as *classifier selection*. Two selection strategies are well known. These are:

- The Direct method
- The "Pool of network" method.

The direct method is made up of neural network aggregate which are error-independent of each other. This is often an informed static selection made in advance. The "pool of network" method is a situation whereby an initial large number [1] of artificial neural systems are initialized, and in the course of experiments, smaller number (usually) of error-independent ANN have been selected by using measures such as error diversity measure.

Alternatively, the inclusion of a classifier in a hierarchy of classifiers may be divided into static and dynamic selection. Static selection mechanisms are those

methods employed in the selection of the based classifier which preclude alteration of composition during experiment. Dynamic selection mechanisms are meant to modify the composition of the ensemble during an experiment. There may be no fixed rule to this because, for example, a feedback of error correlation may convert a static method to a dynamic method.

FACTORIAL SELECTION

A factorial selection of base classifiers can either be dynamic or static depending on experimental setup. Customary selection method employed in choosing component classifiers can be grouped also as static or dynamic selection strategy which depends on whether there is a feedback system or not. Given $n = \sum_{i=1}^{r} n_i$ classes of r distinct types, where n_i are of type i and are otherwise indistinguishable, the number of permutation without repetition, of all n classes is:

$$M_m(n_1, \ldots, n_r) = \frac{n!}{\prod_{i=1}^{r} n_i!} \quad \textbf{(1)}$$

The number M_n is known as a multinormial coefficient. The multinormial coefficient M_m is a closed-form of the coefficient of equation (23) and/or equation (26) of chapter three. A special case is when r = 2. This is a case of binomial coefficient and is denoted by $M_n n_1, \ldots, n_n = {}_nC_r$ where;

$$\frac{n!}{r!(n-r)!} = {}_n C_r \quad \textbf{(2)}$$

Random variables X and Y are independent if, for all x and y;

$$f(x, y) = f_X(x) f_Y(y) \quad \textbf{(3)}$$

where f = the experimental outcome.

f_X = experimental outcome of X;

f_Y = experimental outcome of Y;

x = an element of X;

y = an element of Y.

The statistical selection method [2] exemplified the factorial selection method. An outline of the method is as follows.

In the statistical selection mechanism, n is the number of classes employed in the experiment whereas r represent the number of classes chosen without replacement. Because the objective is to minimize bias, randomization is performed in accordance to equation (2). Two independent randomizations are carried out and the outcome is composed in accordance to equation (3). Setting n = 50 and r = 1 in equation (2);

$$f_X(x) = \frac{n!}{r!(n-r)!} = \frac{50!}{1!.(50-1)!} = \frac{50!}{49!} = 50$$

Similarly,

$$f_Y(y) = \frac{50!}{49!} = 50$$

and

$f(x,y) = 50 + 50 = 100$

In $f_X(x).f_Y(y)$ Table **1**, there are 100 classes in Table **1**, because every entry in the table is a pattern class, and every class is repeated twice. Each row is trained to one component classifier.

The base classifiers are called NTW# (#=0,1,2...). The shuffling and the (re-) occurrence of classes are random and independent. The base ANN denoted by NTW# (where # = 1,2,...) learned the data depicted on Table **1**. Each entry of a row denotes a pattern class, and a whole row is usually trained to one ANN at a time. For example, NTW2 denotes the ANN which is trained on classes 45 as first class, class 26 as second class, class 13 as third class, and so on, until the end of that row. The entries *e.g.* 45, 26 are cases of finger-print files. These files stores finger-prints [3] collected using various forms. The mechanism of classifier selection is termed statistical selection method. It is used in this Multi-Expert System in order to minimize bias and promote independence of component expert system.

Table 1. Randomised input classes. NTW# = Network, where # = 1,2,3,…n.

	CLASSES									
NTW1	40	14	49	50	2	36	12	3	30	16
NTW2	45	26	13	1	39	17	18	47	11	9
NTW3	48	20	41	19	5	32	10	46	34	24
NTW4	25	22	42	33	6	28	27	23	44	29
NTW5	8	37	4	43	21	7	31	15	35	38
NTW6	49	48	22	24	2	39	44	47	3	32
NTW7	42	4	7	14	38	30	45	11	26	29
NTW8	5	16	33	6	10	1	9	50	18	25
NTW9	35	31	12	19	37	23	20	43	34	8
NTW10	15	41	13	36	28	21	27	40	46	17

For base expert systems to make notable contributions in a hierarchical system of ANN, they are expected to be as diverse and independent as possible. As the number of base classifier increases, the advantages of diversity and correlation measure become less pronounced. Lam [4] states that orthogonally, complementarity, and independence of a component neural network usually decide its inclusion in a hierarchical system of ANN. Component ANN selection in Mladenic [5], and Zouari [6] depend on diversity measure whereas the criteria for ANN selection in [7] is due to lack of error correlation among component ANN. Bagging is a Dynamic ANN selection strategy used by Gunter [8] whereas Boosting is used by Freund [9]. The acronym "BAGGING" (Bootstrapping and AGGregatING) refers to a classifier selection method in order to build a hierarchical ANN system. The method randomly select N training samples from a training set S with n replacement (where S > N), and delegate a component ANN to each group of sample drawn. The probability of being selected is the same for all training sample. Boosting distinguishes itself from Bagging in the sense that the probability assigned in favor of difficult-to-recognize pattern classes increases while the probability in favor of easy-to-recognize pattern classes decreases. The most commonly employed variant of Boosting is ADABoost. In ADABoost.M1 [9], for multi-class problems, a component ANN receives a subset of training set drawn. After the selection of the component classifier, the next procedure is the arrangement of the chosen ANNs. Topology refers to the structural organization of component ANN in an MCS. Usual topologies are serial, parallel, cascading, hierarchical topology. The introduction of dynamic (self-) reconfiguration can facilitate the MCS to modify its topology and adapt to new surroundings, new task or both. During experimentation with an MCS, the component ANN utilizes their normal learning and recognition algorithm. In an experimental setup, the EPCN (Chapter 7) have been used on the scheme of Table **1**, whereby all NTW1 to NTW10 [10] are arranged in parallel. The decision to employ a parallel combination is because the component ANN can be parallelized with resulting output similarly ormatted. All output of the component ANN are fuse together since the component ANN are not error correlated and they are diverse. Parallel topology of MCS is usually very resource intensive [7], also computationally. The problem of high computation cost is solved due to the decision to employ RAM-based Weightless MCS which consist of logic neurons and perform mainly logical activities not involving high computational cost as other would alternative MCS.

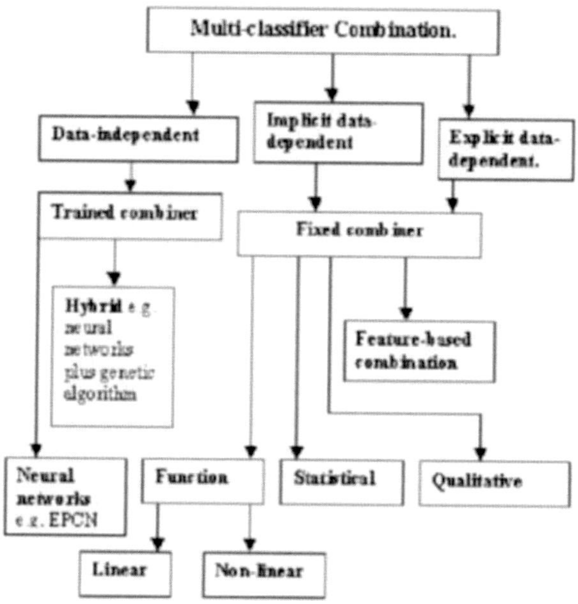

Fig. (1). Multi-expert system fusion; a partial data-driven paradigm.

The parallel method is employed in [7], while the serial topology is used by Austin [11], Dima [12] proposes hierarchical MES and uses a dynamic reconfiguration in the explanation of robot dynamics. The manner in which base ANNs' outputs [13] are composed together is termed multi-experts' fusion. Current research endeavour has facilitated the fusion of multi-expert system *via* their data- dependency, and this is diagrammatically represented in Fig. (**1**).

Every output of each component ANN the EPCN in the MES is a 1-D array of positive integers. The 1-D array, when collected for all output and every component ANN, may be arranged into a multi-dimensional matrix as depicted in equation (4). This process occurs automatically at any time when fusion is taking place.

$$CM(x) := \begin{pmatrix} n(x)_{1,1} & .. & n(x)_{1,j} & .. & n(x)_{1,c} \\ .. & .. & .. & .. & .. \\ n(x)_{i,1} & .. & n(x)_{i,j} & .. & n(x)_{i,c} \\ .. & .. & .. & .. & .. \\ n(x)_{r,1} & .. & n(x)_{r,j} & .. & n(x)_{r,c} \end{pmatrix} \quad \textbf{(4)}$$

Each entry in equation (4), n(x)i,j, is derived from the output of EPCN of the type shown in (Fig. **2**). The resulting multi-dimensional matrix requires an encoding scheme which speaks the language of the trained neural network combiner. An appropriate encoding scheme is necessary for equation (4) to communicate knowledge of input space to the trained combiner.

The majority voting (MV) is suited to conditions whereby common consensus is necessary. Majority voting scheme tend to undermine those network though may be in the minority but do produce more correct result [14], especially in data on which they have been trained on. Secondly, MV normally undermines diversity as a parameter of performance gain, but only mainly consider common consensus [15]. Hansen and Salamon [16] have proved that only if ANNs commit independent errors does MV gives improved result. Tumer and Ghosh [17] contend that error-independence give an indication of a better performing ensemble than a specific fusion mechanism.

Gunter [8] called *objective functions* the functions used in combination. *Qualitative combination* is used by Blue [18]. Duin [19] refers to intelligent combiners as *trained combiner*, and maintains that trained combiners outperformed fixed combiners. Roli and Giacinto [20] calls component classifiers *balanced classifiers* provided they are combined by any of the *fixed combination* method, and have zero or negative correlation. De Carvallo *et al.* [21] combine two RAM-based ANN. Prabhakar [22] categorizes Multi-expert systems with respect to their output.

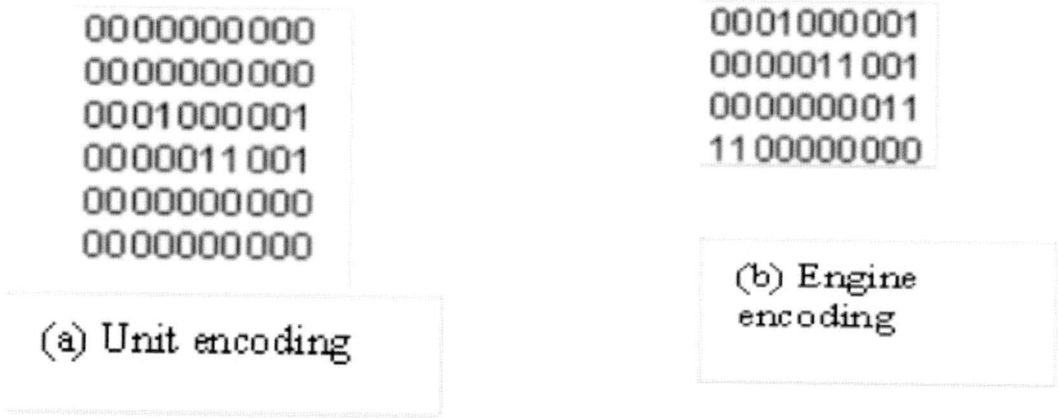

Fig. (2). Encoded information by the gating function f(.), (a) Unit encoding from the combiner unit; (b) Engine encoding from the combiner engine.

The term *Combiner engine* refers to the EPCN combiner [Pc, Mc], and a gating function *f(.)*. The gating function consists of an interpreter and a converter which altogether synthesized the encoding scheme. To elucidate further the meaning of the combiner engine, if identical letter for example “b” is learned to various ANN as belonging to various classes. But in the MES combination stage, and lacking the interpreter, this identical letter “b” will be converted to false and true pattern classes by the converter. For these reasons, an interpreter is essential.

Interpreter:- The role of the interpreter is to take equation (4) and simplify it. This is made possible by the availability of the system parameter data, results, and composite (confusion matrices) output of component ANNs. Based on this premise, a verdict on input data is reached as follows. A weighting scheme is used on the output of the component ANN in case of input overlap. The weighting scheme multiplies only the ANNs’ output that relates to regions of input overlaps.

A weight of zero may switched off a pattern class from a specific ANN component for a while. The interpreter does not possess the capability to eliminate a component ANN; it may only inhibit result output for a while by setting the weight to zero. The inhibition depends on input space overlap, configuration, and, performances on the class concerned. If for example the letter "b" is learned to one ANN as class 1 and to another ANN as class 2, then in the course of the classification procedure, correct recognition by the component ANN demand that the first ANN classifies "b" as class 1 while the second ANN classifies "b" as class 2. The interpreter informs the converter that the outputs from the two base classifiers are correct classifications of "b", and will be weighted by their respective probabilities.

Converter:- It translate the interpreter's whole-numbered output into binary output. The Converter employs an integer constant called division to modify its output. As an illustration, if the output of a base ANN is [10, 10, 65, 25, 10]. The array [10, 10, 65, 25, 10] denote a row of equation (4), and is equivalent to the variable field "decision output" of Table **2**. The array is converted by combiner engine to Fig. (**2b**).

A similar encoding scheme in [23] yields (Fig. **2a**). The general methodology is as follows. Any decimal number, N, is expressible in the form

$$N = \left[\left(d_n \cdot d_{n-1} \cdot \ldots \cdot d_0\right)_{10}\right] \tag{5}$$

where d_i = constituent integer;
and $i = 0,1,2,\ldots,n$

Equation (5) is expandable in a polynomial P(d);

$$P(d) = d_n \cdot 10^n + d_{n-1} \cdot 10^{n-1} + \ldots + d_0 \cdot 10^0 \tag{6}$$

The following algorithm converts equation (6)
to its binary equivalent;

$$b_n = d_n$$

$$b_{n-1} = d_n + d_n \cdot \beta$$

$$b_{n-2} = d_{n-2} + d_{n-1} \cdot \beta$$

....

$$b_0 = d_0 + d_1 \cdot \beta \qquad \textbf{(7)}$$

where b = the base of the decimal number N.
and b_i = binary number; i = 0,1,2,...,n.

<u>Example I</u>. If N = 65, then

$$65 = 6 \cdot 10^1 + 5 \cdot 10^0$$

$$65 = 110_2 \cdot \left(1010^1\right)_2 + 101_2 \cdot \left(1010^0\right)_2$$

$$65 = 110 \cdot 1010 + 101$$

$$65 = 111100 + 101$$

$$65 = 1000001$$

<u>Example II</u>. If N = 25 then

$$25 = 2 \cdot 10^1 + 5 \cdot 10^0$$

$$25 = 10_2 \cdot \left(1010^1\right)_2 + 101_2 \cdot \left(1010^0\right)_2$$

$$25 = 10100_2 + 101_2$$

$$25 = 11001$$

The least probable classes are indicated with low values, *e.g.*; 10 in the vector [10, 10, 65, 25, 10]. The low values are omitted by the *combiner engine*. In the vector [10, 10, 65, 25, 10], 65 occurs in the 3rd position. It is binarised according to equation (5) to (7), and occurs in the 3rd row in Fig. (**2a**), while the same number is binarised and occurs in the 1st row in (Fig. **2b**). The position of 65 in the vector [10, 10, 65, 25, 10] is 3. This position number 3 is binarised by the *combiner engine* to 00000000011 and occurs as the 3rd row in (Fig. **2b**). The pattern concerned here is most probably (the highest probability 0.65) classes three and more probably class four (with probability 0.25). For this reason, 25 is binarised, and it occurs in row 4 in Fig. (**2a**), while in Fig. (**2b**) it occurs in the second position. Both Figs. (*i.e.* (**2a**) and (**2b**)) indicate that the most probable class to be the 3rd class and following this is the 4th class. Secondly, a reversed bit of the most probable class, 3, is also passed on, only by *combiner engine*, to the *converter.* Thus, it is included in Fig. (**2b**) in the 4th row. The reversed bit serves to make the information detectable by the EPCN-combiner. Fig. (**2**) is the form of pattern accepted by EPCN-combiner. The functional activity of the *interpreter* and the *converter* constitute what might be referred to as the *coding scheme* to the EPCN-combiner.

Comparison to Other Similar Coding Scheme for Multi-class Problems

The combination strategy addressed here is comparable to Bayes (trained) combination strategy, and to majority voting (similarities to majority voting are marginal). The fusion method in [10] uses a combiner unit which is similar to the fusion scheme explained in this section. For this reason, contrasts are woven around combiner engine, combiner unit, and MV.

The *combiner engine* has the advantages stated below over *combiner unit* of [23]. The combiner engine encoding produce a smaller pattern size, as compared to combiner unit encoding, and thus these inferences follow:-

- It gives rise to a smaller storage requirement.
- A smaller size of layers in the pre- and main-group (recall that the size of a layer equals the size of input pattern). This indicates a smaller quantity of data being processed at any point in time.
- A favourable change in processing speed because less data may be processed at a given time.

A significance of employing combiner engine instead of combiner unit is that one

EPCN is capable of combining larger class sets in excess of 50 classes, and this fusion prospect does not depend, to a large extent, on a precise structure. The essential dichotomy between the combiner unit and the combiner engine is the employment of an interpreter in place of decision maker. This leads further to the subsequent benefit of the combiner engine over the combiner unit:-

- The interpreter processes more information from each component ANN.
- More effective synchronization among component ANN systems.

THE GROUP METHOD OF SELECTION

It is possible to design an MCS directly from equation (23) of chapter 3. In fact, the Helmholtz machine explained in the previous chapter may also be constructed from equation (26) of chapter 3 directly. Another modelling method of data generator by polynomial is known as the Group Method of Data Handling (GMDH).

Step 1: A polynomial is obtained by expanding equation (23) of chapter 3 in ascending order of variables. Three variables are considered in equation (8) below

$$y = a_0 + \sum_{i=1}^{m} a_1 x_i + \sum_{i=1}^{m}\sum_{j=1}^{n} a_{ij} x_i x_j + \sum_{i=1}^{m}\sum_{j=1}^{n}\sum_{k=1}^{p} a_{ijk} x_i x_j x_k \quad \textbf{(8)}$$

Step 2: The independent m input variables $x_{i,j,or\ k}$ $i = 1,2,3,...,m$ are taken in pairs and a least square polynomial $\overline{y}_n$ of the type:

$$\overline{y}_n = A + Bx_i + Cx_j + Dx_i^2 + Ex_i x_j + Fx_j^2 \quad \textbf{(9)}$$

are formed.

Step 3: The next step is to measure the least square errors between equations (8) and (9):

$$\varepsilon = \sum_{n=1}^{N} \left(y - \overline{y}_n\right)^2 \quad \textbf{(10)}$$

The set $\bar{y}_n$ of equations that give minimal Ó are retained while the rest $\bar{y}_n$ discarded. If m is the number of input variables, we would seek $\binom{m}{2}$ polynomials $\bar{y}_n$ such that (10) is minimum. While equations (8) and (9) may be constructed using a training set, it is essential for equation (10) to be obtained from a testing data set.

Step 4: To obtain the coefficients of (10) $a_{i,j,\ or\ k}$ that correspond to its minimum, differentiate equation (10) with respect to $a_{i,j,\ or\ k}$ and set the result to zero. The expression that correspond to:

$$\frac{\delta\varepsilon}{\delta a_i} = 0; i = 1, 2, \ldots, 5 \tag{11}$$

is an explicit function of input variables that are easily computed.

Steps (1) to (4) constitute the GMDH algorithm. The GMDH is a variant of least square approximation technique. The GMDH may be employed to grow or prune an MCS system. A procedure of how it can be done is now explained.

Assume the system's dynamics can be modelled by Volterra series of Kolmorgorov-Gabor polynomial:

$$y = a_0 + \sum_{i=1}^{m} a_1 x_i + \sum_{i=1}^{m}\sum_{j=1}^{m} a_{ij} x_i x_j + \sum_{i=1}^{m}\sum_{j=1}^{m}\sum_{k=1}^{m} a_{ijk} x_i x_j x_k \tag{12}$$

We wish to find a least square polynomial y_n of the type:

$$y_n = a_0 + a_1 x_{in} + a_2 x_{jn} + a_3 x_{in} x_n + a_4 x_{in}^2 + a_5 x_{jn}^2 \tag{13}$$

that minimize the least square errors:

$$\varepsilon = \sum_{n=1}^{N} (y - y_n)^2 \tag{14}$$

We would expand equation (14) in the y_n variable, differentiate with respect to $a_{i,j,\ or\ k}$; *i, j, or k* =1,2,3,..., and set the result to zero;

$$0 = y + \sum_{i=1}^{m} yx_i + \sum_{j=1}^{m} yx_j + \sum_{i,j=1}^{m} yx_i x_j + \sum_{i=1}^{m} yx_i^2 + \sum_{j=1}^{m} yx_j^2 \quad \textbf{(15)}$$

If y can be approximated by y_n , then substitute equation (13) into equation (15) to replace y. There should be about six equations in this example, each equation representing each term on the RHS of equation (15);

$$y = \sum_{i,j=1}^{m} a_0 + a_1 x_i + a_2 x_j + a_3 x_i x_j + a_4 x_i^2 + a_5 x_j^2 \quad \textbf{(16)}$$

$$\sum_{i=1}^{m} yx_i = \sum_{i,j=1}^{m} a_0 x_i + a_1 x_i^2 + a_2 x_j x_i + a_3 x_i^2 x_j + a_4 x_i^3 + a_5 x_i x_j^2 \quad \textbf{(17)}$$

$$\sum_{j=1}^{m} yx_j = \sum_{i,j=1}^{m} a_0 x_j + a_1 x_i x_j + a_2 x_j^2 + a_3 x_i x_j^2 + a_4 x_i^2 x_j + a_5 x_j^3 \quad \textbf{(18)}$$

$$\sum_{i,j=1}^{m} yx_i x_j = \sum_{i,j=1}^{m} a_0 x_i x_j + a_1 x_i^2 x_j + a_2 x_j^2 x_i + a_3 x_i^2 x_j^2 + a_4 x_i^3 x_j + a_5 x_i x_j^3 \quad \textbf{(19)}$$

$$\sum_{i=1}^{m} yx_i^2 = \sum_{i,j=1}^{m} a_0 x_i^2 + a_1 x_i^3 + a_2 x_j x_i^2 + a_3 x_i^3 x_j + a_4 x_i^4 + a_5 x_i^2 x_j^2 \quad \textbf{(20)}$$

$$\sum_{j=1}^{m} yx_j^2 = \sum_{i,j=1}^{m} a_0 x_j^2 + a_1 x_i x_j^2 + a_2 x_j^3 + a_3 x_i x_j^3 + a_4 x_i^2 x_j^2 + a_5 x_j^4 \quad \textbf{(21)}$$

Given (15) – (21), the $a_{i,j,\ or\ k}$ may be evaluated, which when substituted into equation (13) gives the *polynomial of optimal complexity* [24, 25].

If $\overline{y}_n$ is the computed value y_n, and $\overline{a}_{i,j,\ or\ k}$; *i*, *j*, or *k* =1,2,3,... is the computed value of a_n, then;

$$\overline{y}_n = \overline{a}_0 + \overline{a}_1 x_{in} + \overline{a}_2 x_{jn} + \overline{a}_3 x_{in} x_n + \overline{a}_4 x_{in}^2 + \overline{a}_5 x_{jn}^2 \quad \textbf{(22)}$$

is the least-square polynomial of best fit. Since the GMDH algorithm may not requires a feedback, and a polynomial of optimal complexity is obtained, the GMDH algorithm is termed a self-organizing learning algorithm; and the algorithm is also unsupervised.

Topology of GMDH

A network structure consists of neurons at nodes, and connecting edges being represented by weight coefficients. The network may self-construct layer-by-layer according to the optimal polynomial equation until the squared error achieves a minimum. However the neurons are the same for a layer, and differ from layer to layer. The neurons are normally pre-made, and the network may utilize the pre-made neurons; which neuron type to use depends on which layer is being grown. The first layer is the input layer, while the last layer is the output layer. The output layer preforms the final hard-decision. The second layer neurons often take two inputs each, and produce some soft-decision at output. The third layer neurons takes about four or more input each, and also produce soft-decision at output; and so on and so forth. The stopping criteria is either the squared error is minimum or resources are exhausted. The network has attained the best possible model when the squared errors are minimal. The layers and neurons that contribute to the optimal polynomial result are preserved whereas those layers and neurons that do not contribute to the optimal polynomial are discarded. In order to regulate the activities at each neuron, any of the activation functions of chapter two (in the second section) is suitable. However, for a fuzzy-neuron, two types of activations which are more suitable are the triangular membership function, and Gaussian (fourth section of chapter two) membership function.

Applications of GMDH

Utilizing the architecture of GMDH above in an industrial scenario, the GMDH is able to predict the Natural Gas flow and storage at Bear Paw field in Montana, USA [27].

Another interesting industrial application of the GMDH architecture is the growing of a network that utilizes fuzzy-neurons. Each neuron is an active unit which consist of fuzzy rule-base Tagaki-Sugeno-Kang (TSK) system (see chapter

5), and a soft-decision making unit. The minimum operator "min" is used to fuse the soft-decisions of fuzzy-neurons in each layer before being sent to the subsequent layer. The neuron types also differ in complexity from layer to layer. Except the output layer, the hidden layer neurons all consist of one or more TSK system succeeded by a soft-decision unit. The complexity of these units differs from layer to layer. In Mintrakis [26], this type of fuzzy-neuron is used to grow a network using GMDH algorithm. The network that emerged out of this is used to classify land covered by agriculture in Larisa, Greece. The fuzzy-neurons (see Chapter 3) in the work of [26] utilize Gaussian membership function of neural activation.

CONFLICT OF INTEREST

The author confirm that this chapter contents have no conflict of interest.

ACKNOWLEDGEMENTS

Cited works are appreciated.

REFERENCES

[1] Yang S, Browne A. Expert systems. John Wiley & sons Ltd 2004; 21: pp. (5)243-301.

[2] Dietterich G. Machine-learning research. Four current directions. AI Magazine 1998; 18(4): 97-136.

[3] Maio MD, Jain AK, Prabhakar S. Handbook of fingerprint recognition. Verlag: Springer 2003.

[4] Lam L. Classifier combinations: Implementations and theoretical issues. Springer Verlag 2002; 77-86.

[5] Mladenić D, Brank J, Grobelnik M, Milic-Frayling N. Feature Selection using Linear Classifier Weights: Interaction with classification Models. Sheffield: SIGIR 2004.

[6] Zouari H, Heutte L, Lecourtier Y. Using diversity measure in building classifier ensembles for combination method analysis, Advances in soft Computing. Int Conf Comp Recognit Sys. Springer Berlin Heidelberg 2005; pp. 337-44.

[7] Ranawana R, Palade V. Multi-classifier systems – review and a roadmap for developers. UK: Oxford: University of Oxford Computing Laboratory 2006.

[8] Günter Simon, Bunke Horst. Feature Selection Algorithm for the Generation of Multiple Classifier Systems and their Application to Handwritten Word Recognition. Switzerland: Department of Computer Science, University of Bern 2004.

[9] Freund Y, Schapire R. A decision-theoretical generalisation of on-line learning and application to boosting. J Comp Sys Sci 1997; 55(1): 119-39.

[10] Lorrentz P, Howells WGH, McDonald-Maier KD. A novel weightless neural based Multi-classifier for

large classification. Neural Process Lett 2010; 31(1): 25-44.

[11] Austin. RAM-based neural networks. World Scientific 1998.

[12] Dima Cristian. Sensor and Classifier for outdoor obstacle detection. Pittsburgh, USA: The Robotic Institute Carnegie Mellon University. 2003.

[13] Mitchell Richard. Weightless Neural Networks. University of Reading, Reading, U.K.http://www.personal.rdg.ac.uk/~shsmchlr/ nnetsmsc/nn09weightless.pdf 2006.

[14] Farhan-Khola Serkawt, Howells Gareth. Design of a Genetic Feature Selection Algorithm for Neuron Input Mapping in N-tuple Classifiers. UK: Department of Electronics, University of Kent, CT2 7NT. 2006.

[15] LI Kuncheva. Combining pattern classifier: Methods and algorithm. John Wiley and sons Inc 2004.

[16] LK Hansen, P Salamon . Neural network ensembles. IEEE Trans Pattern Anal Mach Intell. 1990; 12: pp. 993-1001.

[17] K Tumer, J Ghosh. Error correlation in ensemble classifiers. Connect Sci. John Wiley and sons Inc. 1996; 8: pp. 385-404. [http://dx.doi.org/10.1002/0471660264]

[18] JL Blue, GT Candela, PJ Grother, R Chellappa, CL Wilson. Evaluation of pattern classifiers for fingerprint and OCR applications. Pattern Recognit 1994; 27: 485-501. [http://dx.doi.org/10.1109/34.58871]

[19] PW Duin. The combining classifier: to train or not to train? Quebec: ICPR2002 2002.

[20] Roli F, Giacinto G. Hybrid Method in pattern recognition. chapter design of multiple classifier systems. Worldwide Scientific Publishing Co. 2002; pp. 199-226. [http://dx.doi.org/10.1142/9789812778147_0008]

[21] De Carvalho AC. Combining two neural networks for image classification. World Scientific 1998.

[22] Prabhakar S, Jain A, Wang J, Pankanti S, Bolle R. Minutiae verification and classification for fingerprint matching. Int Conf Pattern Recognit 2000; 1: 25-9. [http://dx.doi.org/10.1109/ICPR.2000.905269]

[23] Lorrentz P, Howells WG, McDonald-Maier KD. Design and analysis of a novel weightless neural based Multi-classifier. In: World Congress on Engineering.; 2007; p. 65.

[24] Stanley Farlow J. The GMDH algorithm of Ivakhnenko. Am Stat 1981; 35(4): 210-5.

[25] Ivakhnenko G. Polynomial theory of complex systems. IEEE Trans Syst Man Cybern 1971; 364-78. [http://dx.doi.org/10.1109/TSMC.1971.4308320]

[26] Mitrakis NE, Topaloglou CA, Alexandridis TK, Theocharis JB, Zalidis GC. A Neuro-Fuzzy Multilayered Classifier for Land Cover Image Classification. In: Proceedings of the 5th Mediterranean Conferences on Control and Automation.; Greece. 2007.

[27] James C, Howland III, Mark S. Voss. Natural Gas Prediction Using The Group Method of Data Handling. Montana. Northern Havre, USA: College of Technical Sciences, Montana State University 2003.

CHAPTER 9

Probability-based Neural Network Systems

Abstract: Since Gaussian distribution may be employed as a universal approximator, it is clear that most modelling and optimisation problems could be solved by probability-based ANN systems. For this reason, chapter 9 concentrate on probability-based ANN systems. The first section introduces the random number generator, which has application in Markov-Chain and its hybrid, in subsequent sections. The fifth section describes the Restricted Boltzmann Machine (RBM) in detail. The Boltzmann machine may be a component network of Deep Belief Networks (DBN), which is described in the last section. The chapter has explained many algorithms related to DBN with great intuition, as this may facilitate better understanding and therefore implementation.

Keywords: Annealed Importance Sampling (AIS), Boltzmann machine, Contrastive divergence, Detailed balance, Distribution, Dynamic architecture, Energy function, Ergodic, Gibbs, Hamiltonian, Markov chain, Metropolis-Hasting criteria, Molecular dynamics, Momentum heat-bath, Partition function, Pseudo-random number, Random number, Sampling, Stationary distribution, Time-reversible, Verlet integrator.

INTRODUCTION

Chapter 9 is essentially a description of Bayesian ANN systems. This is because a very large number of ANN systems could be described from probability density consideration and one chapter may not be sufficient to describe them all. The first section describes a random number generator which is required by subsequent sections. For example, Markov chain of the second section may require a random number generator to describe a stochastic sampled path. Subjecting the random walk of a Markov chain to a dynamics gives a hybrid Markov chain of the third section. The first four sections may be essential in order to understand other ANN systems introduced in other sections that follow. The first system that follows is the restricted Boltzmann machine of the fifth section. The (restricted) Boltzmann machine is in the sixth section suitably introduced because it has distinguished

Pierre Lorrentz

itself as probably the most flexible ANN system. It demonstrates a wide range of architectural possibility and more than two learning and/or recognition algorithms may be employed in combination. This possibility may not be commonly found in other ANN systems. An illustration of this is seen in the last section of chapter 9 where deep believe network is introduced.

The random number generator of the first section of chapter 9 may be employed in the generation of uniform distribution, Gaussian distribution, and other distributions. It is then possible to sample from these distribution by Markov process of the second section and/or hybrid Markov chain of the third section of this chapter. Results of hybrid Monte Carlo of chapter 11 may be employed in the Markov chain (or it hybrid) of chapter 8. The (restricted) Boltzmann machine may be developed from scratch by starting from the multinomial series or Generalized factorial of chapter three. Both the (restricted) Boltzmann machine and the hierarchical neural system derivable from it, called the deep believe network, may be employed in industrial framework as explained in chapter 10. Assuming a new integrator is discovered from chapter 11, it may be tested on the Boltzmann machine of chapter 9 and/or in an industrial perspective (the third section) of chapter 10. In any case, the deep believe network of the last section of chapter 9 may be employed in industrial perspective as described in chapter 10.

This chapter has introduced some advanced Bayesian networks and explained their algorithms.

RANDOM-NUMBER GENERATORS

If we sample from a random variable x_i, i = 1, 2, 3,... un-correlated values over certain interval, from a prescribed distribution *e.g.*, uniform distribution, we have generated "random" numbers. For these numbers to be truly random they need to come from a prescribed distribution; but for the numbers to be random only over a specified range, the distribution from which the numbers are sampled from should be close to an ideal true distribution. When the distribution from which the random sample originates is close to the true distribution, and x_i values are such that:

$$x_{i+1} = \alpha x_i + b \pmod{n} \tag{1}$$

then the samples generated are pseudo-random. The device (or algorithm) *i.e.*; implementation of equation (1) that generates the pseudo-random numbers is a pseudo-random-number generator. Values for α and b are constant and positive. The value n determines the ranges (1,n) of random numbers. This (pseudo-) random number generator is suitable for most practical purposes, more so because data samples are normally always processed. The essential constraint to be satisfied is that the distribution from which x_i is sampled from should be arbitrary close (if not exactly equal) to the distribution of interest, over the range (1, n). Dividing the range (1,n) by n gives $\left(\frac{1}{n},1\right) \approx (0,1)$ ≈ (0,1) where n is a sufficient positive large number. So that by a simple division by n, a uniform N(0,1) distribution has been sampled from. From henceforth, a pseudo-random number of the sort described here will be taken as a random number. Also, a corresponding pseudo- random number generator will be assumed throughout as a random-number generator. This is what is normally required in practice. The range of x_i is also sometimes called the period of the x_i random variable. It is essential, for reproduction of random values, to select a number called *seed* around which the random values are produced. To reproduce a specific set of random numbers, set the range (1,n), α, and the corresponding seed of the generator. By using a random-number generator to sample from a distribution, the distribution of choice is said to be sampled at random.

MARKOV CHAIN

If a distribution exist for which no direct access is possible quantitatively, an ideal approach is to sample from the distribution until a sufficient sample is obtained. Taking random samples from partly unknown distribution π(x) is known as Markov Chain (MC) sampling. Taking a random sample from the posterior distribution of partly unknown distribution is called Markov Chain Monte-Carlo (MCMC) sampling. A process is Markov if a next state-space is dependent only on the previous state-space as:

$$\pi(x_{i+1}) = k\pi(x_i) \qquad \textbf{(2)}$$

where the k is called the transition kernel of the Markov process, and $\pi(x_{i+1})$ is a target distribution.

A stochastic sampled path of a Markov chain which is irreducible and aperiodic naturally has a stationary distribution at time $t \rightarrow \infty$. Thus to find the stationary distribution $\pi(x)$of a Markov chain requires an $(n\tau)$−*time* transition kernel k such that;

$$\pi_{t+n\tau} = k_t \pi_t \tag{3}$$

A Markov chain with a stationary distribution $\pi(x)$ is also known as time-reversible if the corresponding transition kernel k satisfy a condition called detailed balance; *i.e.*; if

$$\pi(x)k(x,y) = \pi(y)k(y,x) \tag{4}$$

Conversely, any Markov chain which is time-reversible with a kernel which satisfies the detailed balance (equation (4)) condition must surely have stationary distribution.

HYBRID MARKOV CHAIN (HMC)

A hybrid Markov chain results if the Markov chain is subjected to a dynamics. The HMC is particularly necessary when modelling a system of many coupled degrees of freedom in which a single-variable update is of no meaning. A classical method of design and analysis of such intricate system may not often be possible. But following molecular dynamics evolution which is subjected to a Hamiltonian (a fictitious Hamiltonian to be specific), such a system can be modelled, provided a Markov chain samples from an appropriate distribution [1 - 3]. Details of the procedure occur in three main stages which carry names of:

1. *Momentum Heat-Bath:* An appropriate distribution is formulated from which the Markov chain takes off.
2. *Molecular Dynamic Evolution*: A fake Hamiltonian is fabricated from the quantum field potential energy by the addition of a kinetic energy. So that the theory of classical Hamiltonian applies.
3. *Acceptance:* An acceptance criterion, such as that of Metropolis-Hasting, is applied to accept or reject a proposal configuration which represents the "next step" of the Markov process.

Momentum Heat-Bath

The Gaussian distribution may be used as a universal model predictor. For this reason, it is usual to start sampling from a Gaussian distribution, though other types of distribution may equally be suitable. In any case, we require a probability density function (p. d. f.) of the form:

$$\pi(x) \propto \exp\left(-\frac{y^2}{2}\right) \quad \textbf{(5)}$$

or

$$\pi(x) \propto \exp(-V(x)) \quad \textbf{(6)}$$

where V(x) is a square integrable function, called the “energy” function, and x is a random variable.

If a distribution of type equation (5) is assumed at the start of the experiment, then the Hamiltonian of the energy should also be related to (6) for consistency. The relationship is established be deriving a momentum equation from (5).

$$\pi(x) = k\exp\left(-\frac{y^2}{2}\right);\ \text{k = constant} \quad \textbf{(7)}$$

$$\ln(\pi(x)) = ln(k) + \left(-\frac{y^2}{2}\right)$$

$$2\ln(\pi) = 2\ln(k) - y^2$$

$$-2\ln(\pi) + 2\ln(k) = y^2$$

$$\mp\sqrt{2\ln(\pi)} \pm \sqrt{2\ln(k)} = y$$

where y is the momentum term.

To prevent taking the logarithm of zero distribution, the π is replaced by (1-π) so that:

$$\pm\sqrt{2\ln(1-\pi(x))}\pm\sqrt{2\ln(k)}=y \tag{8}$$

Since $\pm\sqrt{2\ln(k)}$ is a constant which does not contribute to changes in momentum, it automatically drops out when y is added to V(x) field potential energy in order to make the Hamiltonian of the process. For a y momentum, the corresponding kinetic energy E_k is given by equation (9);

$$E_k=\frac{1}{2}\left(\frac{y^2}{m}\right)=\frac{1}{2}\left(y^T m^{-1} y\right) \tag{9}$$

where m = mass of a particle. Combining equation (9) with the potential energy gives the Hamiltonian of any specific particle in the lattice. Though the Hamiltonian is inaccurate (fictitious), it helps to apply the classical method of solution to problems which would otherwise be almost unsolvable. The Hamiltonian now state that:

$$H(\pi,x)=\frac{1}{2}\left[y^T(\pi)m^{-1}y(\pi)\right]+V(x) \tag{10}$$

In summary, particles have been sampled from a distribution, and the particles have been experiencing a hypothetical momentum changes giving rise to the Hamiltonian of equation (10).

Molecular Dynamics

In describing the particle behaviour, we seek numerical solutions of the classical molecular dynamic (MD) equations of motion. Since the Hamiltonian (equation (10)) is known to be conserved, the classical method of Hamiltonian solution applies. Specifically, assume a fictitious time τ, and that the first and second terms of the Hamiltonian are separable. The fictitious time τ, is known as *Markov time-step* which enables the Hamiltonian to be re-written as:

$$H(y(\tau),V(\tau))=H_1(y(\tau))+H_2(V(\tau)) \tag{11}$$

Changes in the field potential V(τ) and momentum y(τ) can be traced by differentiating (11) with respect to τ;

$$\frac{\partial V}{\partial \tau} = \frac{\partial H}{\partial y} = \nabla_y H_1 \tag{12}$$

$$\frac{\partial y}{\partial \tau} = -\frac{\partial H}{\partial V} = -\nabla_V H \tag{13}$$

Both equations (12) and (13) should satisfy

$$\frac{\partial}{\partial \tau}\left(H(y(\tau),V(\tau))\right) = 0 \tag{14}$$

the conservation of Hamiltonian, so that changes in momentum and field potential may be represented by:

$$\text{Field potential: } V \rightarrow V + \epsilon_p \; \nabla_y H_1 \tag{15}$$

$$\text{Momentum: } \quad y \rightarrow y - \epsilon_m \; \nabla_V H_2 \tag{16}$$

The molecular dynamic algorithm consist of repeated application of equation (15) and (16). There are several variations, in software/hardware implementation, of them. One of the most notable is leapfrog algorithm which may utilise the Verlet integrator.

Acceptance Criteria

The random Markov movement now become a type of stochastic dynamic movement away from the previous distribution. Whether or not the present distribution is accepted depends on Metropolis-Hastings acceptance criteria. The acceptance criteria alleviate the bias introduced by the stochastic dynamic movement because the movement is no longer very random. A new configuration is derived from the previous configuration through L iterations each of which make repeated use of equations (15) and (16). One iteration will require a step size of ε_s ; to move through. Iteration at one step is one or more integration process involving the maps specified by equations (15) and (16). The direction λ of one step ε_s ; $\lambda \in \{-1,1\}$ is chosen at random with equal probability. The most popular integration being in use is called the Verlet integrator. The iterations in turn, are arranged in a specific fashion, of which among the most notable is called the leapfrog iteration (or algorithm). Both the verlet integrator (algorithm) and the leapfrog algorithm are presented in the next sub-section. Whichever integrator is used, an L iteration of a molecular dynamic (MD) evolution furnishes a new candidate state configuration by equation (17):

$$\text{MD: } \underbrace{[y(\tau), v(\tau)]}_{old} \rightarrow \underbrace{[y^*(\tau), v^*(\tau)]}_{new} \tag{17}$$

The probability of acceptance of the new state is given by the Metropolis-Hastings (MH) criteria:

$$MH = \min\left(1, \exp\left(-H(y^*, v^*) - H(y, v)\right)\right) \tag{18}$$

The new Hamiltonian $H(y^*,v^*)$ in equation (18) is calculated by substituting the new states (y^*,v^*) into the Hamiltonian dynamic equation (11). If the candidate state is not accepted, the old states (y,v)become the new states.

IMPLEMENTATION ISSUES

1. Verlet Integrator

Assume the time-step is strictly positive $\tau > 0$, so that the temporal dynamical Markov sequence τ_n may be written as:

$$\tau_n = n\tau; \quad n = 1, 2, 3, \ldots \tag{19}$$

The task is to construct a corresponding spatial Markov sequence x_n such that $x_n \approx x(\tau_n)$ as close as possible to the trajectory of the exact solution.

The basic Verlet integration is a central difference approximation to the second-order derivative;

$$\frac{\Delta^2 x_n}{\Delta\tau^2} = \frac{\left(\dfrac{x_{n+1} - x_n}{\Delta\tau} - \dfrac{x_n - x_{n-1}}{\Delta\tau}\right)}{\Delta\tau} = \frac{x_{n+1} - 2x_n + x_{n-1}}{\Delta\tau^2} = a_n \tag{20}$$

That is: $x_{n+1} = 2x_n + x_{n-1} + a_n\Delta\tau^2$ **(21)**

The Verlet position x_{n+1} approximation to the Markov position sequence is the most widely used algorithm to model the trajectory of the exact solution. This is because of the time symmetry inherent in Verlet integration reduces the level of errors which may be expressed as a Taylor's polynomial.

$$x(\tau + \Delta\tau) = x(\tau) + v(\tau)\Delta\tau + \frac{a(\tau)\Delta\tau^2}{2} + \frac{b(\tau)\Delta\tau^3}{6} + O\left(\Delta\tau^4\right) \tag{22}$$

$$x(\tau - \Delta\tau) = x(\tau) - v(\tau)\Delta\tau + \frac{a(\tau)\Delta\tau^2}{2} - \frac{b(\tau)\Delta\tau^3}{6} + O\left(\Delta\tau^4\right) \tag{23}$$

Adding these two expressions together;

$$x(\tau + \Delta\tau) + x(\tau - \Delta\tau) = 2x(\tau) + a_n\Delta\tau^2 + O\left(\Delta\tau^4\right) \tag{24}$$

where by $v(\tau)$= velocity; $a(\tau)$= acceleration; $b(\tau)$= the jerk.

From the equations above, it may be seen that the order of accuracy is $O(\Delta\tau^4)$, which is one order more accurate than Euler's integration, or the simple Taylor's expansion method.

The Verlet iteration requires adequate initial conditions. The designer decides on the time $\Delta\tau$ step-size and the initial position x_0. Both the time-step size $\Delta\tau$ and the initial position x_0 may then decide the first position x_1 by Taylor's expansion;

$$x_1 = x_0 + v_0\Delta\tau + \frac{1}{2}a_0\Delta\tau^2 + O(\Delta\tau^3) \tag{25}$$

Setting $v_0 = 0;\quad x_1 = x_0 + \frac{1}{2}a_0\Delta\tau^2 + O(\Delta\tau^3)$ **(26)**

After deducting both x_0 and x_1, the normal Verlet iteration may begin. For large n, the errors accrue from only one step, the first step, is not significant. It may even be removed as part of burn-in period. The Verlet algorithm explained here is sometimes referred to as position-Verlet algorithm.

2. Velocity Verlet

Since velocity is sometimes required and is not part of the basic Verlet method, this section introduces the velocity Verlet method; it states:

$$x(\tau+\Delta\tau)=x(\tau)+v\Delta\tau+\frac{1}{2}a\Delta\tau^2 \tag{27}$$

$$v(\tau+\Delta\tau)=v(\tau)+\frac{a(\tau)+a(\tau+\Delta\tau)}{2}\Delta\tau \tag{28}$$

For stochastic dynamic Markov chain, the momentum and the velocity are updated. It follows that:

$$\text{Momentum, } M_I:\ p(\tau+\Delta\tau)=p(\tau)-\frac{\Delta\tau}{2}\frac{dE}{dx}\left(x(\tau)\right) \tag{29}$$

$$i\in I;\quad i=0,\ 1,\ 2....$$

$$\text{Velocity, } V_I:\ v(\tau+\Delta\tau)=v(\tau)+\frac{p\left(\tau+\dfrac{\Delta\tau}{2}\right)}{M_i} \tag{30}$$

$$\text{Momentum, } M_I:\ p(\tau+\Delta\tau)=p(\tau+\frac{\Delta\tau}{2})-\frac{\Delta\tau}{2}\frac{dE}{dx}\left(x(\tau+\Delta\tau)\right) \tag{31}$$

Equations (29) to (31) is a procedural implementation of (15) and (16), and are called leapfrog algorithm. The Mi is the "particle mass" that appears in the Hamiltonian equation (11) – the value is set from system's configuration.

The errors on the velocity Verlet is the same order as that on position Verlet integration. Both velocity Verlet and Leapfrog iteration are one-order better than the semi-implicit Euler method. Since the target distribution is an ergodic distribution, the value of $\Delta\tau$ may be randomly perturbed. Random perturbation of $\Delta\tau$ prevent periodic return to regions that encourage ergodicity. By employing stochastic dynamic Hamiltonian, and moving in direction that maximises Δx , we prevent correlation effects, and avoid random walks which are too short and/or repetitive. Using the stochastic dynamic Hamiltonian in Markov processes also prevent paths that are too long because the Hamiltonian is coupled with an acceptance criterion which drops drastically if Δx leads to larger errors.

Verlet integrator is an algorithm obtained by implementing equations (27), (29), (28), and (31) in that order. The arrangement of integration of the form:

$$M_I\left(\frac{\Delta\tau}{2}\right)V_I(\Delta\tau)M_I\left(\frac{\Delta\tau}{2}\right) \tag{32}$$

is the Leapfrog algorithm. One other interesting arrangement of integral is:

$$M_I(\varepsilon\Delta\tau)V_I\left(\frac{\Delta\tau}{2}\right)M_I((1-2\varepsilon)\Delta\tau)V_I\left(\frac{\Delta\tau}{2}\right)M_I(\varepsilon\Delta\tau) \tag{33}$$

known as Omelyan integrator. The Omelyan integrator leads to a significant improvement of numerical solution over leapfrog integrator. These integrators are exact in that they conserve both phase space measure and time reversibility.

RESTRICTED BOLTZMANN MACHINE

Gibbs Sampling

Given n^x, x^{n+1} is generated by the following procedure:

1. $x_1^{n+1} \xleftarrow[generate]{} x_1^n$: from the conditional probability of x_1 if $x_2^n, x_3^n, \ldots, x_m^n$ is given;
2. $x_2^{n+1} \xleftarrow[generate]{} x_2^n$: from the conditional probability of x_2 if $x_1^{n+1}, x_3^n, \ldots, x_m^n$ is given;

3. $x_j^{n+1} \xleftarrow{generate} x_j^n$: from the conditional probability of x_j if $x_1^{n+1}, x_2^{n+1}, \ldots, x_{j-1}^{n+1}, x_{j+1}^n, \ldots, x_m^n$ is given;

4. $x_m^{n+1} \xleftarrow{generate} x_m^n$: from the conditional probability of x_m if $x_1^{n+1}, x_2^{n+1}, \ldots, x_{m-1}^{n+1}$ is given;

It is noteworthy that Gibbs sampling depends on the conditional probability $\pi(x_1 \mid x_2,\ldots,x_m)$ of a distribution π being considered. And that the Markov chain given in the Gibbs algorithm leaves the distribution invariant if and only if each transition does.

The Restricted Boltzmann Machine (RBM)

A Boltzmann machine is a two-layered network that consists of a visible v_i layer and a hidden h_j layer. The visible v_i, ($i = 0, 1, 2 \ldots$) layer and a hidden h_j layer are connected by weight w_{ij} ($j = 0, 1, 2 \ldots$). The restriction between neurons (units) of the visible layer maintains independence of initial parameters as a result of lack of connection between them. The connection between visible layer and the hidden layer is expressed as an energy $E(v_i, h_j)$ of the form:

$$E(v_i, h_j) = -\left[\sum_i v_i a_i + \sum_j b_j h_j + \sum_{i,j} a_i^T w_{ij} b_j\right] \tag{34}$$

The energy, in standard form, almost always consists of three terms; the exact expression of each of these three terms is dependent on data distribution. From data distribution, the network assigns a probability distribution to every possible pairs of visible and hidden neuron. The probability distribution $p(v_i, h_j)$ is expressed by:

$$p(v_i, h_j) = \frac{\exp(-(E(v_i, h_j)))}{Z} \tag{35}$$

$$\text{where;} \quad Z = \sum_{v_i, h_j} \exp(-(E(v_i, h_j))) \tag{36}$$

Z is a partition function.

The probability distribution of the visible neuron is given by summing (35) over all hidden neuron;

$$p(v_i) = \frac{1}{Z}\sum_j \exp\left(-\left(E(v_i, h_j)\right)\right) \quad \textbf{(37)}$$

Similarly, the probability distribution of the hidden neuron is obtained by summing (35) over all visible neuron;

$$p(h_j) = \frac{1}{Z}\sum_i \exp\left(-\left(E(v_i, h_j)\right)\right) \quad \textbf{(38)}$$

To follow the changes in probability distribution over the neurons, the logarithm of equation (37) and (38) are observed. The derivatives of the logarithm express the changes. Since the biases, a_i and b_j are effectively constant, the changes are due to the weight connections between the neurons. By substituting equation (33) into (37) and taking the log derivatives, we obtain:

$$\frac{\partial \log\left(p(v_i)\right)}{\partial w_{ij}} = \langle v_i h_j \rangle_{data} - \langle v_i h_j \rangle_{model} \quad \textbf{(39)}$$

after some algebra. The right-hand side (RHS) of equation (39) represent expected values; *i.e.*; the $\langle v_i h_j \rangle_{data}$ means to calculate the expected value of $v_i h_j$ from the given data points i and j; the $\langle v_i h_j \rangle_{model}$ means to calculate the expected values of $v_i h_j$ from resulting model (data) points i and j. Given specific network architecture with constant biases, the difference (contrast) between data and the model may only be represented through changes in weight Δw_{ij} given by:

$$\Delta w_{ij} = \lambda\left[\langle v_i h_j \rangle_{data} - \langle v_i h_j \rangle_{model}\right] \quad \textbf{(40)}$$

where λ = learning rate.

Thus given V-dimensional visible biases, and a H-dimensional hidden biases, an

RBM is defined as a network θ_{RBM} given by;

$$\theta_{RBM} = (W,h,v) \quad \textbf{(41)}$$

A deep belief network (DBN) may be defined by a sequence of RBMs given as in equation (42);

$$\{\theta_{RBM}\} = \{(W,h,v)\} \quad \textbf{(42)}$$

In DBN, the $\theta_{RBM} = (W,h,v)$ define the parameters of each network. The dimension of the weights for each network is (VxH)-dimension, and $w_{ij} \in W;\ h_j \in h;\ v_i \in v$.

An RBM requires an activation function for learning. The activation function determines which neuron turns on and which neuron turns off. Two most popular activation functions with respect to RBM are the sigmoid, and softmax activation functions. An illustration with sigmoid activation follows. On the visible layer v, a neuron v_i is selected at random and the (binary) state of the associated hidden neuron h_j is set to 1 with probability:

$$p(h_j = 1 \mid v_i) = \sigma\left(b_j + \sum_i v_i w_{ij}\right) \quad \textbf{(43)}$$

$$\text{where} \quad \sigma(x) = \frac{1}{1+e^{-x}} \quad \textbf{(44)}$$

Similarly, on the hidden layer h, a neuron h_j is selected at random and the (binary) state of the associated visible neuron v_i is set to 1 with a probability given by:

$$p(v_i = 1 \mid h_h) = \sigma\left(a_i + \sum_j h_j w_{ij}\right) \quad \textbf{(45)}$$

The learning algorithm employs the Gibbs Sampling algorithm, coupled with equation (43) and (45) in alternation for activation. This alternating Gibbs sampling, using equation (43) on the visible neuron and equation (45) on the hidden neuron of RBM, is the principle behind the contrastive divergence learning algorithm [4]. Some other two-step alternating Markov Chain sampling *e.g.*; hybrid Markov Chain (HMC) of the previous section, may also be used. So also the Maximization-Expectation (E-M) algorithm and its variants may also well be employed for learning by using equation (43) and (45) for neuron activation in this example. One may note that RBM is very flexible to learning algorithms. After some iterations of alternating Gibbs sampling, the expected value of $\langle v_i h_j \rangle_{model}$ of equation (40) may then be calculated.

Energy Dynamics and Learning

For images and speech signals, a better energy function for RBM is:

$$E(v_i, h_j) = \sum_i \frac{(v_i - a_i)^2}{2\sigma_i^2} - \sum_j b_j h_j - \sum_{i,j} \frac{v_i h_j}{\sigma_i} w_{ij} \quad \textbf{(46)}$$

This is because it accommodates the Gaussian signal of standard deviation σ_i of the input. If it is desired that the RBM support Gaussian signal both on hidden and visible neurons, then equation (46) should be modified to:

$$E(v_i, h_j) = \sum_i \frac{(v_i - a_i)^2}{2\sigma_i^2} - \sum_j \frac{(h_j - b_j)^2}{2\sigma_j^2} - \sum_{i,j} \frac{v_i h_j}{\sigma_i \sigma_j} w_{ij} \quad \textbf{(47)}$$

The equation (46) is much stable and suitable for images and speech signals.

Among variety of learning algorithms utilised by RBM, the maximum likelihood (ML) [5] and the Contrastive Divergence (CD) learning algorithm are the most widely used. In view of the ML, the RBM θ_{RBM} search for and selects the system parameters θ that assigns the highest probability (*i.e.* lowest energy) to the observed data. This is equivalent to searching for a set of system parameters that minimize the Kullback-leibler (KL) divergence:

$$KL(\pi_e \mid \pi_\theta) = \sum_{x_i \in x} \pi_e \left(\log(\pi_e(x)) - \log(\pi_\theta(x))\right) \quad \textbf{(48)}$$

between the empirical distribution $\pi_e(x)$ and the target distribution $\pi_\theta(x)$. Equation (48) is addressed as explained previously (see equations (39) and (40)) by differentiation of equation (48), setting the result to zero, and finding Δw_{ij} of (39) the set of weights that makes the observed data more likely, in addition to the observed biases. If on the other hand one likes to train the network with a contrastive divergence algorithm, one will look for the set of parameters θ_{RBM} that minimizes the difference between two KL functions. This scenario could be quantified by:

$$f_{CD}(\theta(x)) = \sum_{x_i \in x} \pi_e(x) \log\left(\frac{\pi_e(x)}{\pi_\theta(x)}\right) - \sum_{x_i \in x} \pi_e^t(x) \log\left(\frac{\pi_e^t(x)}{\pi_\theta(x)}\right) \quad \textbf{(49)}$$

Where $\pi_e^t(x)$ is the distribution obtained by application of a t-step standard Gibbs sampling to the empirical distribution $\pi_e^t(x)$. In both equations (47) and (48), the expected values of the RHS are only required. In cases where the expected values are tedious, a stochastic approximation works well in practice.

A DEEP BELIEF NETWORK OF BOLTZMANN MACHINES

The expected value of KL divergence (*e.g.*; equation (48)) may be calculated by using the mean-field algorithm. Let θ_{BM}^τ be the present parameter, and x^τ the present state of a Boltzmann machine (BM), the $(\theta_{BM}^\tau, x^\tau)$ are updated in sequence using a transition operator $T_\theta\ (x^{\tau+1}, x^\tau)$ which leaves the distribution π_θ invariant. That is:

$$x^{\tau+1} := T_\theta(x^{\tau+1}, x^\tau) \quad \textbf{(50)}$$

transition leave π_θ invariant, provided the transition kernel T_θ converges. The main conditions for convergence are:

1. To decrease the learning rate λ gradually with time *e.g.*; by setting $\lambda = k\frac{1}{t}$;
2. The sequence of parameters $|\theta_{BM}|$ is bounded;
3. The Markov chain, governed by the transition kernel T_θ is ergodic.

When a (restricted) Boltzmann Machine is fully connected, equation (41) may be re-written as:

$$\theta_{BN} = \left((W; h; v), (M; h), (N; v) \right) \quad \textbf{(51)}$$

where N = visible-to-visible v unit interaction weights;

M = hidden-to-hidden h unit interaction weight.

W = visible-to-hidden connection weights.

Equation (51) reflects full weight connections, at constant biases, of neurons both between layers and within layers. For an RBM, N and M are zero because of lack of connection within layers. A Deep Belief network consisting of Boltzmann Machines may be seen from equation (51) as a cascade of BMs:

$$\{\theta_{BM}\} = \{\left((W; h; v), (M; h), (N; v) \right)\} \quad \textbf{(52)}$$

The dynamics (or energy) corresponding to (51) and (52) is:

$$E(v, h, \theta) = -\sum_{v,h} \left(v^T W h + \frac{v^T N v}{2} + \frac{h^T M h}{2} \right) \quad \textbf{(53)}$$

at constant biases.

The probability that a hidden layer neuron h_j is turned on given the states of other units is:

$$p\left(h_j = 1 \mid v, h_{\#/j}\right) = \sigma\left(\sum_{i=1}^{D} W_{ij} v_i + \sum_{m=\#/j}^{P} M_{jm} h_j \right) \quad \textbf{(54)}$$

where #/j = other states excluding j.

Similarly, the probability that a visible unit v_i is turned on given the state of other units is:

$$p(v_i = 1 | h, v_{\#/i}) = \sigma\left(\sum_{j=1}^{P} W_{ij} h_j + \sum_{k=\#/i}^{D} N_{ik} v_j\right) \tag{55}$$

The connection weights W, N, M are updated algorithmically (the algorithm will be given shortly) as learning proceeds. Learning performs a gradient ascent in the log-likelihood similar to equation (38), which yields:

$$\Delta W = \sigma\left(E\left(p_{data}(vh^T)\right) + E\left(p_{model}(vh^T)\right)\right) \tag{56}$$

$$\Delta N = \sigma\left(E\left(p_{data}(vv^T)\right) + E\left(p_{model}(vv^T)\right)\right) \tag{57}$$

$$\Delta M = \sigma\left(E\left(p_{data}(hh^T)\right) + E\left(p_{model}(hh^T)\right)\right) \tag{58}$$

All at constant biases.

Assuming an independent posteriori distribution $\pi_{PS}(h,\mu)$ over the hidden units;

$$\pi_{PS}(h, \mu) = \prod_{j=1}^{P} \pi_{PS}(h_j) \tag{59}$$

where $(h_j = 1) = \mu_j$;

μ_j = number of unit; and

P = number of hidden unit

The log probability over the visible unit may be lower-bounded as:

$$\ln(p(v;\theta)) \geq \frac{1}{2}\left[\sum_{i,k} N_{ik} v_i k_k + \sum_{j,m} M_{jm} \mu_j \mu_m\right] + \frac{1}{2}\sum_{i,j} W_{ij} v_i \mu_j - Z(\theta)$$
$$+\sum_j \left[\mu_j \ln(\mu_j) + (1-\mu_j)\ln(1-\mu_j)\right] \tag{60}$$

Learning aims to maximize the lower-bound of the RHS of equation (60) with respect to the mean μ_j for fixed parameter θ. Maximization results in a mean field fixed-point equation;

$$\mu_j \xleftarrow[j]{} \sigma\left(\sum_j W_{ij} v_i + \sum_{m,\#/j} M_{mj} \mu_m\right) \quad \textbf{(61)}$$

which converges faster to μ_j mean than other alternatives available for mean μ_j update. Combining equations (50), (61), and Gibbs (Markov chain) sampling gives the Boltzmann Machine learning algorithm:

Boltzmann Machine Learning Algorithm

Given: a training data D vectors $\{v\}_{i=1}^{D}$;

Initialize: the parameters θ to random value;

Initialize the visible and the hidden units (the fantasy particles) $(v^{0,1}, h^{0,1})...(v^{0,m}, h^{0,m})$ of M values to random numbers;

Initialize the means μ_j to random numbers;

- For t = 0 to t = # (number of iteration)
  For each training data v_i ; i = 0,1,2,…,D
    - Run mean-field fixed-point equation (61) to obtain μ_j
    - Set $\mu_{\tau,j} = \mu_j$
- For each set of initialized $(v^{0,1}, h^{0,1})...(v^{0,m}, h^{0,,m})$ perform a Markov chain (Gibbs) sampling as follows:

$\{v^{0,1}, h^{0,1}\}...\{v^{0,m}, h^{0,m}\} \xrightarrow{T_e \text{ Gibbs samplinng}} \{v^{1,1}, h^{1,1}\}...\{v^{1,m}, h^{1,m}\}$; repeat of all τ;

$$\{v^{\tau,1}, h^{\tau,1}\}...\{v^{\tau,m}, h^{\tau,m}\} \xrightarrow{T_e \text{ Gibbs samplinng}} \{v^{\tau+1,1}, h^{\tau+1,1}\}...\{v^{\tau+1,m}, h^{\tau+1,m}\}$$

- Update the weight W^{τ};

$$W^{\tau} = W^{\tau-1} + \lambda\left[\frac{1}{D}\sum_{n=1}^{D} v^n (\mu^n)^T - \frac{1}{H}\sum_{m=1}^{H} v^{\tau,m} (h^{\tau,m})^T\right] \quad \textbf{(62)}$$

- Similarly update N and M weights

- Decrease the learning rate λ

The Partition Function: Annealed Importance Sampling (AIS)

The partition function Z cannot be calculated exactly, but can be estimated. To this end, assume a deep-belief network consist of two Boltzmann machines A and B each with its parameter θ_A and θ_B respectively. Taking the ratios of probabilities $p(v,\theta_A)$ and $p(v,\theta_B)$ over the visible v units;

$$\frac{p(v,\theta_A)}{p(v,\theta_B)} = \frac{p^*(v,\theta_A)}{p^*(v,\theta_B)}\frac{Z(\theta_B)}{Z(\theta_A)} \tag{63}$$

From equation (62);

$$\frac{Z(\theta_B)}{Z(\theta_A)} = \frac{p(v,\theta_A)}{p(v,\theta_B)}\frac{p^*(v,\theta_B)}{p^*(v,\theta_A)} \quad \text{or} \quad \frac{Z(\theta_B)}{Z(\theta_A)} = \frac{p_B^*(v)}{p_A^*(v)}\frac{p_A(v)}{p_B(v)} \tag{64}$$

$$\frac{Z(\theta_B)}{Z(\theta_A)} = \frac{p_B^*(v)}{p_A^*(v)}\frac{p_A(v)}{p_B(v)} = \frac{\int p_B^*(v)\partial v}{Z_A}$$

$$\frac{\int p_B^*(v)\partial v}{Z_A} = \int \frac{p_B^*(v)}{p_A^*(v)} p_A^*(v)\partial v = E_{p_A}\left[\frac{p_B^*(v)}{p_A^*(v)}\right]$$

where E_{p_A} expected value of P_A

Equation (64) may be estimated by taking certain C steps of stochastic approximation;

$$\frac{Z_A}{Z_B} = \frac{1}{C}\sum_{i=1}^{C}\frac{p_B^*(v_i)}{p_A^*(v_i)} = \frac{1}{C}\sum_{i=1}^{C} w_{(i)} \tag{65}$$

The following story describes how the C-steps may be taken:

a. Define a sequence of probability distribution $p_0, p_1, \ldots, p_k$ such that $p_0 = p_A$ and $p_k = p_B$. If the probability distribution sequence satisfy the following condition:

   - $p_i(v) \neq 0$ imply $p_{i-1} \neq 0$; ($i = 0, 1, 2, \ldots, K - 1$ $i \in K$)

- $p_i(v)$ is easily computable;
- For each i = 0,1,2,…,k-1, it is possible to sample v' from v using a transition operator

$$T_i(v',v) \text{ by: } p_i(v') = \int T_i(v',v)\, p_i(v) dv \tag{66}$$

that leaves $p_i(v)$ invariant.

- Independent samples may be also drawn from p_A.

b. Partition the interval (0,1) as: $0 = \beta_0 < \beta_1 < ... < \beta_k = 1$; and define;

$$p_i(v) \propto \left(p_A^*(v)\right)^{1-\beta_i} \left(p_B^*(v)\right)^{\beta_i} \tag{67}$$

Let equation (67) be defined as a sequence of intermediate probability distribution. Then the annealed importance sampling procedure follows. Generate $v_1, v_2, ..., v_k$ as follows.

- Sample v_1 from $P_0 = P_A$;
- Gibbs sample v_i from v_{i-1} using the transition kernel T_{i-1} from i = 0 to $i = K - 1$.

$$w_{(i)} = \frac{p_1^*(v_1)}{p_0^*(v_1)} \frac{p_2^*(v_2)}{p_1^*(v_2)} \cdots \frac{p_{k-1}^*(v_{k-1})}{p_{k-2}^*(v_{k-1})} \frac{p_k^*(v_k)}{p_{k-1}^*(v_k)} \tag{68}$$

After C iterations of the AIS, the importance weight $w^{(i)}$ may be substituted into equation (64) in order to calculate the partition function. It may be noticed that AIS is an example of stochastic approximation procedure described previously.

Pre-Training of Deep Belief Network

To equation (54) and (55) we add one more conditional probability:

$$p(h_j^{(2)} = 1 \mid h^{(1)}) = \sigma\left(\sum_m W_{im}^{(2)} h_i^{(1)}\right) \tag{69}$$

Equation (69) represents connection (turn-on) between two hidden layers 1 and 2.

The same expression, with indices 1 and 2 replaced by different set of indices, exist when there are more than two layers. In that case, the adjacent pairs of hidden layers under consideration will have their indices replacing 1 and 2 in equation (69). For a Deep Belief Network (DBN) consisting of units of BM, the BM learning algorithm may be used for learning with (54), (55), and (69) for turning on/off the neurons. To save time, it may be worthwhile initializing the hidden layers of a DBN to sensible weight connections; this is known as pre-training. As seen from the dynamics (or energy) equation (53), the half suggests either to double certain weights or half something else. This is because the first visible (v_1) - hidden (h_1) - hidden (h_2) layers of a DBN are normally un-directed. This means that the hidden layer h_1 will be traversed twice while the visible layer v_1 and the hidden layer h_2 traversed once in a single iteration. The visible layer distribution $p(v, h_1 | W^{(1)})$ is initialized from given data. Then the weights $W^{(2)} = W^{(1)T}$ are set and $W^{(2)}$ are fixed at that value. The Boltzmann Machine comprising the first two layers v_1 and h_1 of the DBN are trained by the usual BM learning algorithm already described (see Fig. **1**). This training produces a first fantasy model distribution of $\left\langle v_i h_1^T \right\rangle_{model}$. The fantasy model becomes data for the subsequent hidden h_2 layer. Then freeze $W^{(1)T}$ and allow $W^{(2)}$ to change values by using the BM learning algorithm. This procedure can be repeated for as many hidden layer as desired, and is summarised as follows.

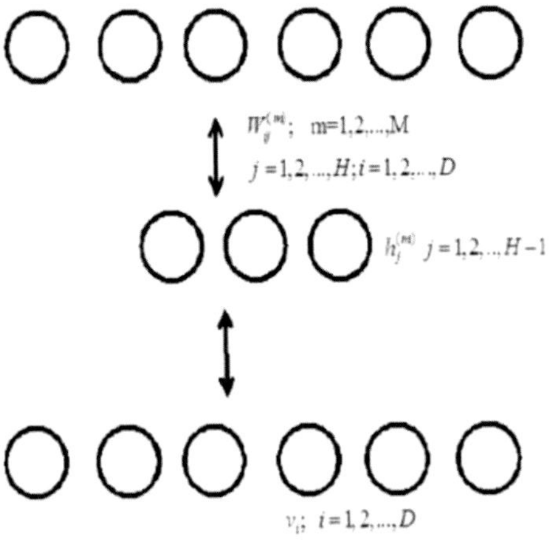

Fig. (1). A deep belief network which consists of ith Boltzmann machines as component.

- Train a normal BM with its learning algorithm. Set the $W^{(1)T}$ produced to $W^{(2)}$.
- Freeze the first layer weights $W^{(1)T}$ and associated parameters, and use $p(h_1 | v_1, W^{(1)})$ as data for the next h_2 hidden layer.
- Repeat for as many hidden h_j layers as desired.

The doubling of weights only affects the first and the last layers of DBN during learning. The pre-training of a DBN produced a sensible approximate inference at the first single iteration, and is also a suitable parameter initialization strategy for the mean-field method.

Dynamic Biases of a DBN

The case whereby the biases are dynamic (*i.e.*; non-constant) as opposed to static, is now introduced. Alongside of biasing a DBN with a label, gating of DBN is also presented. A stereo-type application area of a gated DBN is in autonomous image processing and video coding; as in a robot.

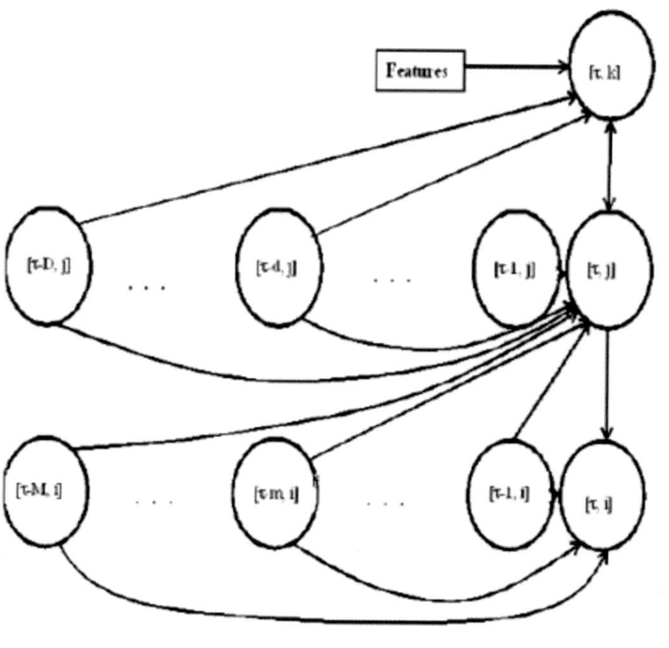

Fig. (2). A schematics of dynamic deep belief network.

The first Boltzmann machine is usually gated, whereas the subsequent Boltzmann

Machine may not be gated. A gated DBN may be viewed as a gated regression by hidden layer, or as modulated filters whereby the inputs (visible units) of the first BM gates the interaction between the hidden and the output layer as shown in Fig. (**2**). When the first BM of a DBN behaves as regressive filters, subsequent BM is also conditioned on information from the time past τ_i; $i = -K, 1-K, 2-K, \ldots$. A one-hot encoding on the style $y_{k\tau}$ of an object produces features $y_{p\tau}$ given as:

$$y_{k\tau} = \sum_{p} S_{pk} \cdot y_{p\tau} \tag{70}$$

where S_{pk} = style labels,

and $y_{k\tau}$ = *one−hot* encoded feature.

The features of a style plus the (class) label may bias and/or gates the interaction between the first visible unit and the first hidden unit. A Gaussian noise with $\sigma_i = 1$ may be added to the visible units. Then the effective energy/dynamics equation of the BM, when normalized, becomes:

$$E(v, h \mid x, \theta) = -\left[\sum_{i,j,k} W_{ijk} v_i h_j x_k + \sum_{i,j} c_{ij} v_i h_j + \sum_{i} a_i v_i + \sum_{j} b_j h_j\right]; \tag{71}$$

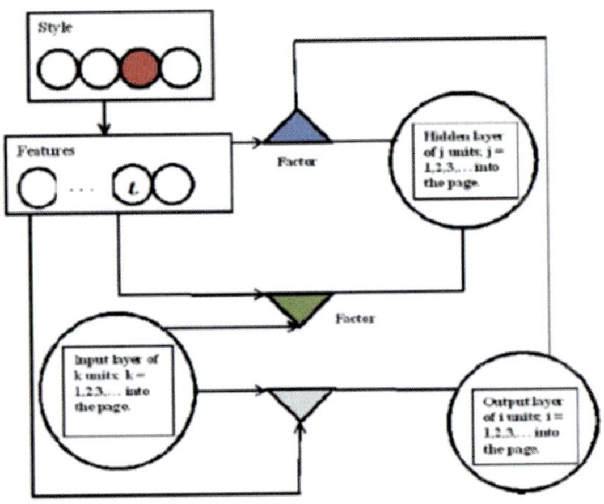

Fig. (3). A schematics of a DBN showing dynamic factored components.

Having the dynamics (or energy) equation (71), Fig. (**2**) defines a joint probability distribution over $v_{\#<\tau,i}$ visible units, and also over h_j hidden units conditional on the past D (or M) observations. To aid computation and tractability, the weight W_{ijk} may be factorize into three factor as shown in Fig. (**3**) (triangles in Fig. (**3**)); given by equation (72).

$$W_{ijk} = \sum_f W_{if} W_{jf} W_{kf} \tag{72}$$

So that $$\sum_{i,j,k} W_{ijk} v_i h_j y_k = \sum_{i,j,k} \sum_f W_{if}^{v} W_{jf}^{h} W_{kf}^{x} v_i h_j y_k \tag{73}$$

Similarly, the biases may be factorized as:

$$a_{\tau i} = a_i + \left[\sum_m A_{im}^{v}\right]\left[\sum_g A_{gm}^{v_{\#<\tau}} v_{g,\#<\tau}\right]\left[\sum_k A_{km}^{y} y_{k\tau}\right] \tag{74}$$

$$b_{j\tau} = b_j + \left[\sum_n B_{jn}^{h}\right]\left[\sum_g B_{gn}^{v_{\#<\tau}} v_{g,\#<\tau}\right]\left[\sum_k B_{kn}^{y} y_{k\tau}\right] \tag{75}$$

In equations (74) and (75), the a_i and b_j represent the static components of the biases while the second terms represent the dynamic components factored as shown in Fig. (**3**). The dynamic factored components (triangles in Fig. (**3**)) are gates/biases to the visible and hidden connections. By using, in equation (46), one or more of the weight factorization equations (72) to (75) above, and $\sigma = 1$ from Gaussian noise, the new energy becomes;

$$E\left(v_{\tau,i}, h_{\tau,j} \mid v_{\#<\tau,i}, y_{\tau}, \theta\right) = \frac{1}{2}\sum_i \left(\left(v_{\tau i} - a_{\tau i}\right)^2\right) - \sum_{i,j,k}\sum_f W_{if}^{v} W_{jf}^{h} W_{kf}^{x} v_{\tau i} h_{\tau j} y_{\tau k} - \sum_j b_{\tau j} h_{\tau j} \tag{76}$$

Equation (76) is the energy required to train the gated DBN. The gated DBN may be trained as given above which include greedy pre-training, and the contrastive divergence of distributions that made use of equation (75). The learning requires that weights W_{ijk} and biases A and B be updated at certain interval. The interval may be after K-steps (*e.g.*; K = M or D in Fig. (**2**)) of alternating Gibbs sampling, after τ_i time-steps, or any other cycle determined by the designer. The interaction weights ΔX_{qr} are updated as:

$$\Delta X_{qr} = KL.\left[\sum_{\tau}\left(\left\langle \alpha_{q,\tau}\beta_{r,\tau}\gamma_{r,\tau}\right\rangle_{data} - \left\langle \alpha_{q,\tau}\beta_{r,\tau}\gamma_{r,\tau}\right\rangle_{K-Gibbs}\right)\right] \quad \textbf{(77)}$$

where KL = a constant of the Kuhlback-Leibler divergence;

$\alpha_{q,\tau}\beta_{r,\tau}\gamma_{r,\tau}$ = the factor terms

The biases a and b are updated similarly. Example of a weight update ΔW_{if}^{v} using equation (77) is given by equation (78):

$$\Delta W_{if}^{v} = KL.\left[\sum_{\tau}\left(\left\langle v_{i,\tau}\sum_{j} W_{jf}^{h} h_{j\tau}\sum_{k} W_{kf}^{y} y_{k\tau}\right\rangle_{data} - \left\langle v_{i\tau}\sum_{j} W_{jf}^{h} h_{j\tau}\sum_{k} W_{kf}^{y} y_{k\tau}\right\rangle_{K-Gibbs}\right)\right] \quad \textbf{(78)}$$

Example of a bias update ΔA_{km}^{y} using equation (77) is given by equation (79);

$$\Delta A_{km}^{y} = KL.\left[\sum_{\tau}\left(\left\langle y_{k,\tau}\sum_{i} A_{im}^{v} v_{i\tau}\sum_{g} A_{gm}^{v_{\#<\tau}} v_{g,\#<\tau}\right\rangle_{data} - \left\langle y_{k,\tau}\sum_{i} A_{im}^{v} v_{i\tau}\sum_{g} A_{gm}^{v_{\#<\tau}} v_{g,\#<\tau}\right\rangle_{K-Gibbs}\right)\right] \quad \textbf{(79)}$$

where the subscript " $\# < \tau$ " stand for "some interval of time smaller than τ ".

The feature weights ΔS_{pk} are updated differently as given by equation (80):

$$\Delta S_{pk} = LF.\left[\sum_{\tau}\left(\left\langle C_{k,\tau} y_{p,\tau}\right\rangle_{data} - \left\langle C_{k,\tau} y_{p,\tau}\right\rangle_{K-Gibbs}\right)\right] \quad \textbf{(80)}$$

Learning the feature weights may be accomplished by a back propagation algorithm (see chapter 7) or by recursive least-square algorithm (see chapter 6). For a biased/gated DBN consisting of Boltzmann machine as units, the first unit is essentially prepared as explained. Subsequent units may be a normal BM, RBM, or CRBM without biasing and/or gating. During the design of variants of a gated DBN, it may be essential or as part of the greedy pre-training, to freeze the first fantasy pattern produced by the first gated BM for several epochs, so that subsequent BMs may extract meaningful structure of object of interest. This removes also most correlated weights from weight matrices. It is not uncommon for learning to take days. As such, the greedy pre-training may/has become a permanent procedure employed in learning a homogenous DBN consisting of BM as units. At present, a dynamic procedure for growing or pruning such a DBN does not yet exist because of intractable parameters. Many intractable parameters (*e.g.*; the partition functions) prevents the formulation of a dynamic complexity algorithm which may guide the pruning or growing of the DBN. Secondly, distributions involved are mainly conditional multiplicative, conditional exponential and/or factorial. Their composition is estimated subjectively, for otherwise may render many dynamic architecture of BM unstable. But for any specific (modelling) problem, a specific architecture of a (conditional restricted) Boltzmann Machine can be implemented and made a unit for an associated DBN, as described.

CONFLICT OF INTEREST

The author confirm that this chapter contents have no conflict of interest.

ACKNOWLEDGEMENTS

Cited work are appreciated.

REFERENCES

[1] Blanes S, Casas F, Sanz-Serna JM. Numerical integrators for the Hybrid Monte Carlo method. Valencia: Universidad de Valencia, Jaume 2013.

[2] Stephen P. Markov chain Monte Carlo method and its application. Statistician. Bristol, UK: Brooks University of Bristol 1998; 47: pp. (Part 1)69-100. [http://dx.doi.org/10.1111/1467-9884.00117]

[3] Simon D, Kennedy AD, Brian JP, Duncan R. Hybrid Monte Carlo. Physics Letters, 0370-2693/87/$ 0350 ©. Elsevier Science Publishers B.V. 1987; 195.(2)

[4] Geofrey Hinton. A Practical Guide to Training Restricted Boltzmann Machines. UTML TR 2010-003, Copyright © Geofrey Hinton 2010. Toronto: Version 1 Department of Computer Science, University of Toronto 2010.

[5] Dempster AP, Laird NM, Rubin DB. Maximum likelihood from incomplete data *via* the EM algorithm. J R Stat Soc, B 1977; 39(1): 1-38.

Artificial Neural Systems, **2015**, 198-216

CHAPTER 10

Emerging Networks

Abstract: Considering the possible availability of non-volatile memory element, chapter 10 has presented a memristive neural network in its first section. Generally, the chapter aims to present those neural systems that, at present, exist as proof of concept, some of which are undergoing industrial tests. For this reason, quantum neural networks are described in relative detail, and without losing its generality. A category of Bayesian network commonly known as Deep Belief Networks (DBN) is revisited, this time to illustrate their industrial tests. This chapter has provided some informational resources on the present state of ANNs′ development. It has also striven to bridge the gap between researches, developments, and applications.

Keywords: Amplifier, Bridge Circuit, Coupling Strength, Doublet Generator, Entanglement, Green Function, Hierarchical Bayesian Network, K_{th} phonon, Memristance, Probability Density, OFF-state, ON-state, Period, Polarization, Pulse, Q-dot, Schroedinger Equation, Synapses, Time-slice, Transconductance, Transistor.

INTRODUCTION

After having explored the meaning of memristance in chapter 5, the memristance is used in the first section of this chapter to compute synapsis. A quantum neural system based on quantum principles is described in the second section. This follows because methods of producing quantum gates have already been explained. The Deep Believe Network (DBN) of the last section of chapter 10 may be regarded as the application of DBN that is described in the previous chapter.

Chapter 5 has given sufficient description of memristance which is required for the synaptic computation of the first section of this chapter. Similarly, the sections that describe quantum logic and quantum algebra of chapter 5 contain sufficient information for qu-gate primitives which may be used for quantum expert system of the second section of this chapter. The Bayesian networks of chapters 7 and 9

Pierre Lorrentz

may be components of a deep believe network which in the third section of this chapter is set in industrial perspective.

Chapter 10 has explained emerging networks in considerable detail, and also describe how deep believe networks may be employed in industries.

MEMRISTIC NEURAL NETWORKS

The making of memristive (resistance based on memristor) primitives have been introduced in chapter 5. The design of a memristive artificial synapse is introduced here by using the memristor primitives of chapter 5. The memristive artificial synapses consist of five memristor and one differential amplifier. A ciruit composed with five memristances and one differential amplifier in order to generate a synapse, is termed memristive synaptic circuit. The memristive synaptic circuit described is able to set both positive and negative weights.

We assume that the reader is familiar with high-school or undergraduate Wheatstone Bridge, and amplifier. The first step is simply to replace the resistances of the bridge-circuit with memristances, and connect the circuit as shown in Fig. (**1**). Fig. (**1**) essentially functions as an artificial synaptic circuit as follows.

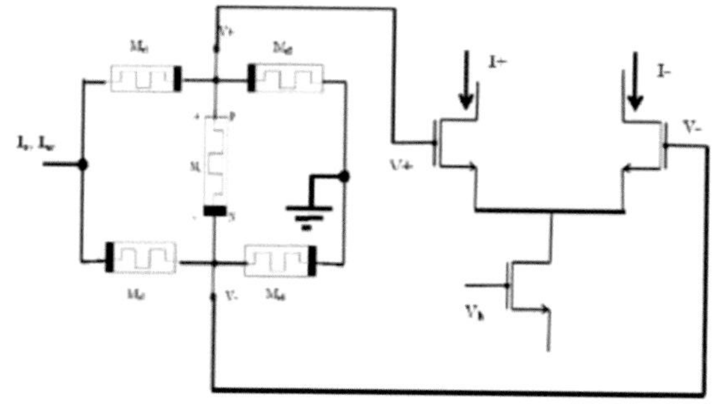

Fig. (1). A diagram to demonstrate the use of memristors in a synaptic circuit.

The memristance M_w at the centre is the weight memristance, and M_{r1}, M_{r2}, M_{r3}, and M_{r4} acts in pairs, similar to bridge circuit, to give the weight a sign. The sign is either positive (+) or negative (-). A positive signal (broken signal, Fig. (**2**)) increases memristances M_{r1} and M_{r4}, whereas the same pulse decreases the memristances M_{r2} and M_{r3}. This result in [M_{r1},M_{r4}] switching to ON-state and [M_{r2},M_{r3}] switching to OFF-state.So that current flows through M_{r1}, M_w, M_{r4} in that order, leading to increasing V+ value and decreasing V- value of voltages. A negative strong pulse (dotted signal, Fig. (**2**)) decreases the memristances M_{r1} and M_{r4}, whereas it increases the memristances M_{r2} and M_{r3}. This switches [M_{r1},M_{r4}] to OFF-state, and [M_{r2},M_{r3}] to ON-state, such that current flows in opposite direction through M_{r2}, M_w, M_{r3}, in that order.But when the conventional direction of left-t--right current flow is maintained, the voltage shown on Fig. (**1**) and Fig. (**2**) gets the opposite signs. The effect is a small positive voltage on the lower side of Fig. (**1**) and Fig. (**2**), and large negative voltage on the upper side of Fig. (**1**) and Fig. (**2**), giving a net negative voltage as shown on Table **1**.

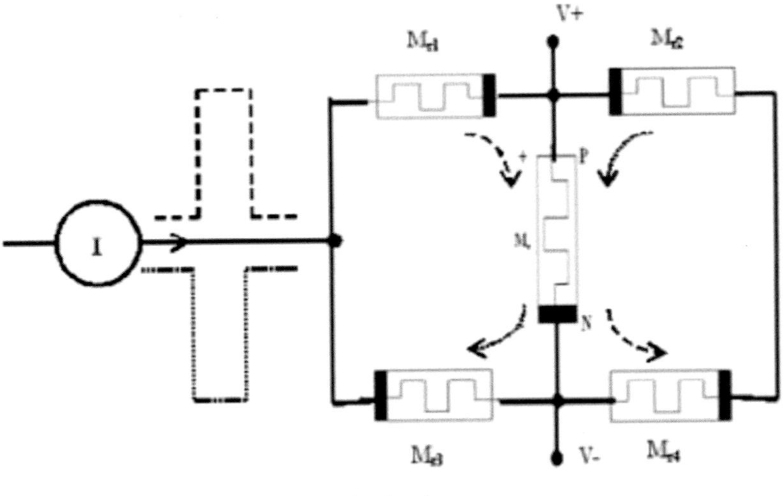

Fig. (2). The functionality of a memristive synaptic circuit.

Table 1. A tabular explanation of the switching circuit.

Applied wave-pulses	**Memristance configuration**	**Current sign**	**Voltage sign [(V+)-(V-)]**	**Sign of weights M_w**
Positive wave-pules (broken line; Fig. (**2**))	Mr1 = Mr4 = min.	+	+	+
	Mr2 = Mr3 = max.	-	-	
Negative wave-pulses (dotted line; Fig. (**2**))	Mr1 = Mr4 = max.	+	-	-
	Mr2 = Mr3 = min.	-	+	

Thus M_w gets a negative sign on weights, so also the net voltage. To set the value of the weight, a small pulse of a corresponding sign on weight is utilised to bias the circuit until the value of M_w reaches the desired value.The switching itself is achieved by a doublet generator [1], shown in Fig. (**3**), which may employs a pulse of zero net area. Usage of a doublet generator for switching prevents depreciation of weight M_w with time.

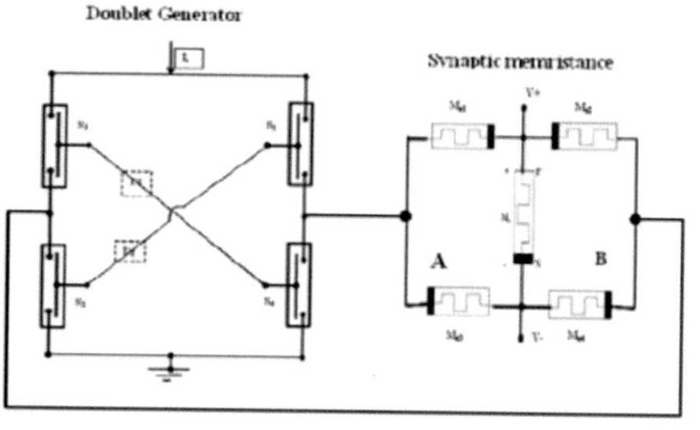

Fig. (3). The doublet generator is a signal source for the switching.

It consists of four switches, which operate in two pairs D_1 (S_3,S_4) and D_2(S_1,S_2); where D_2 and D_2 are pulses that act on switches.The pulses D_1 and D_2 act concurrently, that is; $D_1(S_3,S_4)$ turns S_3 and S_4 ON, while $D_2(S_1,S_2)$ turns S_1 and S_2 OFF. This is shown on the timing diagram of Fig. (**4a**) from which it can be seen that each pulse act for a half $(\frac{1}{2}T_d)$ period.

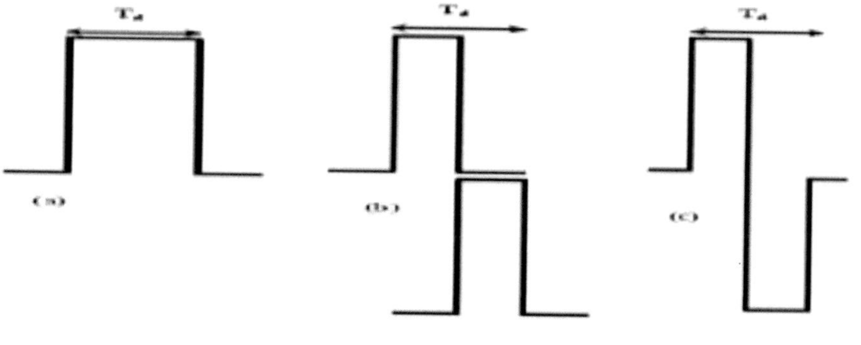

Fig. (4). Various types of a typical timeslice.

Fig. (**4**) is the timing diagram obtainable from Fig. (**3**). Assume the input Is signal is posive. For a half $\tau = \frac{1}{2}T_d$ period when D_1 (S_3,S_4) is ON and positive, then $D_2(S_1,S_2)$ is OFF and flat at zero-level. Current then flows from A to B. For the next half $\tau = \frac{1}{2}T_d$ period when $D_1(S_3,S_4)$ is OFF and $D_2(S_1,S_2)$ is ON, the same current flows from B to A; resulting in opposite polarity. This phenomenon is termed positive doublet and is schematized in (Fig. **4b**). Now assume the input I_s signal to be negative; then the pulse $D_2(S_1,S_2)$ turn the switches S_1 and S_2 ON (lower negative crest of Fig. (**4c**) for an half $\tau = \frac{1}{2}T_d$ period. On the other hand, the pulseD_1 (S_3,S_4) turn the switches S_3 and S_4 OFF for an half $\tau = \frac{1}{2}T_d$ period (upper crest of (Fig. **4c**)). This phenomenon is termed negative doublet. In any case, the period T_d of a doublet must be determined to achieve the desired switching.

If the voltage v_d across M_w applies, then

$$v_d = i_s M_w \tag{1}$$

The voltage v_d produces a differential current i_d given by equation (2):

$$i_d = g_m v_d = g_m i_s M_w \tag{2}$$

Where g_m = transconductance of the transistor of the amplifier.

The voltage across M_{r2} or M_{r4} termed v_{cm} also produce a current flow called the the common-mode current i_{cm} given by:

$$i_{cm} = \frac{g_m v_{cm}}{1 + g_m r_o} \tag{3}$$

If the effective memristance across M_{r2} and M_{r4} be represented by $(M_{r4} + M_{r4})_{\text{eff}}$, then;

$$(M_{r2} + M_{r4})_{eff} = M_w \tag{4}$$

and therefore:

$$v_{cm} = i_s\left(M_{r2} + M_{r4}\right)_{eff} = i_s M_w \quad \textbf{(5)}$$

Substituting equation (5) into (3):

$$i_{cm} = \frac{g_m i_s\left(M_{r2} + M_{r4}\right)_{eff}}{1 + g_m r_o} = \frac{g_m i_s M_w}{1 + g_m r_o} \quad \textbf{(6)}$$

The current i_o that appears at the output of the amplifier is the sum of

$$i_o = i_d + i_{cm} = \left(g_m i_s M_w\right) + \left(\frac{g_m i_s M_w}{1 + g_m r_o}\right) \quad \textbf{(7)}$$

the common-mode current (equation (6)) and the differential current (equation (2)) giving the resulting equation (7). Re-expressing equation (7) by factoring gives:

$$i_o = \left(g_m + \frac{g_m}{1 + g_m r_o}\right) i_s M_w \quad \textbf{(8)}$$

Knowing the output current i_o and device parameters, the weight M_w is set by current source i_s . This is true only if equation (4) holds. Because memristor are much more compact and resilient to weight drifts, it may be the best option in the neuromorphic neural (chapter 5) networks design in future.

QUANTUM EXPERT SYSTEMS

Building of a quantum neural networks' equivalent of a classical neural network requires a mapping of the classical NN to quantum domain. Primitives and quantum logic of chapter 5 can achieve this. One may also be interested in mapping of a classical learning algorithm to its corresponding quantum algorithm. Chapter 5 has provided most essential units and gates required to implement the corresponding quantum learning algorithm. Any of these maps depends most wholly on a specific neural network considered, and there are multitudes of classical neural networks. For these reasons, mapping of classical neural networks to quantum NNs is considered accomplished. In this section however, considered will be the quantum NNs developed from quantum mechanical principles with an applied practical quantum learning algorithm. The quantum architecture of the neural network is considerably general and generic such that both static and dynamic growing and/or pruning of the quantum NN is possible. This enables and enhances very wide problem application domains for the quantum neural networks.

A general architecture for a quantum neural network is any suitable substrate in which quantum mechanical effect can be observed with considerable accuracy, *e.g.*, Gallium Arsenide (GaAS). A specific architecture of a quantum neural network may consist of multiple cells. A cell may be considered as an independent unit whose replication produces the quantum neural networks. We would consider a cell to be Fig. (**3b**) of chapter 4 with an additional dot at the centre of the cube. Such cube will be referred to as five (5) – quantum – dot (abbreviated as "5 q--) unit cell. The 5 q-dot neural network unit requires initialization similar to any other neural network. The number of quantum dots (q- dots) for a unit may not be five, but any simple number of dots (atoms/molecules) at initialization is suitable. Since an arbitrary quantum neural network unit cell is usually an N q-dot molecule, where N is any positive integer, the number of atoms for a unit cell may be left to vary.

Initialization

The 5 q-dot molecule may be coupled to a suitable substrate lattice by optical phonons [2]. Let the 5 q-dot cell have a dynamic state variable x_d, external input i_{ed}, internal constant c_d. Each dot is connected to its neighbours through a synaptic input I_d^N. The synaptic input I_d^N may be related to states x_d, external input i_{ed} within a sphere N_d centred on d, by a synaptic law which may be summarised in equation (9):

$$I_d^N = \sum_{\lambda} D_d^{\lambda} x_d + \sum_{\lambda} E_d^{\lambda} f\left(x_d, x_{d+\lambda}\right) + \sum_{\lambda} F_d^{\lambda} c_d \tag{9}$$

where D_d^λ, E_d^λ, and F_d^λ are constants; and the $f\ (x_d, x_{d+\lambda})$ is a function of states. The optical phonons give rise to an influence function which may guide the states of the 5 q-dot unit. Two electrons are then introduced into the 5 q-dot molecule. These two electrons will settle at dot-sites so that entropy within the 5 q-dot cell is maximized. The final positions of these two electrons (in absence of external energy) correspond to ±1 polarization of the unit cell. Measurement of the polarization ensures there is no entanglement.

Behaviour

Assume the quantum state of the 5 q-dot molecule to be span by two basic independent states $|\psi_1\rangle$ and $|\psi_2\rangle$; any other state $|\psi_a\rangle$ may be specified by equation (10) as

$$|\psi_a\rangle = \alpha_1|\psi_1\rangle + \alpha_2|\psi_2\rangle \quad \textbf{(10)}$$

a linear combinations of the two states. The $|\psi_a\rangle$ state is subject to the constraints of equation (11):

$$1 = |\alpha_1|^2 + |\alpha_2|^2;\ |\alpha_1|^2 - |\alpha_2|^2 = P;\ \ P \le |1| \quad \textbf{(11)}$$

where P = polarization of the 5 q-dot molecule having two electrons.

There is no special reason to start with N = 5 of an N q-dot molecule, because equations (10) and (11) may always be expressed to take N into account. Several experimentations, including [3], have however given better result when $4 \le N \le 6$. So that throughout this section, N set to 5 is assumed for better illustration, and then we have our 5 q-dot molecule. A quantum neural network, when subjected to an external potential $V(r)$; $r \in X$; $X = x \perp y \perp z$ behaves in respect of Schroedinger equation (12):

$$i\frac{h}{2\pi}\frac{\partial \psi_a}{\partial \tau} = -\frac{1}{2m}\left(\frac{h}{2\pi}\right)^2 \nabla^2\psi + V(r)\psi \quad \textbf{(12)}$$

where h = Planck's constant; and $\hbar = \frac{h}{2\pi}$

The dynamic equation (12) of a quantum neural network describes the time evolution $i\hbar\frac{\partial\psi}{\partial\tau}$ of the 5 q-dot unit (For an introduction, see the last section of chapter 3, and the third section of chapter 5).The behaviour of the 5 q-dot molecule may be made unique by specifying on the cube a normalization condition of:

$$\int\int\int\left|\psi(r,\tau)\right|^2\partial x\partial y\partial z = 1 \quad \textbf{(13)}$$

where $\int|\psi(r,\tau)|^2$ = squared amplitude *i.e.*; probability density for the location of the electrons. And by specifying the initial potential state:

$$V(r_0)=\text{K}.\, I_d^N \quad \textbf{(14)}$$

Since the two terms on the right-hand-side (RHS) of (12) contain ψ , and both terms are derived from a system that effectively collapse any entanglement and de-cohere in the presence of $V(r)$, then equation (12) may be expressed as:

$$i\hbar\frac{\partial\psi}{\partial\tau}\left|\psi_a\right\rangle = H_d\left|\psi_a\right\rangle \quad \textbf{(15)}$$

where H_d is the Hamiltonian of the system; it is of the form:

$$H_d = \begin{bmatrix} E_0 - \frac{1}{2}P_{qd}E_{qd} & -E_t \\ -E_t & E_0 + \frac{1}{2}P_{qd}E_{qd} \end{bmatrix} \quad \textbf{(16)}$$

In equation (16), E_{qd} is the energy of adjacent fully polarized quantum dot, $-E_t$ is the interdot tunnelling energy, P_{qd} is the polarization on one quantum dot, and E_0 is the ground-state (initial) energy. In short, the Hamiltonian describes the values and distribution of energy within the q-dot neural network.We are interested in those set of ψ_a that solves equation (12) (or its equivalent equation (15). The set of ψ_a that solves equation (15) describe the quantum neural network's behavior with respect to time. To describe any ψ_a , equation (10) is generalized as a Green function$G(r,\tau)$;

$$G(r,\tau)=\sum_{N}|\psi_a\rangle=\sum_{n=0}^{N-1}\alpha_n|\psi_n\rangle \tag{17}$$

where $\alpha_n = \alpha_1,\alpha_2,\alpha_3...$ are constants, and ψ_n are basic quantum state called eigenfunction of equation (15).

As a boundary condition for the dynamic equation (15) of N q-dot neural network, the condition equation (13) is relaxed to include all relevant dimensions,

$$D(r(\tau))=\lim_{N\to\infty}\left[\int_{1}^{N}\partial x_1\partial x_2...\partial x_N\right]\ll\infty \tag{18}$$

and that equation (18) be finite and small even when the number of neurons (or dots) tends to infinity. The initial (condition) state $\psi(r,0)$ is specified by equation (19) as

$$\psi(r,0)=f\left(r,\tau,I_d^N,V(r_0),c_d\right) \tag{19}$$

a function $f\ (r,\tau,{}^{\tau=\frac{1}{2}T_d},V(r_0),c_d\ )$ which account for initialization parameters, initial phonons, and initial potential energy (*i.e.*; initial field). Then the solution to equation (15) may be expressed as:

$$|\psi_a\rangle=K.|\psi_0(r)\rangle e^{(-H_d)} \tag{20}$$

where K = constant.

The solution to equation (15) may alternatively be expressed in term of a Green function $G(r,\tau)$ as in equation (21):

$$|\psi_a\rangle = G(r,\tau)|\psi_0(r)\rangle \quad \textbf{(21)}$$

The Green function is given by:

$$G(r,\tau) = D(r(\tau)).\left[\left(\frac{m}{2\pi i\Delta\tau}\right)^{\frac{(N-1)}{2}}\right].\exp\left[\left(\frac{i\Delta\tau}{\hbar}\right)\sum_{j=0}^{N-1}\frac{m}{2}\left(\frac{r_{j-1}-r_j}{\Delta\tau}\right)^2 - V(r_j)\right] \quad \textbf{(22)}$$

Putting equation (18) into (22);

$$G(r,\tau) = \lim_{N\to\infty}\left[\int_1^N \partial x_1 \partial x_2 \ldots \partial x_N\right].\left[\left(\frac{m}{2\pi i\Delta\tau}\right)^{\frac{(N-1)}{2}}\right].\exp\left[\left(\frac{i\Delta\tau}{\hbar}\right)\sum_{j=0}^{N-1}\frac{m}{2}\left(\frac{r_{j-1}-r_j}{\Delta\tau}\right)^2 - V(r_j)\right] \quad \textbf{(23)}$$

Substituting equation (23) into (21) gives:

$$|\psi_a\rangle = \lim_{N\to\infty}\left[\int_1^N \partial x_1 \partial x_2 \ldots \partial x_N\right].\left[\left(\frac{m}{2\pi i\Delta\tau}\right)^{\frac{(N-1)}{2}}\right].|\psi_0(r)\rangle.\exp\left[\left(\frac{i\Delta\tau}{\hbar}\right)\sum_{j=0}^{N-1}\frac{m}{2}\left(\frac{r_{j-1}-r_j}{\Delta\tau}\right)^2 - V(r_j)\right] \quad \textbf{(24)}$$

The kinetic energy term $\left(\frac{r_{j-1}-r_j}{\Delta\tau}\right)^2$ and the exponential of $\left(\frac{m}{2\pi i\Delta\tau}\right)$ in equation (24) are the non-linearity typical of neural networks' computations.Each of the possible neural states N contribute to the final measured state by an amount which depent on $V(r)$and variations in $V(r)$, the potential energy.Physically therefore:

1. $V(r)$ can be varied by time-varying electric field E_1;
2. The 5 q-dot molecule (N = 5) can be coupled to a lattice substrate (as its environment) of GaAs;
3. The optical phonons I^N_d is at our disposal as input to the coupled system. The coupling parameter must be small *e.g.*; 0.081 for GaAs;
4. The N may not tend to infinity but satify:

$$N\Delta\tau = T \quad \textbf{(25)}$$

The state $|\psi_a\rangle$ of equation (24) may now be re-written to consider the practical and physical resources available to the 5 q-dot molecule (the quantum neural network). In order to achieve this, the potential energy $V(r)$ is given by:

$$V(r) = E_l \sigma_z (j\Delta\tau) \quad \textbf{(26)}$$

where E_l = Elecrtic field, and σ_z ($j\Delta\tau$)= polarization at time slice ($j\Delta\tau$).

The kinetic energy term E_k also gives:

$$E_k = K.\sigma_x (j\Delta\tau) \quad \textbf{(27)}$$

where K = a constant multiplied by the tunnelling amplitude; and σ_x($j\Delta\tau$)= Pauli matrices at time slice ($j\Delta\tau$).

The effect of the optical phonons is expressed by the influence function (see equation (9)) $\tau = \frac{1}{2}T_d$ which may explicit be written as:

$$I_d^N(\sigma_z(\tau)) = \int \prod_k D(r(\tau)).\exp\left[\int_0^T \left(\frac{i}{\hbar}\partial\tau\right) \sum_k \left(\frac{m_k}{2}\alpha_k^2(\tau) + \frac{m_k\omega_k^2}{2}\alpha_k^2(\tau) + \lambda_k \alpha_k(\tau)\sigma_z(\tau)\right)\right] \quad \textbf{(28)}$$

Combining equations (20) to (23) with (25) to (28), and substituting into the state equation (24) gives:

$$|\psi_a\rangle_T = \sum_{\sigma_z(j\Delta\tau)} \left[I_d^N(\sigma_z(\tau)).|\psi(\sigma_z(0),0)\rangle\right] \exp\left[\frac{i}{\hbar}\sum_j K.\sigma_z(j\Delta\tau) + \in(j\Delta\tau).\sigma_z(j\Delta\tau)\right] \quad \textbf{(29)}$$

Since we may only need to observe the system for a period $N\Delta\tau = T$ which has been decretized, summation may replace integration.The problem now reduces to how one may physically vary the phonons. This may be done by taking equation (28) into consideration; α_k is the position of the kth harmonic oscillator (kth phonon), m_k is its mass (mass – energy conversion holds!), and λ_k is the coupling strength of the kth phonons – electrons system coupling.The I^N_d may be simplified further. Since the time is decretized in ($j\Delta\tau$), the integral of I^N_d in equation (28) may be replaced by summation leading to:

$$I_d^N(\sigma_z(\tau)) = \exp\left[\sum_j \sum_j \sigma_z(j\Delta\tau).\chi_{qtm}(j\Delta\tau).\sigma_z(j\Delta\tau)\right] \quad \textbf{(30)}$$

Where:

$$\chi_{qtm}(j\Delta\tau) = \sum_k \frac{\lambda_k^2}{2m_k\omega_k} \operatorname{cosec}\left(\frac{\beta_k\omega_k}{2}\right)\left[\cosh\left(\frac{\beta_k\omega_k}{2}\right)\cos(\omega_k\tau) + i\sinh\left(\frac{\beta_k\omega_k}{2}\right)\sin(\omega_k\tau)\right] \quad \textbf{(31)}$$

The learning parameters may now be specified from (20) through to (31) as follows:

1. The coupling strength λ_k to each of the kth bath oscillator.
2. The electric field E_l.
3. The frequency ω_k of the oscillator.

By exiting multiple phonons, the coupling strength λ_k may be changed. By changing the phonons' frequency of excitation, the frequency ω_k of oscillation may be varied. The electric field E_l may also be varied directly.

The 5 q-dot NN is a fully connected neural network because every neuron is connected to other neurons, and any edge may be traversed forward and backward in time.

Learning Algorithm

The computed probability amplitude

$$\left\|\left(+\left|\psi_a\right\rangle_T\right)\right\|^2 = \left\|\left(+\left|\psi(\sigma_z(N\Delta\tau), T)\right\rangle\right)\right\|^2 \quad \textbf{(32)}$$

is the amplitude to be observed. Equation (32) may be calculated from (29). Assuming a simple quantum gradient descent algorithm is employed in training the network, the corresponding error function ζ is given by:

$$\mathfrak{L} = \frac{1}{4}\left[\left\| \left(+ |\psi_a\rangle_T \right) \right\|^2 - \left\| \left(+ |\psi_a\rangle_T \right)_{tg} \right\|^2 \right]^2 \tag{33}$$

By differentiating the Lagrangian equation (33) with respect to a particular parameter of interest (*e.g.*; the coupling strength λ_k of the system to a phonon bat h), it gives;

$$\frac{\delta \mathfrak{L}}{\delta \lambda_k} = \frac{1}{2}\left[\left[\left\| \left(+ |\psi_a\rangle_T \right) \right\|^2 - \left\| \left(+ |\psi_a\rangle_T \right)_{tg} \right\|^2 \right]^2 \right] . 2\,\mathrm{Re}\left[\frac{\partial \left(+ |\psi_a\rangle_T \right)}{\lambda_k} \left(+ |\psi_a\rangle_T^{*} \right) \right] \tag{34}$$

The equation (34) is used to learn a new coupling strength λ_k^{new} in the direction which minimizes the error; given as:

$$\lambda_k^{new} = \lambda_k^{old} - \eta \frac{\delta \mathfrak{L}}{\delta \lambda_k} \tag{35}$$

where η = learning parameter.

Thus the 5 q-dot neural network may learn, recognise, predict, and model other systems and devices by using a quantum gradient descent algorithm. The N q-dot system is not limited to gradient descent algorithm. Any other algorithm may be employed in learning as long as the probability amplitude is available and amendable by the learning algorithm. It may be noted that equation (34) and (35) is considerably general to learning paradigms. It is also noteworthy that N, the number of neurons, is constrained by the dynamic equation only; that is, by the problem specification only. The problem specification (the dynamics) may easily modify the substrate and phonons bath, *via* system parameters, in which the N q-dot lies, thereby changing the architectural complexity and/or the functionality of the N q-dot neural system as explained. Outputs of this system consist of both classical and quantum values, this follows by realising that everyday classical system are just because there is no quantum phenomena observed.

DEEP BELIEF NETWORKS (DBN) IN INDUSTRY

Junk and spam filtering is intricately linked to words and context recognition. Bayesian filters of junk emails are well known. Research and development of Deep Belief Network (DBN) using Restricted Boltzmann Machine (RBM) for word and digits recognition is at an advanced stage to the extent that such DBN may be available commercially from industries. Processing databases for word and digit recognition by DBN follows the usual method which the reader must have been familiar with. But for speech and acoustics recognition, an effective method which has often proved useful is now presented.

Among many ways of preparing the speech and acoustic data, it is better to represent the acoustics as R^{th}-order Mel Frequency Cepstral Coefficient (MFCC) and energy, where R is a number. Also the first and second order temporal derivatives should be added. These put the acoustics data in line with the appropriate learning dynamics (of chapter 8) formulation. The acoustics MFCC data may be normalize to have zero mean and unit variance. This idea is supported by Mohammed [4] research results and is currently being explored by G. Dahl, Microsoft Inc. [5] for industrial usefulness.

At present, DBN that employs RBM as components is not suitable for online and/or live speeches and acoustics. For static stored acoustics data, initialization and learning of data by DBN (with component BM) normally takes many hours to many days even when graphic cards and GPU (Graphic Processing Unit) is employed.

Another difficulty faced by deep belief networks that employs RBM as component is lack of growing/pruning (scalability) capability of the network. Knowledge on how this may be accomplished is still very rare; so are the resources for it. Most DBN (with RBM as components) are normally pre-made and pre-trained before the normal learning, and the corresponding recognition or prediction. Dynamic and/or autonomous growing/pruning of this DBN network is for both present and future research possibilities. Dynamic and/or autonomous growing/pruning of this DBN network with RBM as components is therefore, at present, very rare if not impossible.

An important area of growing interest is the employment of DBN (with RBM as components) in control engineering. In respect of control engineering, a Bayesian network BN may be defined as an acyclic graph:

$$BN = (N, E); \quad E \in [N-1] \tag{36}$$

where $E \in [N - 1]$represent the edges in one dimension, and N the nodes or vertices.

For every vertex v; $v \in N$, corresponds one-to-one a random variable x; $x \in X$, with an associated (joint) probability distribution $P(X)$. Since the vertices are essentially independent [6] with mutual edge connections, the probability $P(X)$ is a product of conditional probabilities;

$$P(X) = \prod_{v \in N} P\left(X_v \mid X_{\pi(v)}\right) \tag{37}$$

where $\pi(v)$ = probability distribution on v.

Because sums of equation (37) are possible, (37) and (36) trivially generalizes to multi-dimension. The conditional probability (37) also lends itself easily to factorization in respect of the nodes (vertices) v, meaning that P(X) of equation (37) may be seen as a collection of local conditional probability distributions. Assuming the nodes of a Bayesian network is indexed with respect to time, it is known as a *temporal Bayesian Network.* All nodes having the same time index form a *time-slice.* A Bayesian Network in one time-slice forms a *static Bayesian Network.* A *dynamic Bayesian Network* is a sequence of static Bayesian Network indexed with respect to time. It is also a *dynamic Bayesian Network* if the nodes and parameters of the Bayes Network are parameterized not with respect to time but with respect to some other random variable. The illustration here employs time as index for the vertices and parameters. When discussing the dynamics of the system under consideration, we assume that the system is Markovian and stationary. The stationarity assumption is often relaxed in practice because we do not wait for infinite time to elapse. In order to design a Bayesian Network for control, four main types of nodes may be considered, these are:

1. Control Variables C: These are input variable used to control the device under consideration.
2. Hidden nodes, H: These are vertices from which data may not be directly extracted, and data may also not be directly given. The hidden nodes H model high-order relationship between parameters and high-order relationship in data.
3. Sensor (data) nodes, S: Sensor variables (may also be called vertices) S obtain data, *via* sensing, and quantify information on the states of hidden nodes.
4. Target nodes, T: These nodes consist of reference values or set-points of the variables that are under the control of the Bayesian Network.

Based on these node types, and for n time-slices, a Bayesian Network may have an associated joint probability distribution of the form:

$$P(C_1, H_1, S_1, T_1; C_2, H_2, S_2, T_2; \ldots; C_n, H_n, S_n, T_n) \tag{38}$$

In the language of control system, a hierarchical Bayesian network with hidden layers H_i; $i = 1,2,\ldots,n$ is influenced by a feedback controller through the control inputs C_i, where the C_i forms the visible layer of the network. The influence of the feedback controller is obtained by comparing the sensed data (variable) S_i with the target data (variable) T_i. After a t-times Markovian step, the joint probability distribution may be modified with the t-times sensor data $S_1,\ldots,S_t$, and control values of $C_1,\ldots,C_t$. This is done by updating the conditional probability distribution as:

$$P(T_1,\ldots,T_n; H_1,\ldots,H_n; S_{t+1},\ldots,S_n; C_{t+1},\ldots,C_n \mid S_1,\ldots,S_t; C_1,\ldots,C_t) \tag{39}$$

A control engineering question is to estimate a target T_k variable, that is, to compute $P_t(T_k)$ for an arbitrary k from the conditional probability distribution (39). If (38) and/or (39) can be sampled from reliably to predict $P_t(T_k)$, then the controller is able to reason about the future target T_f :

$$T_f = T_{t+1}, \ldots, T_{t+l}; \quad (t+l) \leq n \tag{40}$$

given a possible choice of future control C_f;

$$C_f = C_{t+1},\dots,C_{t+q};\quad (t+q)\leq n \tag{41}$$

where q and l depends on control dynamics.

This method of control is relatively general to include almost all control problems encountered in control engineering. A specific industrial application is given in Hommersom [7] where it has been employed successfully for an adaptive industrial printing system which yield a 9% productivity increase compared to the rule-based method.

CONFLICT OF INTEREST

The author confirm that this chapter contents have no conflict of interest.

ACKNOWLEDGEMENTS

Cited works are appreciated.

REFERENCES

[1] Kim H, Sah MP, Changju Y, Roska T, Chua LO. Neural synaptic weighting with a pulse-based memristor circuit. IEEE Trans Cct Sys-I 2012; 59(1): 148-58.

[2] Toth G, Craig LS, Douglas TP, *et al.* Neural networks. Superlattices Microstruct 1996; 20(4): 473. [http://dx.doi.org/10.1006/spmi.1996.0104]

[3] Behrman EC, Niemel J, Steck JE, Skinner SR. A Quantum Dot Neural Network Wichita. USA: Wichita State University 1996.

[4] Mohamed A, Dahl GE, Hinton G. Acoustic modeling using deep belief networks. IEEE Trans Audio Speech Lang Process 2012; 20(1): 14-22. [http://dx.doi.org/10.1109/TASL.2011.2109382]

[5] Dahl George, Yu Dong, Deng Li, Acero Alex. Context-dependent Pre-trained Deep neural networks for large vocabulary speech recognition. IEEE Trans Audio Speech Lang Process 2012; 20(1): 30-42. [Special Issue] [http://dx.doi.org/10.1109/TASL.2011.2134090]

[6] Wasserman PD. Neural Computing Theory and Practice. New York: Van Nostrand Reinhold 1965.

[7] Evers S, Hommersom A, Lucas P, Cochior C, van den Bosch PP. Reasoning with uncertainty about

system behaviour: making printing systems adaptive. In: Basten T, Hamberg R, Reckers F, Verriet J, Eds. Model-Based Design of Adaptive Embedded Systems. Berlin: Springer 2013; pp. 125-58. [http://dx.doi.org/10.1007/978-1-4614-4821-1_5]

CHAPTER 11

Research and Developments in Neural Networks

Abstract: Two categories of ANN systems are able to model any intelligent Expert in great detail. These are Bayesian network, and neuromorphic network. Both are hampered by lack of adequate resources and lack of human knowledge. Research and development on these two categories of ANN systems is the subject of this chapter. The first section of chapter 11, on Bayesian network, specifically describes Hybrid Monte Carlo (HMC) and associated algorithms, after which areas of possible researches are highlighted. The second section is on neuromorphic network. It presents the current state of industrial development. The chapter has taken care to omit those conceptual developments which may not be achievable in near future. Illustration of the recent neuromorphic design has been given in concluding the second section. The chapter has provided research and development information resources on two advanced ANN systems.

Keywords: Average error, CMOS, Comlex-conjugate Eigenvalue, Efficacy, Hamiltonian system, Harmonic oscillator, Hybrid Monte Carlo (HMC), Leapfrog algorithm, Long-Term Depression (LTD), Long-Term Potentiation (LTP), Markov-Chain Monte Carlo (MCMC), Multi-dimensional matrix, Omyleyan integrator, Pulse-Width Modulation (PWM), Random-number generator, Shadow Hamiltonian, Simplectic, Spike-Timing-Dependent-Plasticity (STDP) computation, Titanium dioxide, Verlet velocity.

INTRODUCTION

The first section of chapter 11 explore the possibility of improving hybrid Markov chain through search for more efficient integrator for hybrid Monte Carlo algorithm. The second section presents a complete neuromorphic network. Without this, the book may not have completed an industrial illustration of a neuromorphic network.

Section one of this chapter considers various types of integrators which may be employed in Bayesian networks of chapters 7 and 9. While the second section

Pierre Lorrentz

presents a general framework of neuromorphic network to which the euromorphic networks of chapter 6 and 5 applies.

This chapter has provided some ways of extending neuromorphic networks, and improving Bayesian ANN systems.

EXTENSION OF HYBRID MONTE CARLO

At each stage of the Markov chain HMC, a numerical integration of a Hamiltonian system of differential equation is required. The integration relies often heavily on Verlet's algorithm. Since much of the computation done by Markov chain HMC is the integration of the Hamiltonian system of differential equation, the efficiency and exact-ness of Verlet algorithm is of paramount importance. A single integration stage requires a step size h in Verlet integrator (see chapter 9 for details), which is expected to be sufficiently large and to promote stability of the HMC algorithm. We therefore would not seek an order of accuracy as h tends to zero. Rather h dictates a region of stability when inserted into a function that models the behaviour of the integrator of choice as the Markov chain progresses. This function may be denoted by f(h).

HMC may be defined as a Markov chain which samples from a probability distribution in $\mathbb{R}^d$ with a density function π *(v);*

$$\pi(v) \propto \exp(-V(v)) \quad \textbf{(1)}$$

where v = velocity, and *V (v);* = potential energy.

A kinetic energy term is added to equation (1). The kinetic energy term consist of momentum p and a mass matrix M in a Hamiltonian $H(v, p)$ energy of equation (2);

$$H(v, p) = \frac{1}{2} p^T M^{-1} p + V(v) \quad \textbf{(2)}$$

In view of the energy (2), another probability distribution $\prod(v,p)$ is also defined as:

$$\prod(v,p) = K.\exp(-H(v,p)) \tag{3}$$

$$\prod(v,p) = K.\exp\left(-\frac{1}{2}p^T M^{-1} p\right).\exp(-V(v))$$

The K of equation (3) is a scaling constant, whereas p and v are stochastic and independent. The momentum p has a Gaussian N(0, M) distribution. Markov chain sampling by HMC from $v^{(n)}$ and $p^{(n)}$ is expected to be symplectic (*e.g.*; volume preserving), and ergodic. This means that a map

$$\psi:\left(v^n,p^n\right)\rightarrow\left(v^*,p^*\right) \tag{4}$$

is such that

$$\det\left\|\psi'(v,p)\right\| = 1 \tag{5}$$

Hybrid Monte Carlo (HMC) Algorithm

1) Given: $v^{(0)} \in \mathbb{R}^d$; $N \geq 1$; $n = 0$

2) Sample $p^{(n)} \sim N(0,M)$; calculate $\left(v^*,p^*\right) = \psi\left(v^{(n)},p^{(n)}\right)$

3) Compute $a^{(n)} = \min\left(1,\exp\left(H(v^{(n)},p^{(n)}) - H\left(v^*,p^*\right)\right)\right)$

4) Sample $u^{(n)} = U(0,1)$; if $a^{(n)} > u^{(n)}$; set

   $v^{(n+1)} = v^*$; otherserwise set $v^{(n+1)} = v^{(n)}$

5) Set $u = u + 1$; if $n = N$ stop otherwise go to step 1.

Fig. (1). Normal HMC.

Hybrid Monte Carlo satisfies these criteria, and has been introduced in chapter 9.

Its algorithm is given here in Fig. (**1**). This section will describe in considerable detail, the integrator that may be involved. To introduce the integrators we seek the solutions v and p to equation (2) which are independent and satisfy equation (6).

$$\frac{\partial}{\partial t} H\left(v(t), p(t)\right) = 0 \tag{6}$$

This implies that a such solution should make H(v, p) separable. The solution set v, and p should satisfy equation (5) in addition. If v and p are independent, then H(v, p) may separate as in equation (7):

$$\frac{\partial v}{\partial t} = \nabla_p H(v, p); \quad \frac{\partial p}{\partial t} = -\nabla_v H(v, p) \tag{7}$$

Verlet's velocity Algorithm

1) Given that $\left(v^{(n)}, p^{(n)}\right) \in \mathbb{R}^d; I \geq 1; h > 0$

2) Let $v = v^{(v)}; p = p^{(n)}; i = 0;$

3) Calculate $\nabla_v V(v)$; and let $p = p - \left(\frac{h}{2} . \nabla_v V(v)\right)$

4) Let $v = v + \left(hM^{-1}p\right)$; and $i = i + 1$

5) If $i < I$; calculate $\nabla_v V(v)$; and let $p = p - (h . \nabla_v V(v))$, then go to step 3.

   Otherwise go to step 6

6) Let $v^* = v$; calculate $\nabla_v V(v)$; and let $p = p - \left(\frac{h}{2} . \nabla_v V(v)\right)$; end

Fig. (2). Velocity verlet's algorithm.

We require a solution to (7) capable of performing the map of equation (4) when v and p, which are solutions of (7), are substituted into the map $\psi(v, p)$. Having an initial conditions as $v^{(n)}$ and $p^{(n)}$, Verlet algorithm provide the map ψ ($v^{(n)}$, $p^{(n)}$). Having equation (7) with initial conditions of $v = v^{(n)}$; $p = p^{(n)}$;$i = 0$; Verlet algorithm of Fig. (**2**) performs the mapping ψ

$$\psi : \{v^n . p^n\} \rightarrow \{v_I . p_I\} \qquad \textbf{(8)}$$

which satisfy all aforementioned criteria. The main iteration steps of Verlet algorithm are:

$$\left.\begin{array}{l} p_{i+1/2} = p_i - \dfrac{h}{2}\nabla_v V(v_i); \;\; i = 0,1,2,....,(I-1) \\ v_{i+1} = v_i + hM^{-1} p_{i+1/2} \\ p_{i+1} = p_{i+1/2} - \dfrac{h}{2}\nabla_v V(v_{i+1}) \end{array}\right\} \qquad \textbf{(9)}$$

By employment of Verlet's velocity algorithm (equation (9)) in the basic HMC Fig. (**1**), the Markov chain no longer have the random-walk nature but a walk subjected to a prescribed Hamiltonian. Thus such HMC is given the name Markov Chain Monte Carlo (MCMC). MCMC is still a hybrid because it is no longer the original Markov Chain. The name Monte Carlo [1, 2] is the founder of the algorithm.

<u>*Example: Harmonic Oscillator*</u>

Consider the Hamiltonian:

$$H(v, p) = \frac{p^2}{2} + \frac{v^2}{2} \qquad \textbf{(10)}$$

By equation (7);

$$\frac{\partial v}{\partial t} = \nabla_p H; \quad \frac{\partial p}{\partial t} = -\nabla_v H$$

$$\nabla_p H = \frac{2}{2} p = p; \quad -\nabla_v H = \frac{-2}{2} v = -v$$

That is; $\begin{bmatrix} \frac{\partial v}{\partial t} \\ \frac{\partial p}{\partial t} \end{bmatrix} = \begin{bmatrix} p(t) \\ -v(t) \end{bmatrix};$ and solving this elementary equation gives:

$$\begin{bmatrix} p(t) \\ v(t) \end{bmatrix} = \begin{bmatrix} \cos(t) & \sin(t) \\ -\sin(t) & \cos(t) \end{bmatrix} \begin{bmatrix} v(0) \\ p(0) \end{bmatrix} \quad \mathbf{(11)}$$

If the role of v and p are interchanged in equation (9), we would have position Verlet integrator as in equation (12) below.

$$\left.\begin{aligned} v_{i+1/2} &= q_i + \frac{h}{2} M^{-1} p_i; \quad i = 0, 1, 2, \ldots, (I-1) \\ p_{i+1} &= p_i - h \nabla_v (v_{i+1/2}) \\ v_{i+1} &= v_{i+1/2} + \frac{h}{2} M^{-1} p_{i+1} \end{aligned}\right\} \quad \mathbf{(12)}$$

Equation (9) or (12), when employed in Fig. (**2**) and combined with HMC of Fig. (**1**), the random walk of the Markov chain is biased in a direction which is a solution to the Hamiltonian dynamics (equation) of the system. A question is whether there are other suitable integrators apart from Verlet for sufficiently large step-size h? The answer is yes; if equation (11) of the harmonic oscillator is generalized, and satisfy the given crireria. It is suprising to note that every solution of the type (11) that satisfies the criteria may be written in form of (12) and/or (9); we denote such mapping by ψ henceforth.

A one-step (i+1)h map: $\psi_h : (v_i, p_i) \rightarrow (v_{i+1}, p_{i+1})$ may be written as:

$$\psi_h = \varphi^A_{h/2}\varphi^B_h\varphi^A_{h/2} \qquad \textbf{(13)}$$

where $\varphi^A_{h/2}$ denotes the first term on the right-hand-side (RHS) of equation (9) or (12);

φ^B_h denotes the second term on the RHS of equation (9) or (12);

$\varphi^A_{h/2}$ denotes the third term on the RHS of equation (9) or (12);

A matrix of type (11) may also be factorized to give (9), (12), or (13), provided they are symplectic, ergodic, and reversible. When designed with care, the RHS of (13) may only approximate the left-hand-side (LHS). General design errors are not considered here, but those errors which make the solution (13) inexact. It has been proved by other designers ([2, 3] and their references) that Verlet integrator is an exact solution. After $(i+1)h \subseteq I$; $i = 0,1,2,...$ iterations, the first little iteration may be discarded (called the burn-in period) to remove dependence on the choice of initialization data. The correlation effect typical of random-walk of a normal Markov chain has been extensively reduced by the Hamiltonian dynamics. Since

$$\psi_I \approx \left\{\varphi^A_{h/2}\varphi^B_h\varphi^A_{h/2}\right\} = \varphi^H_I \qquad \textbf{(14)}$$

the energy error, which may be denoted by $\Delta(v, p)$, is given by:

$$\Delta(v, p) = H\left(\psi_I(v, p)\right) - H\left(\varphi^H_I(v, p)\right) \qquad \textbf{(15)}$$

as a result of (14); it determines the acceptance probability of a proposed distribution on v^* and p^* (see Fig. (**1**) and Fig. (**2**)). Note that the energy error is not feedback to bias the Markov chain Monte Carlo movement, but substituted into the acceptance criteria (of Metropolis-Hastings). It is nevertheless interesting to know that starting from ($v^{(n)}$, $p^{(n)}$) distribution, the aim is to obtain φ_I^H but achieve ψ_I instead. Since the interest lies in the generator of $v^{(n)}$ and $p^{(n)}$, one may therefore compare the energy H ($\psi_I(v, p)$) with that of $H(v, p)$, and attempt to place an upper bound on the expected error $E(\Delta)$ as follows.

$$E_b\left(\Delta(v,p)\right) = \int \Delta(v,p).\exp\left(-H(v,p)\right)\partial v \partial p \tag{16}$$

$$E_f\left(\Delta(v,p)\right) = -\int \Delta(v,p).\exp\left(-H(\psi(v,p))\right)\partial v \partial p \tag{17}$$

Adding (16) to (17) and dividing by 2 to get the average E_{av} ($\Delta(v, p)$) energy;

$$\begin{gathered} E_{av}\left(\Delta(v,p)\right) = \frac{1}{2}\int \Delta(v,p).\left[\exp\left(-H(v,p)\right) - H(\psi(v,p))\right]\partial v \partial p \\ \left[\exp\left(-H(v,p)\right) - H(\psi(v,p))\right] = \left[1-\exp\left(-\Delta(v,p)\right)\right].\exp\left(-H(v,p)\right) \end{gathered} \tag{18}$$

$$E_{av}\left(\Delta(v,p)\right) = \frac{1}{2}\int \Delta(v,p).\left[1-\exp\left(-\Delta(v,p)\right)\right].\exp\left(-H(v,p)\right)\partial v \partial p \tag{19}$$

Set $x = (\Delta(v, p))$

$$\begin{gathered} \left(1-e^{-x}\right) = \left(x - \frac{x^2}{2!} + \frac{x^3}{3!} - \frac{x^4}{4!} + \dots\right) \\ x\left(1-e^{-x}\right) = x\left(x - \frac{x^2}{2!} + \frac{x^3}{3!} - \frac{x^4}{4!} + \dots\right) = \left(x^2 - \frac{x^3}{2!} + \frac{x^4}{3!} - \frac{x^5}{4!} + \dots\right) \\ \left(x^2 - \frac{x^3}{2!} + \frac{x^4}{3!} - \frac{x^5}{4!} + \dots\right) < x^2 \end{gathered} \tag{20}$$

Using (20) in (18);

$$\left[1-\exp\left(-\Delta(v,p)\right)\right].\Delta(v,p) < \Delta^2(v,p) \tag{21}$$

Putting (21) into (19)

$$E_{av}\left(\Delta(v,p)\right) \leq \int \Delta^2(v,p).\exp\left(-H(v,p)\right)\partial v \partial p \quad \textbf{(22)}$$

Thus the average error is of the order of Δ^2 from equation (22). The expected error is bounded above by Δ^2. We now seek those families of integrators similar to Verlets' which solves the Hamiltonian (7) for large step-size h. For an arbitrary seperable Hamiltonian dynamics, the RHS of (14) is expressible as a positive definite symmetric matrix, example of which is equation (11). Generalization of equation (11) may be written as:

$$\begin{bmatrix} p(t) \\ v(t) \end{bmatrix} = M_{PS} \begin{bmatrix} v(0) \\ p(0) \end{bmatrix} \quad \textbf{(23)}$$

where $M_{PS} = \begin{bmatrix} A & B \\ C & D \end{bmatrix}$

E,g,; $\begin{bmatrix} A & B \\ C & D \end{bmatrix} = \begin{bmatrix} \cos(t) & \sin(t) \\ -\sin(t) & \cos(t) \end{bmatrix}$ from equation (11)

The matrix M_{PS} of equation (23) is the multi-dimensional matrix in quest, and subscript "ps" denotes "positive symmetric". The constraint of equation (5) also dictates that M_{PS} is unitary. Values ascribe to A, B, C, and D depends on algorithm employed to determine them. The unitary condition of equation (5) inplies:

$$AD - BC = 1 \quad \textbf{(24)}$$

Since values of A, B, C, and D depends on h and $i \subseteq I$, then the A, B, C, and D may be indexed to reflect this. Reversibility implies that $\|A\| = \|D\|$. So that attention may now be focused on the numerical values ascribe to A in particular as the leading term of the matrix. There are four main situations on M_{PS} :

1. If h is determined such that $\det(M_{PS}) > 1$then the spectra radius of $M_{PS} > 1$, and the system is unstable.

2. If an h is found such that $\|A\| < 1$, then M_{PS} has a complex conjugate eigenvalues and the powers of M_{PS} is bounded. The integrator is stable because the eigenvalues have a unit modulus; so also the complex conjugate.

3. If $\|A\| = 1$ and B = C = 0; then $M_{PS} = \pm I$. This scenario implies stability.

4. If however $\|A\| = 1$ but $\|B\| + \|C\| > 0$ then the powers of M_{PS} is linearly dependent on i. This is a case of weak stability.

Any designer in quest of a new integrator may preferably look at regions of point (2) above since most integrators there are likely to be stable. Regions of points (1) and (4) may not be fruitful. In region (3), there is likely to be very few choices of integrators. Verlet integrator is an example of integrator from region (2).

It is possible to modify a Hamiltonian dynamics slightly so that:

$$\psi_I = \varphi_I^H \tag{25}$$

The modified Hamiltonian dynamics is known as shadow Hamiltonian. Whenever equation (25) holds, the numerical integrator becomes an exact solution of the shadow Hamiltonian.

Example 2: Shadow Hamiltonian

For all h such that $\|A\| < 1$, introduce an angular variable $\theta_h \in R$ such that $A_h = D_h = \cos(\theta_h)$, $\sin(\theta_h) \neq 0$. Define a variable χ_h as:

$$\chi_h = \frac{B_h}{\sin(\theta_h)} \tag{26}$$

The M_{PS} matrix whose example is equation (11) may be re-written as:

$$M_{PS} = \begin{bmatrix} \cos(\theta_h) & \chi_h \sin(\theta_h) \\ -1/\chi_h \sin(\theta_h) & \cos(\theta_h) \end{bmatrix} \quad \textbf{(27)}$$

Equation (27) is the integrator of a Hamiltonian H_s given by equation (28).

$$H_s = \frac{\theta_h}{2h}\left(\chi_h p^2 + \frac{v^2}{\chi_h}\right) \quad \textbf{(28)}$$

The Hamiltonian H_s is a shadow of Hamiltonian H(v, p); *i.e.*; H_s is equation (10) modified by h and χ_h . For H_s , equation (25) holds, therefore equation (27) is an exact integrator. When $\theta_h = h$, the angular frequency of rotation of the numerical solution equals the true angular rotation of the harmonic oscillator exactly. A second special case is when $\chi_h = 1$, the energy error is essentially zero. By using the analogy of example 2 on region $\|A\| < 1$ Sergio Blanes [2] presents several expamples of exact integrators. Surprisingly (or not), most of them are multiples of Verlet integrator. A well-known integrator is the Leapfrog algorithm. Another exact integrator derived from region $\|A\| < 1$ is Omyleyan integrator [4] which offers some performance advantages over Verlet integrator for some problems. A Matlab code of Leapfrog integrator may be found in [4].

NEUROMORPHIC NETWORKS II

Considerable efforts have been successful in mapping natural neurons to either hardware or software or both. There have been few efforts at morphing a neuron directly; most of these efforts have had very little success. The main success today lies in the discovery of Spike-Timing-Dependent-Plasticity (STDP) computation (see chapter 6). This section described the first successful attempt at morphing a neuron (source of the term "neuromorphic") directly onto hardware. This follows from the possibility of sandwitching Titanium Dioxide, TiO_2, between two crosshair nanowires to make a memristor. The neuromorphic neuron consists of one or more CMOS nodes with memristive crosshair nanowire as edges. One or more of these neuromorphic neurons execute STDP computation which is believed to be the basis of learning in an original biological neural system. This section assumes the reader may be familiar with neuromorphic network (of chapter 6) and memristive circuit (of chapter 5). In chapter 6, the Hodgkin-Huxley (HH) model gives the dynamics of a neuromorphic neuron, and it was shown by equation (15) of chapter 6 that the sigmoidal function is a suitable candidate in expressing the behaviour of the neuron as time progresses. The neuromorphic neuron therefore may accept most existing learning laws, especially those whose time evolution may be written in terms of sigmoid function. Another condition is that the learning law should contain both an excitatory term and an inhibitory term. The simplest learning algorithm which possesses both excitatory and inhibitory terms is the gated steepest descent devised by Grossberg [5].

The gated steepest descent states that change in weight $\frac{\partial w_{ij}}{\partial t}$ with respect to time t is given by:

$$\frac{\partial w_{ij}}{\partial t} = C_j \cdot \left(-\frac{1}{\tau} w_{ij} + kC_i(x_i) \right) \tag{29}$$

where k = learning rate; 1/τ = time constant; C_j and C_j the "activity" function of the internal state of a node.

The C_j and C_i may be derived by comparing equation (29) above with equation (16) of chapter of chapter 6. If a node has internal state y_i and input x_i, then the change $\frac{\partial y_j}{\partial t}$ in internal state of the node with respect to time may be represented by:

$$\frac{\partial y_j}{\partial t} = -\frac{1}{\tau} y_j + S\left(\sum_i w_{ij} x_i + \sum_k w_{jk} . y_k \right) \tag{30}$$

where S = sigmoid function; y_k = received states of connected nodes.

In equation (30) above, the first term represents an inhibitory term while the second term the excitatory terms. The right-hand-side (RHS) of equations (29), (30) of this section, and (16) of chapter 6 may be converted, by purely mathematical reformulation, to multiples of hyperbolic sine wave. For such hyperbolic sine wave, an equivalent memristance can be found whose current-voltage characteristics exhibit approximately the same behaviour. Thus for an arbitrary weight w,

$$\frac{\partial w}{\partial t} = Nw\sinh(Mv) \tag{31}$$

where v = voltage.

where v = voltage.

Values of matrices N and M may be determined by comparing equation (31) with equation (16) of chapter 6 after its conversion to hyperbolic sine function. When both conductance and voltage are negative, the RHS of equation (31) is negative, when both conductance and voltage are positive, the RHS of equation (31) is positive. This motivates the definition of a spike to consist of a positive pulse followed by negative pulse, because it constitutes a period of hyperbolic sine wave. Nodes of a neuromorphic network communicate with other nodes by sending and receiving spikes. A spike may be a conductance change $\frac{\partial g}{\partial t}$ against voltage characteristics of a memristor. The characteristic is idealised in STDP computation. The STDP has been directly confirmed experimentally in some brains of living organism. It causes synaptic efficacy or weight change as a function of relative spike time of a pre-synaptic and post-synaptic neuron. If pre-precedes post-synapsis, the synapse increases in efficacy, this is called the Long-Term-Potentiation (LTP). But if pre- succeeds post-synapsis, there is a decrease in efficacy, which is known as Long-Term-Depression (LTD). Interestingly, both LTP and LTD can be approximated by decaying exponential functions.

Communications between CMOS-based nodes occur through memristive synapses by using Time Division Multiplexing (TDM) thereby forming a modulated communication channels between a pre-synaptic neuron and post-synaptic neuron. The time division may generically consist of five timeslots as shown in Fig. (**3**). Information in each timeslot is encoded using Pulse-Width-Modulation (PWM). If a neuron spikes, both the LTP and LTD timing circuits are initialized.

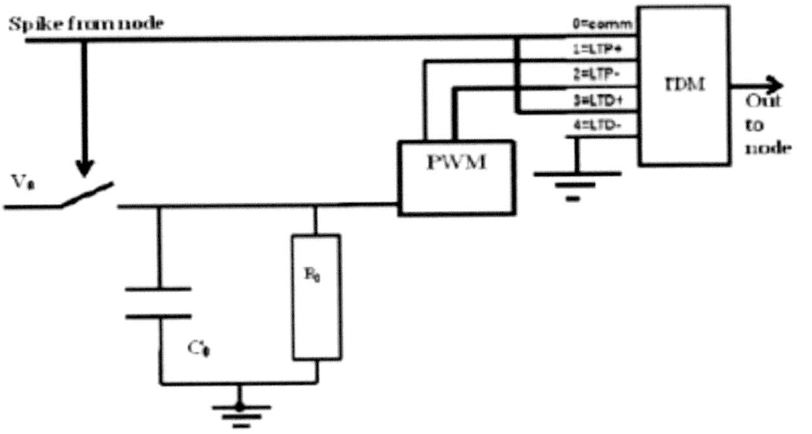

Fig. (3). LTP and associated TDM circuit.

The timing circuits contain a resistance and a capacitance in parallel which are used to implements the exponential decay curve characteristics of an STDP. The state of the neuron meant for communication are sent *via* the timeslots and modulated by PWM unit (see Fig. (**3**) and Fig. (**4**)). A neuron's input and output ports are essentially at zero volts when idle. But when it spikes, the spiking neuron sends LTP to its output port and LTD to its input port. Both LTP and LTD signals are pulse-width modulated, and subsequently weighted by the memristive synapses along the edges. The comm (0) port of TDM communicates spikes from pre- to post-synapses for inner products and/or matrix product computations. The LTP+ (1) and LTP- (2) timeslots communicate timing information from pre- to post-synapses using PWM. Both LTP+ and LTP- have equal time span and opposite polarity as this minimizes any conductance changes induced by signals.

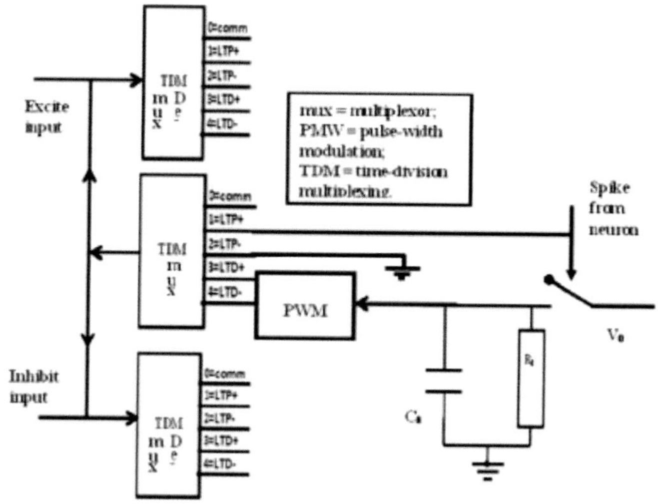

Fig. (4). LTD and associated TDM circuit.

Similarly, the LTD+ (3) and LTD- (4) timeslots communicate the LTD time-based signals from post to pre-synapsis using PWM. Also both LTD+ and LTD- have equal time span and opposite polarity within a frame. This reduces any conductance variation effects. In a spiking neuron, both LTP- and LTD- always transmit to a virtual ground, while LTP+ and LTD+ transmit to a voltage of opposite polarity which may exceed the threshold voltage. The LTP+ and LTD+ voltage polarization of synapses causes a voltage change across that synapse. A spiking neuron closes the switch of Fig. (**3**) causing the capacitance C_0 to charge to a voltage V_0 ; it concurrently drives the comm (0) port of the TDM to output. When the voltage across C_0 reaches V_0 , it causes the circuit to break open the switch. The switch opens thereby causing the capacitance to discharge through the resistance R_0 . The value of C_0 in parallel with R_0 represents the time constant of an exponential decay of the LTP timing curve. The voltage across the capacitance also drives the PWM to encode that voltage. The resulting LTP+ pulse and its negative counterpart LTP- pulse are driven to their respective ports. A spiking neuron also closes the switch of Fig. (**4**), thereby causing the capacitor to charge to an initial voltage V_0 . The capacitance C_0 in parallel with R_0 resistance determines the time-constant of the LTD exponential decay curve. The voltage across the capacitor also drives the PWM to encode that voltage.

The resulting LTD+ pulse and its counterpart LTD- are driven to input 3 and 4 respectively. The LPT+ (1) port of the same TDM is at this time driven by a negative pulse while the LPT- (2) is virtually grounded. Whether or not a neuron will spike is dependent on the internal state of that neuron, which in turn depends on the learning dynamics of the neural system. The closest learning dynamics to a natural biological brain is that of Hodgkings-Huxley (HH) formalism (see chapter 6). The HH algorithm may be implemented as the neural processing (learning) module of a neuromorphic neural network as shown in Fig. (**5**).

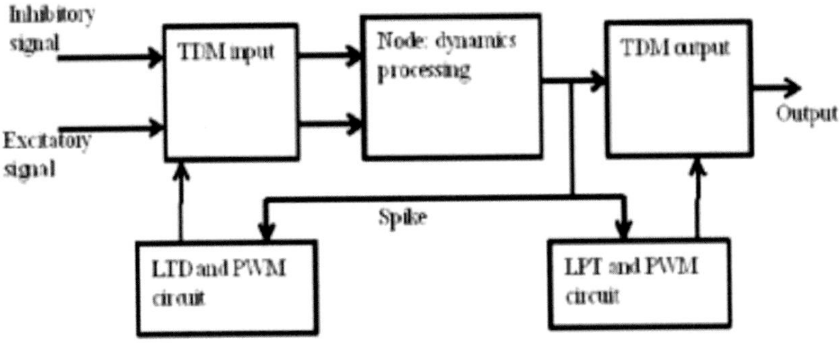

Fig. (5). A block diagram of a neuromorphic neuron

On a compact (Nano-) scale, the Hewlett-Packard Laboratory [5, 6] is researching into, and developing a generic framework of neuromorphic neural network. It is also noteworthy that the exposition of this section is easily amenable to any neuromorphic network provided the learning dynamics contain both the excitatory and inhibitory terms.

CONCLUSION

The book is entitled "Artificial Neural Network" so that anyone attempting to adopt the book might be initially interested in the subject matter. Though it is not an exhaustive coverage of Artificial Neural Network (ANN), but it has contributed somewhat in a way by starting from a biological natural neuron in chapter 1. In the same chapter 1, the first artificial neuron was designed based directly on the principles of natural biological neuron. In an attempt to represent various types of biological neurons artificially, chapter 2 introduces Integrate-and-fire neuron, and Stein Model of artificial neurons. Apart from these two, chapter 2 also has explained methods (*e.g.* of Generating Functions) which account for neuronal functionalities that are not common. Chapter 3 regard neurons from a fuzzy-logic perspective. The chapter has explained also, the principles of ANN analysis and design. Natural evolution and selection was introduced in chapter 4. Genetic Algorithm (GA), and Particle Swam optimization (PSO) are examples of algorithms derived from natural evolution and selection; these are applied to (and/or with) ANN and illustrated with application examples. The applications motivate the subsequent formal definition of ANN system in the same chapter 4. The chapter 4 was concluded with ways of independently and formally accessing the performances of an ANN system. Knowing (or not knowing) what the future hold, chapter 5 presents quantum algebra and quantum neural network in a general perspective. For the same reason, the section on quantum neural network was followed by an introduction to non-volatile memory element (the memristance). A non-volatile memory element may facilitate the design of artificial neuromorphic neural network at a very high performance level. Anyone with a full understanding of chapters one to five may be able to design an ANN system from first principle.

Part II of the book may be regarded as the active (practice) part whereby chapter 6 starts off with contemporary learning dynamics. That is, the main and usual driving forces behind an ANN which makes it behave intelligently and autonomously (also called the learning algorithm) are explained. The learning algorithms lead to the presentation of several ANN systems that employs them in chapter 6. Notable algorithm is the back-propagation algorithm, and Radial Basis Function. Chapter 7 on the other hand delved into categorization of ANN systems, and described examples of each category. The last section of chapter 7 presented several algorithmic evaluation methods of ANN systems. These algorithms are in considerable details. In order to provide a reasonable solution to complex problems, chapter 8 has described how ANNs may be combined, dependent on the problem's complexity, to produce a suitable ANNs' hierarchical architecture and an optimal solution. Two main selection methods of ANNs were discussed in considerable detail in chapter 8. These are the factorial selection method and the Group Method of Data Handling (GMDH). Natural problems do not come properly posed. Types of ANNs capable of gaining insight into such problem are the probability-based (or density-based) neural networks. For this reason, chapter 9 has described probability-based ANN systems. The ANN systems described in chapter 9 may sample data of unknown sources and disaster sources (for examples) directly in order to properly represent that source. The probability- based ANNs may also adapt (grow/prune) itself, sample data from known sources, and solve properly posed problems. Chapter 10 has described two main types of dense and large ANN systems which are quantum neural network and Deep Believe Network (DBN). Their implementation, adaptation, and use are described in considerable detail. Chapter 11 consider ways of improving large and dense ANN systems in order to facilitate their implementation. Two main types of ANNs in this category were considered; they are Bayesian Network and Neuromorphic network. On the part of Bayesian network, certain integration algorithms are considered for improvement. For the neuromorphic network, the fabrication procedures to meet specification may be more involving. Though simulations of DBN and Neuromorphic Network systems may be performed, but such systems may not yet be physically manufactured to autonomously do work (*e.g.*; in real-time). Chapter 11 consider these as areas of research and development in neural network.

CONFLICT OF INTEREST

The author confirm that this chapter contents have no conflict of interest.

ACKNOWLEDGEMENTS

Cited works are appreciated.

REFERENCES

[1] Simon D, Kennedy AD, Brian JP, Duncan R. Hyride monte carlo. Phy Lett 1987; 195(2): 216-22. Elsevier Science Publishers B.V.

[2] Blanes Sergio, Casas Fernando, JM Sanz-Serna . Numerical integrators for the Hybrid Monte Carlo method. Valencia: Universitat Politecnica de Valencia 2013.

[3] Stephen P. Markov chain Monte Carlo method and its application. Bristol: Brooks University of Bristol, UK. Statistician 1998; 47(Part 1): 69-100. [http://dx.doi.org/10.1111/1467-9884.00117]

[4] Ian Nabney T. Netlab: Algorithms for Pattern Recognition. Springer 2004. ISBN: 1-85233-440-1

[5] Snider GS. Self-organized computation with unreliable, memristive nanodevices. California, USA: Hewlett-Packard Laboratories 2007; p. 1501.

[6] Snider GS. Spike-Timing-Dependent Learning in Memristive nanodevices. California, USA: Hewlett-Packard Laboratories 2008; p. 1501.

SUBJECT INDEX

Pierre Lorrentz

Made in the USA
San Bernardino,
CA

58482930R00137